Teach Yourself
VISUALLY™
Office 2010

Visual

by Kate Shoup

WILEY

Wiley Publishing, Inc.

Teach Yourself VISUALLY™
Office 2010

Published by
Wiley Publishing, Inc.
10475 Crosspoint Boulevard
Indianapolis, IN 46256
www.wiley.com

Published simultaneously in Canada

Library of Congress Control Number: 2010922553

ISBN: 978-0-470-57193-4

Manufactured in the United States of America

10 9 8 7 6 5 4 3 2 1

Trademark Acknowledgments

Disclaimer

In order to get this information to you in a timely manner, this book was based on a pre-release version of Microsoft Office 2010. There may be some minor changes between the screenshots in this book and what you see on your desktop. As always, Microsoft has the final word on how programs look and function; if you have any questions or see any discrepancies, consult the online help for further information about the software.

Contact Us

For general information on our other products and services please contact our Customer Care Department within the U.S. at 877-762-2974, outside the U.S. at 317-572-3993 or fax 317-572-4002.

For technical support please visit www.wiley.com/techsupport.

WILEY

Wiley Publishing, Inc.

Sales
Contact Wiley
at (877) 762-2974 or
fax (317) 572-4002.

Credits

Executive Editor
Jody Lefevere

Sr. Project Editor
Sarah Hellert

Technical Editor
Vince Averello

Copy Editor
Scott Tullis

Editorial Director
Robyn Siesky

Business Manager
Amy Knies

Sr. Marketing Manager
Sandy Smith

Vice President and Executive Group Publisher
Richard Swadley

Vice President and Executive Publisher
Barry Pruett

Sr. Project Coordinator
Lynsey Stanford

Graphics and Production Specialists
Andrea Hornberger
Jennifer Mayberry
Christine Williams

Quality Control Technician
John Greenough

Proofreader
Context Editorial Services

Indexer
Potomac Indexing, LLC

Screen Artists
Ana Carrillo
Jill A. Proll
Ron Terry

Illustrators
Ronda David-Burroughs
Cheryl Grubbs

About the Author

During the course of her career, freelance writer/editor **Kate Shoup** has authored 20 books and edited scores more. Recent titles include *Windows 7 Digital Classroom, Teach Yourself VISUALLY Outlook 2007, Office 2007: Top 100 Simplified Tips & Tricks, Internet Visual Quick Tips,* and *Windows Vista Visual Encyclopedia*. She has also co-written a feature-length screenplay (and starred in the ensuing film) and worked as the sports editor for *NUVO Newsweekly*. When not working, Kate loves to ski (she was once nationally ranked), read, and ride her motorcycle — and she plays a mean game of 9-ball. Kate lives in Indianapolis with her daughter and their dog.

Author's Acknowledgments

Thanks go out to publisher Barry Pruett and to executive editor Jody Lefevere for allowing me the opportunity to tackle this exciting project; to project editor Sarah Hellert for her dedication and patience in guiding this project from start to finish; to copy editor Scott Tullis for ensuring that all the i's were dotted and t's were crossed; to technical editor Vince Averello for skillfully checking each step and offering valuable input along the way; and finally to the production team at Wiley for their able efforts in creating such a visual masterpiece. Thanks, too, to my beautiful and brilliant daughter, Heidi Welsh; to my incredible parents, Barb and Steve Shoup; to my wonderful sister, Jenny Shoup; to my brother-in-law, Jim Plant; to my nephew, Jake Plant. Special thanks to Francois DuBois. Finally, much love and strength to Tom Plant and his lovely family.

How to Use This Book

Who Needs This Book?

This book is for the reader who has never used this particular technology or software application. It is also for readers who want to expand their knowledge.

The Conventions in This Book

❶ Steps

This book uses a step-by-step format to guide you easily through each task. Numbered steps are actions you must do; bulleted steps clarify a point, step, or optional feature; and indented steps give you the result.

❷ Notes

Notes give additional information — special conditions that may occur during an operation, a situation that you want to avoid, or a cross reference to a related area of the book.

❸ Icons and buttons

Icons and buttons show you exactly what you need to click to perform a step.

❹ Tips

Tips offer additional information, including warnings and shortcuts.

❺ Bold

Bold type shows command names, options, and text or numbers you must type.

❻ Italics

Italic type introduces and defines a new term.

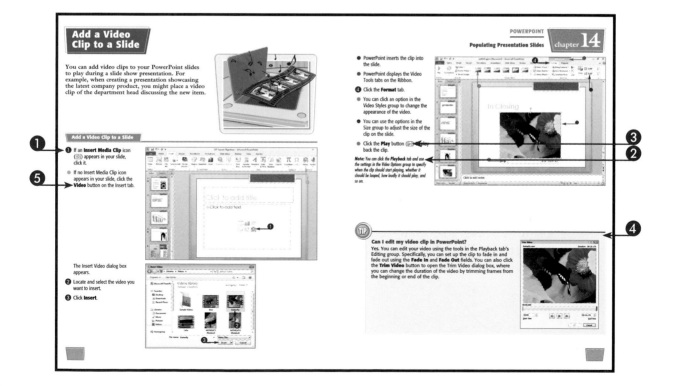

Table of Contents

 **chapter 4** **Working with Office Files Online**

WORD

 **chapter 5** **Adding Text**

Table of Contents

chapter 6 · Formatting Text

chapter 7 · Adding Extra Touches

Table of Contents

 **chapter 10** Worksheet Basics

 **chapter 11** Working with Formulas and Functions

POWERPOINT

Table of Contents

chapter 16

Database Basics

Table of Contents

OUTLOOK

chapter 18 — Organizing with Outlook

chapter 19 E-mailing with Outlook

PUBLISHER

chapter 20 Publisher Basics

Table of Contents

chapter 21 — Fine-Tuning a Publication

ONE NOTE

chapter 22 — Taking Notes with OneNote

chapter 23

Organizing and Sharing Notes

Office
Features

The Office 2010 applications share a common look and feel. You can find many of the same features in each program, such as the Ribbon, Quick Access toolbar, program window controls, and File tab. Many of the tasks you perform, such as creating and working with files, share the same processes and features throughout the Office suite. In this part, you learn how to navigate the common Office features and basic tasks.

Start and Exit Office Applications

Before you can begin working with a Microsoft Office program, you must open the program. Then, when you finish your work, you can close the program. If applicable, you can save your work before exiting a program completely.

Start and Exit Office Applications

Start an Office Application

1 Click **Start**.

2 Click **All Programs**. The All Programs menu option changes to a Back menu option.

3 Click **Microsoft Office**.

4 Click the name of the program that you want to open.

● The program that you selected opens in a new window.

Note: See the next section to learn how to identify different areas of the program window.

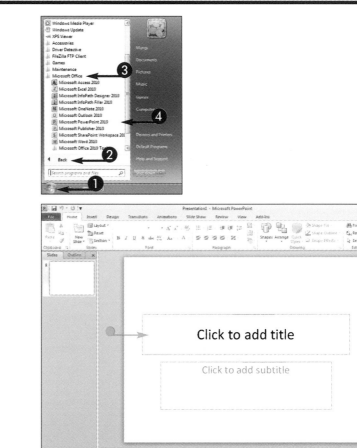

Exit an Office Application

1 Click the **Close** button ().

● You can also click the **File** tab and then click **Exit**.

If you have not yet saved your work, the program prompts you to do so before exiting.

2 Click **Save**.

The program window closes.

● If you click **Don't Save**, the program closes without saving your data.

● If you click **Cancel**, the program window remains open.

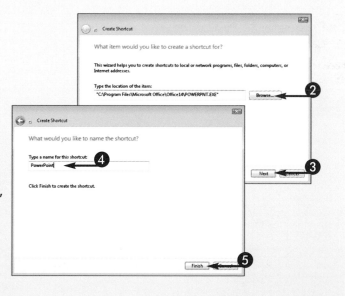

TIP

Can I create a shortcut icon for an Office application?

Yes. You can create a shortcut icon that appears on the Windows desktop. Whenever you want to open the program, you can simply double-click the shortcut icon. Follow these steps to create a shortcut icon:

1 Right-click over a blank area of the desktop and click **New** and then **Shortcut**.

The Create Shortcut dialog box appears.

2 Click **Browse**, navigate to the Office program, click the filename, and click **OK**.

3 Click **Next**.

4 Type a name for the shortcut.

5 Click **Finish**.

The new shortcut icon appears on the desktop.

Navigate the Program Windows

All Office programs share a common appearance and many of the same features, such as a Ribbon, a Quick Launch toolbar, and scroll bars. When you learn your way around one Office program, you can easily use the same skills to navigate the others. If you are new to Office, you should take a moment and familiarize yourself with the types of on-screen elements that you can expect to encounter.

Title Bar

Displays the name of the open file and the Office program.

Quick Access Toolbar

Displays quick access buttons to the Save, Undo, and Redo commands.

File Tab Menu

Click to display a menu of file commands, such as New and Open.

Ribbon

Displays groups of related commands in tabs. Each tab offers buttons for performing common tasks.

Status Bar

Displays information about the current worksheet or file.

Program Window Controls

Use these buttons to minimize the program window, restore the window to full size, or close the window.

Formula Bar

This appears only in Excel. Use this bar to type and edit formulas and perform calculations on your worksheet data.

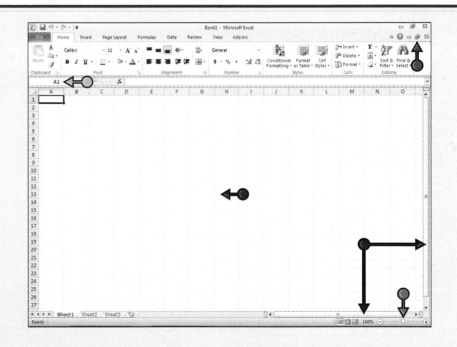

Work Area

The area where you add and work with data in a program. Depending on the Office program, the work area may be a document, a worksheet, or a slide.

Document Window Controls

Use these buttons to minimize or restore the current document within the program window.

Zoom Controls

Use this feature to zoom your view of a document.

Scroll Bars

Use the vertical and horizontal scroll bars to scroll through the item shown in the work area, such as a document or worksheet.

Work with the Ribbon

Instead of the menus and toolbars found in earlier versions of Office, Office 2010 features the Ribbon, which offers an intuitive way to locate commands. The Ribbon is grouped into tabs, and each tab holds a set of related commands. (Some tabs appear only when needed, such as when you are working with a particular object in a document.)

Work with the Ribbon

Use the Ribbon

1 Click a tab.

The tab organizes related tasks and commands into logical groups.

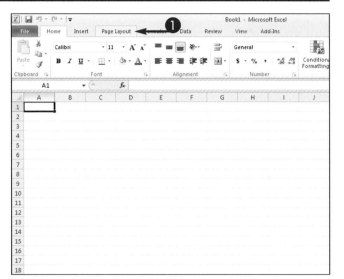

2 Click a button to activate a command or feature.

● Buttons with arrows display additional commands.

● With some groups of commands, you can click the corner group button (⬜) to display a dialog box of additional settings.

When you position the mouse pointer over Live Preview options on the Ribbon, you see the results in the document before applying the command.

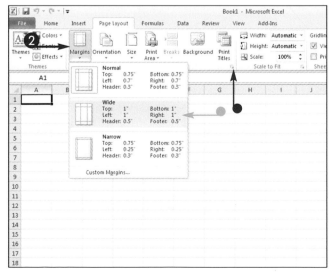

Minimize the Ribbon

1 Double-click a tab name.

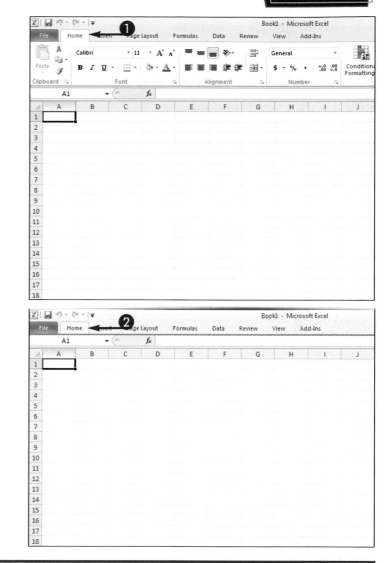

The Ribbon is minimized.

2 Double-click the tab name again to maximize the Ribbon.

Is there a way I can keep the Ribbon minimized?

Yes. You can keep the Ribbon minimized and click a tab when you need to use a command. Follow these steps:

1 Right-click a tab on the Ribbon.

2 Click **Minimize the Ribbon**.

The program's Ribbon is minimized at the top of the screen.

To use a Ribbon while it is minimized, simply click the tab containing the tools that you want to access to reveal it.

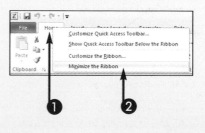

Customize the Quick Access Toolbar

The Quick Access toolbar, located in the top left corner of the program window, offers quick access to the Save, Undo, and Redo commands. If you want, you can customize this toolbar to include other commands, such as the Quick Print command or another command you use often. You can also choose to display the toolbar above or below the Ribbon.

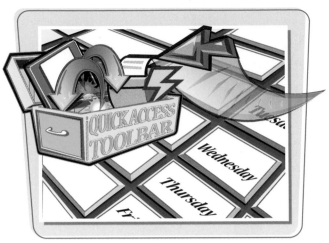

Customize the Quick Access Toolbar

① Click the **Customize Quick Access Toolbar** button (⊡).

② Click **More Commands**.

● You can click any of the common commands to add them to the toolbar.

● You can click **Show Below the Ribbon** if you want to display the toolbar below the Ribbon.

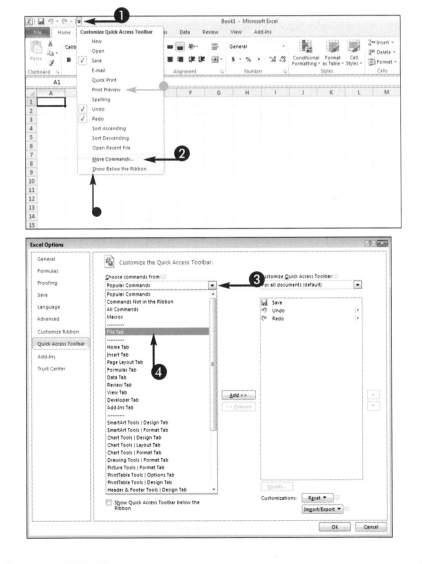

The Options dialog box opens with the Customize options displayed.

③ Click the **Choose commands from** ⊡.

④ Click a command group.

5 Click the command that you want to add to the toolbar.

6 Click the **Add** button.

● Office adds the command.

You can repeat Steps **3** and **6** to move additional buttons to the toolbar.

7 Click **OK**.

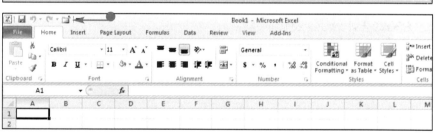

● The new command appears on the Quick Access toolbar.

TIPS

How do I remove a button from the Quick Access toolbar?

To remove a command, reopen the program's Options dialog box by following the steps in this section, click the command name in the list box on the right, click the **Remove** button, and click **OK**. The button no longer appears on the toolbar.

Are there other ways to customize the Quick Access toolbar?

Yes. You can add commands to the toolbar directly from the Ribbon. Simply click the tab containing the command that you want to add, right-click the command, and then click **Add to Quick Access Toolbar**. The command is immediately added as a button on the toolbar.

Find Help with Office

You can use the Office Help tools to assist you when you run into a problem or need more information about a particular task. The Help window offers tools that enable you to search for topics that you want to learn more about. With an Internet connection, you can access Microsoft's online help files for even more information.

Find Help with Office

① Click the **Help** button ().

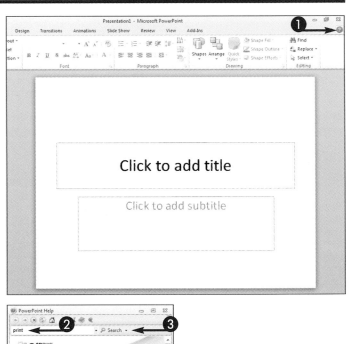

The Help window opens.

② Type a word or phrase that you want to learn more about.

③ Click the **Search** button.

You can also press `Enter` to start the search.

Note: *You must be connected to the Internet to access Microsoft's online help files.*

● The results window displays a list of possible matches.

④ Click a link to learn more about a topic.

● The Help window displays the article, enabling you to read more about the topic.

● You can use the **Back** and **Forward** buttons (◄ and ►) to move back and forth between help topics.

● You can click the **Print** button (🖨) to print the information.

⑤ Click ✕ to close the window.

TIPS

Can I use the Help feature if I am offline?
Yes. You can still access the help files that are installed with the program. However, the online resources offer you more help topics, as well as links to demos and other help tools.

Where can I find a table of contents for the help files?
You can click the **Home** button (🏠) on the Help window's toolbar to quickly display the table of contents for the Office program that you are using. You can click a help category to display subtopics of help information. You can click an article to view more about a topic. Many articles include links to related articles.

Create a New File

Suppose you want to create a new file in Office 2010 — a Word document, an Excel workbook, an Access database, a PowerPoint presentation, a Publisher publication, or an Outlook item. In every Office 2010 program but Outlook, you create a new file using the Getting Started screen. In Outlook, you create a new item from the Ribbon.

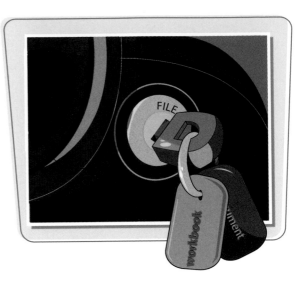

Create a New Word, Excel, PowerPoint, Access, or Publisher File

① Click the **File** tab.

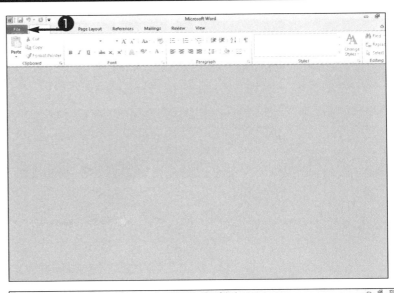

② Click **New**.

The New screen appears.

③ Click the type of file that you want to create.

④ Click **Create**.

The new file opens.

Note: Another way to create a new file is to press Ctrl + N . *Office creates a new file using the default settings.*

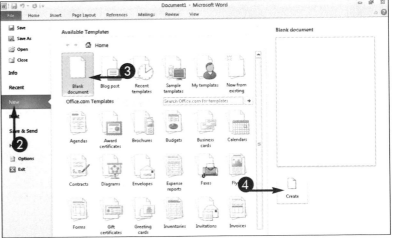

Create a New Outlook Item

① In the lower left corner of the Outlook window, click the type of item you want to create — Mail, Calendar, Contacts, or Task.

② Click the **New *Type*** button. For example, if you are creating a Mail item , the button is labeled New E-mail. If you are creating a Calendar item, the button is labeled New Appointment, New Meeting, and so on.

The new item opens.

TIPS

How do I create a new file based on a template?

Many Office programs allow you to create a new file from a template — that is, a preformatted layout. For example, in Word, you can choose from templates for letters, faxes, memos, reports, and more. Simply click the template that you want to apply in the New screen. You can also create your own templates by saving an existing file in the program's template format.

Where can I find more templates to use with my Microsoft Office programs?

You can find more Office templates online. To do so, click a template category under Office.com Templates in the New screen. Office displays a list of available templates in the selected category; double-click one to download the template and apply it to a new file. (Note that you must be connected to the Internet to access Office templates online.)

Save a File

If you want to be able to refer to the data in a file at some later time, you must save the file. You should also frequently save any file you are working on in case of a power failure or computer crash. When you save a file, you can give it a unique filename and store it in the folder or drive of your choice.

① Click the **File** tab.

● For subsequent saves, you can click the **Save** button (🖫) on the Quick Access toolbar to quickly save the file.

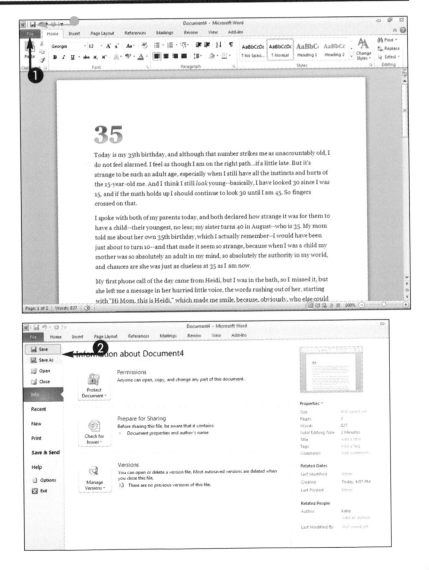

The document's Info screen appears.

② Click **Save** or **Save As**.

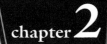
The Save As dialog box appears.

Note: Another way to save a file is to press Ctrl + S . If this is the first time the file has been saved, Office launches the Save As dialog box.

③ In the Navigation pane, click the library in which you want to save the file (here, Documents).

④ In the file list, navigate to the folder in which you want to save the file.

⑤ Type a name for the file in the **File name** field.

⑥ Click **Save**.

● The Office program saves the file and the new filename appears on the program window's title bar.

Can I save a file using a different file type?
Each Office program saves to a default file type. For example, a Word document uses the DOCX file format. If you want to save the file in a format compatible with previous versions of Office, you must save it in the appropriate format, such as Word 97-2003 Document for previous versions of Word. To save a file in a different format, click the **Save as Type** in the Save As dialog box and choose the desired format from the list that appears. Alternatively, with the file open, click the **File** tab, click **Share**, click **Change File Type**, and choose the desired file type from the options that appear.

Open a File

In addition to creating new files, you can open files that you have created and saved previously in order to continue adding data or to edit existing data. Regardless of whether you store a file in a folder on your computer's hard drive or on a CD, you can easily access files using the Open screen.

Open a File

1 Click the **File** tab.

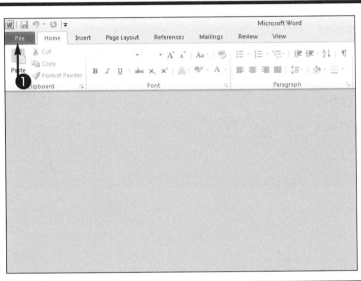

● If the file you want to open is listed under Recent Documents, you can click it to open it.

2 Click the **Open** button.

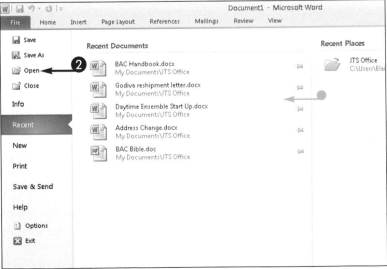

The Open dialog box appears.

Note: *Another way to launch the Open dialog box is to press* **Ctrl** + **O**.

③ In the Navigation pane, click the library in which the file you want to open has been saved (here, Documents).

④ In the file list, locate and click the folder in which the file you want to open has been saved.

⑤ Click **Open**.

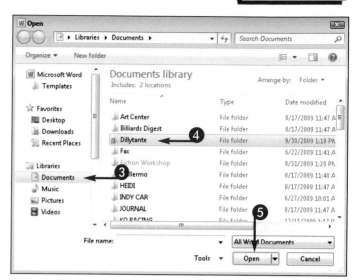

⑥ Click the name of the file that you want to open.

⑦ Click **Open**.

The file opens in the program window.

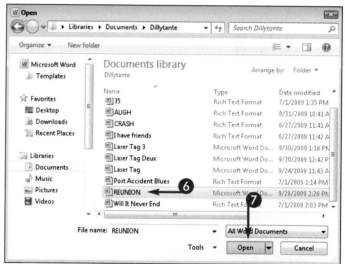

How do I close an open file?

Closing an open file is simple. Just click the **File** tab and click **Close** in the screen that appears. When you do, Office closes the open file but leaves the program window open. To close both the open file and the program window, click the ▣ button in the upper right corner of the program window. When you close unnecessary files and programs, you free up processing power on your computer.

What if I cannot find my file?

If you are not sure where your file was saved, you can use the Search box in the upper right corner of the Open dialog box to locate it. Simply open the folder in which you believe the file was saved and type the file's name in the Search box. Alternatively, search by author, file type, or date modified.

Print a File

If a printer is connected to your computer, you can print your Office files. For example, you might distribute printouts of a file as handouts in a meeting. You can send a file directly to the printer using the default settings or you can open the Office application's Print screen to change these settings. (Printer settings vary slightly among Office programs.)

Print a File

1 Click the **File** tab.

2 Click **Print**.

The Print screen appears.

Note: *Another way to open the Print screen is to press* Ctrl + P .

● You can specify the number of copies to print using the **Copies** spin box.

● You can choose a printer from the **Printer** drop-down list.

● You can choose to print a selection from the file or specific pages using the available settings in the Settings list.

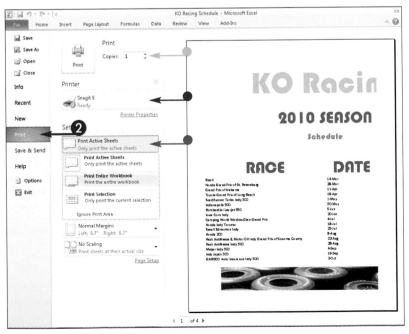

● You can access additional print options under Settings.

● View a preview of the printed file here.

③ Click **Print**.

The Office program sends the file to the printer for printing.

How do I print using default settings?

If you do not need to change any of your default print settings, such as the printer used or the number of copies, you can simply click the **Quick Print** button (🖶) on the Quick Access toolbar. If the Quick Print button does not appear on your Quick Access toolbar, you can add it. To do so, click the **Customize Quick Access Toolbar** button (▾) to the right of the Quick Access toolbar. A list of commands you can add to the toolbar appears; click **Quick Print** to add the Quick Print button (🖶) to the Quick Access toolbar. (Notice that you can also add a Print Preview button to the Quick Access toolbar; clicking that button opens the Print screen.)

Check Your File for Hidden or Personal Data

If you plan to share an Office document with others via e-mail or by some other digital method, you should first remove any personal, company, or other private information stored in the document's metadata or in the document itself. To locate and remove this data, you can use Office's Document Inspector.

Check Your File for Hidden or Personal Data

① With the document you want to check for sensitive information open, click the **File** tab.

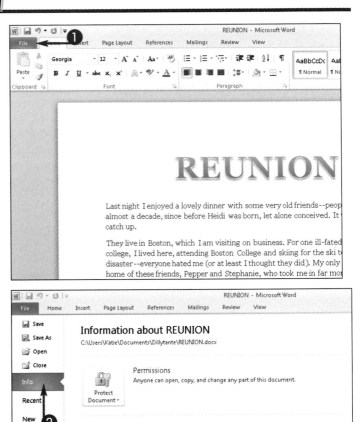

② If necessary, click **Info**.

③ Click **Check for Issues**.

④ Click **Inspect Document**.

The Document Inspector dialog box opens.

5 Ensure that the check box next to each type of content you want to inspect is checked.

6 Click **Inspect**.

Document Inspector determines whether any sensitive information appears in the document.

● If Document Inspector locates sensitive information in the document, it flags it.

7 Click **Remove All**.

Document Inspector removes the sensitive information.

8 Click **Close**.

TIPS

What if I am not sure whether I want to remove the information flagged by the Document Inspector?

If you are not sure whether you want to remove the information flagged by the Document Inspector, cancel the inspection and use the appropriate Office tools to view the information. For example, if document properties are flagged, then view the document properties to see whether you want to eliminate them from the document.

Can I undo changes made by the Document Inspector?

You cannot undo the effects of removing information with the Document Inspector. You can, however, restore the removed information by closing the document without saving the changes made by the inspection process.

E-mail a File

You can share a file with others via e-mail. One approach is to open Outlook, create a new e-mail message, and add the file as an attachment (discussed later). Alternatively, you can initiate the send operation with the program you used to create the file (covered here). Note that to open the file, recipients must have the appropriate software on their computer.

E-mail a File

① With the document you want to share via e-mail open, click the **File** tab.

② Click **Save & Send**.

③ Click **Send Using E-Mail**.

The Send Using E-Mail screen opens.

④ Click **Send as Attachment**.

Office launches an Outlook New Message window.

● The name of your file appears in the New Message window's Subject line.

● The file is attached to the message.

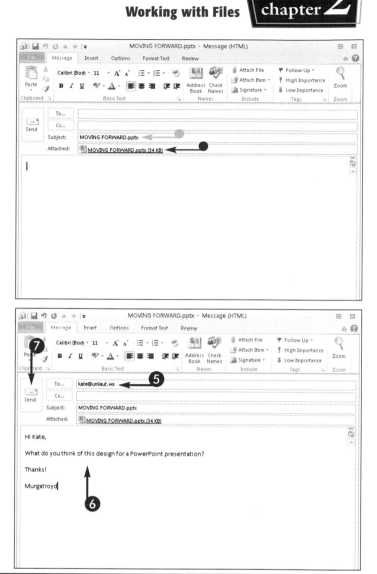

5 Type the message recipient's e-mail address in the **To** field.

6 Type your text in the body of the message.

7 Click **Send**.

What if my recipient does not have the necessary software to open the file?

Suppose you need to share an Office file, but your recipient does not have Office on his or her computer. In that case, you can send the file in PDF or XPS format. When you use these formats, files look the same on almost any computer, with fonts, formatting, and images remaining consistent. The tradeoff, however, is that unlike an Office file, the contents of PDF and XPS files are not easily changed — meaning your recipient cannot edit the file. As long as no edits are required, you can send a PDF or XPS version of your file by following the steps in this section, but choosing **Attach a PDF copy of this *file* to an e-mail** or **Attach a XPS copy of this *file* to an e-mail** in the Send Using E-Mail screen (refer to Step **4**) instead of Attach a Copy of This *File* to an E-mail.

You can select data in your file to perform different tasks, such as formatting or copying and pasting. Depending on what program you are using, Office offers several different selection techniques. For example, in Word, PowerPoint, and Publisher, you can use your mouse pointer or your keyboard to select a single character, a word, a sentence, a paragraph, or all the data in the file.

Select Data

Click and Drag to Select Data

1 Click to one side of the word or character that you want to select.

2 Drag the cursor across the text that you want to select.

Word selects any characters that you drag across.

You can use this technique to select characters, words, sentences, and paragraphs.

To deselect selected text, simply click anywhere outside the text or press any arrow key on your keyboard.

Note: *This technique also works for selecting images in your Office files. In addition, you can select images by simply clicking them.*

REUNION

Last night I enjoyed a lovely dinner with some very old friends--people I hadn't seen in almost a decade, since before Heidi was born, let alone conceived. It was wonderful to catch up.

They live in Boston, which I am visiting on business. For one ill-fated semester in college, I lived here, attending Boston College and skiing for the ski team there. It was a disaster--everyone hated me (or at least I thought they did). My only refuge was at the home of these friends, Pepper and Stephanie, who took me in far more often than they probably would have liked. The house was plenty full without me. Pepper's mother had been recently divorced, and she had moved in with Pepper and Stephanie and their toddler daughter, Laura, as had two of Pepper's younger brothers, one of whom was about my age. But they never made me feel anything less than completely welcome. They were my family during a time when I desperately needed one.

REUNION

Last night I enjoyed a lovely dinner with some very old friends--people I hadn't seen in almost a decade, since before Heidi was born, let alone conceived. It was wonderful to catch up.

They live in Boston, which I am visiting on business. For one ill-fated semester in college, I lived here, attending Boston College and skiing for the ski team there. It was a disaster--everyone hated me (or at least I thought they did). My only refuge was at the home of these friends, Pepper and Stephanie, who took me in far more often than they probably would have liked. The house was plenty full without me. Pepper's mother had been recently divorced, and she had moved in with Pepper and Stephanie and their toddler daughter, Laura, as had two of Pepper's younger brothers, one of whom was about my age. But they never made me feel anything less than completely welcome. They were my family during a time when I desperately needed one.

Select Text with a Mouse Click

1 Double-click anywhere inside a word that you want to select.

Word selects the text.

You can also triple-click anywhere inside a paragraph to select the paragraph.

REUNION

Last night I enjoyed a lovely dinner with some very old friends--people I hadn't seen in almost a decade, since before Heidi was born, let alone conceived. It was wonderful to catch up.

They live in Boston, which I am visiting on business. For one ill-fated semester in college, I lived here, attending Boston College and skiing for the ski team there. It was a disaster--everyone hated me (or at least I thought they did). My only refuge was at the home of these friends, Pepper and Stephanie, who took me in far more often than they probably would have liked. The house was plenty full without me. Pepper's mother had been recently divorced, and she had moved in with Pepper and Stephanie and their toddler daughter, Laura, as had two of Pepper's younger brothers, one of whom was about my age. But they never made me feel anything less than completely welcome. They were my family during a time when I desperately needed one.

Select Text from the Margin

Note: *This technique works only in Word.*

1 Click in the left margin.

Word selects the entire line of text next to where you clicked.

You can double-click inside the left margin to select a paragraph.

You can triple-click inside the left margin to select all of the text in the document.

REUNION

Last night I enjoyed a lovely dinner with some very old friends--people I hadn't seen in almost a decade, since before Heidi was born, let alone conceived. It was wonderful to catch up.

They live in Boston, which I am visiting on business. For one ill-fated semester in college, I lived here, attending Boston College and skiing for the ski team there. It was a disaster--everyone hated me (or at least I thought they did). My only refuge was at the home of these friends, Pepper and Stephanie, who took me in far more often than they probably would have liked. The house was plenty full without me. Pepper's mother had been recently divorced, and she had moved in with Pepper and Stephanie and their toddler daughter, Laura, as had two of Pepper's younger brothers, one of whom was about my age. But they never made me feel anything less than completely welcome. They were my family during a time when I desperately needed one.

TIPS

Can I also use my keyboard to select text?

Yes. You can use keyboard shortcuts to select text in your file. To select a single word, press `Ctrl` + `Shift` + `←` or `Ctrl` + `Shift` + `→`. To select a paragraph from the cursor down or up, press `Ctrl` + `Shift` + `↓` or `Ctrl` + `Shift` + `↑`. To select all of the text from the cursor onward, press `Ctrl` + `Shift` + `End`. To select all of the text above the current cursor location, press `Ctrl` + `Shift` + `Home`. To select all the text in the file, press `Ctrl` + `A`.

How do I select data in Excel?

To select data in Excel, click the cell that contains the data. To select data in a range of cells, click in the upper left corner of the range, and then drag down and to the right until all the cells you want to select are highlighted. To select multiple cells that are not part of a continuous series, press `Ctrl` as you click each cell you want to select.

Cut, Copy, and Paste Data

You can use the Cut, Copy, and Paste commands to move or copy data within a program or to a different program. For example, you might copy a picture from Word and paste it in a PowerPoint slide. The Copy command makes a duplicate of the selected data, whereas the Cut command removes the data from the original location.

Cut, Copy, and Paste Data

Drag and Drop Data

① Select the data that you want to cut or copy.

② Click and drag the data to a new location.

The ↖ changes to ↘.

To copy the data as you drag it, you can press and hold **Ctrl**.

REUNION

Last night I enjoyed a lovely dinner with some very old friends--people I hadn't seen in almost a decade, since before Heidi was born, let alone conceived. It was wonderful to catch up.

They live in Boston, which I am visiting on business. For one ill-fated semester in college, I lived here, attending Boston College and skiing for the ski team there. It was a disaster--everyone hated me (or at least I thought they did). My only refuge was at the home of these friends, Pepper and Stephanie, who took me in far more often than they probably would have liked. The house was plenty full without me. Pepper's mother had been recently divorced, and she had moved in with Pepper and Stephanie and their toddler daughter, Laura, as had two of Pepper's younger brothers, one of whom was about my age. But they never made me feel anything less than completely welcome. They were my family during a time when I desperately needed one.

③ Release the mouse to drop the data in place.

The data appears in the new location.

REUNION

Last night I enjoyed a lovely dinner with some very old friends--people I hadn't seen in almost a decade, since before Heidi was born, let alone conceived. It was wonderful to catch up.

They live in Boston, which I am visiting on business. For one ill-fated semester in college, I lived here, attending Boston College and skiing for the ski team there. It was a disaster--everyone hated me (or at least I thought they did). My only refuge was at the home of these friends, Pepper and Stephanie, who took me in far more often than they probably would have liked. Pepper's mother had been recently divorced, and she had moved in with Pepper and Stephanie and their toddler daughter, Laura, as had two of Pepper's younger brothers, one of whom was about my age. The house was plenty full without me. But they never made me feel anything less than completely welcome. They were my fam(Ctrl) ▾ g a time when I desperately needed one.

Cut and Copy Data

1 Select the data that you want to cut or copy.

2 Click the **Home** tab.

3 Click the **Cut** button (✂) to move data or the **Copy** button (📋) to copy data.

Note: *You can also press* Ctrl + X *to cut data or* Ctrl + C *to copy data.*

The data is stored in the Windows Clipboard.

4 Click the point where you want to insert the cut or copied data.

You can also open another file into which you can paste the data.

5 On the Home tab, click the **Paste** button. Alternatively, to preview how the text will look before you paste it, click the down arrow below the Paste button and position your mouse pointer over any of the three buttons that appear.

Note: *You can also press* Ctrl + V *to paste data.*

● The data appears in the new location.

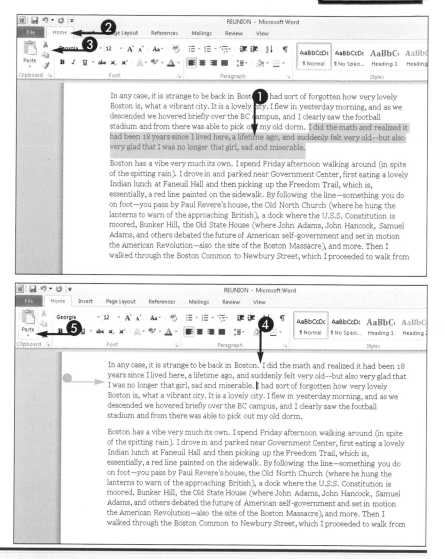

TIPS

When I paste cut or copied data, an icon appears. What is it?

The Paste Options smart tag (📋) may appear when you paste cut or copied data. Click the smart tag to view various Paste-related buttons: Keep Source Formatting (🖋), Merge Formatting (🖌), and Keep Text Only (🄰). You can click one of these buttons to activate it. Alternatively, ignore the tag; eventually, it disappears.

Can I cut or copy multiple pieces of data?

Yes. You can cut or copy multiple pieces of data, and open the Office Clipboard task pane to paste the data. The Office Clipboard holds up to 24 items. You can paste them in whatever order you choose, or you can opt to paste them all at the same time. To display the task pane, click the corner group button (🔲) in the Clipboard group on the Ribbon's Home tab. The Office Clipboard is just one of many task panes available in the Office programs.

View Multiple Files

You can display different views of a file or view multiple files at once. For example, you might view two Word documents side by side to compare how they are formatted or view two Excel workbooks to compare data. In addition, you can split a particularly long file into two scrollable panes to view different portions of it.

View Multiple Files

1. Open two or more files.

2. Click the **View** tab.

3. Click **Arrange All**.

Note: In Excel, the Arrange Windows dialog box opens, and you can select how you want to display multiple files.

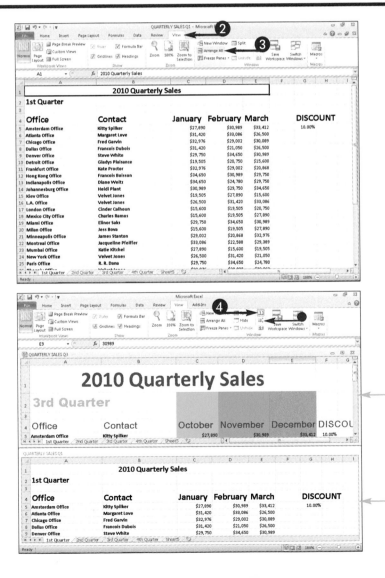

● Both files appear on-screen.

4. Click the **View Side by Side** button ( ) on the View menu to switch between viewing the open files side by side and stacked one on top of the other.

● You can click the **Synchronous Scrolling** button ( ) to scroll both files at the same time.

● The files appear side by side.

● You can click the **Close** button () to close a file.

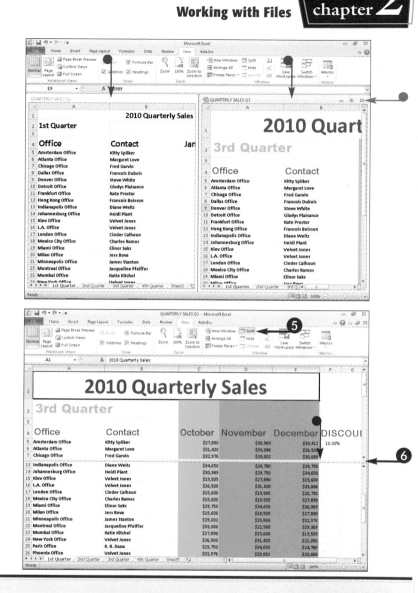

5 To split a single file into scrollable panes, click the **Split** button.

● A horizontal bar appears over the file.

6 Drag the bar up or down to resize the panes, and click to set the bar in place when the panes are the desired size.

*Note: To return the page to a full document again, click the **Split** button again.*

TIPS

What does the Switch Windows button do?

If you open two or more files, you can click the **Switch Windows** button on the View tab to view a list of every open file in the current Office program. You can then choose a file in the list to view it. You might use this feature to quickly display a file that you want to edit.

How do I redisplay full windows again?

Each open file has a set of window controls — Minimize (□), Maximize (□), Restore (□), and Close (✕) — to control the individual document window. If you use the Arrange All command to display several open files at once, you can click the **Maximize** button (□) in the upper right corner of a file's pane to open the file to its full window size again.

Insert Clip Art

You can add interest to your Office files by inserting clip art images in them. Clip art is simply predrawn artwork. Word, Excel, PowerPoint, Publisher, and Outlook install with the Office clip art collection. In addition, you can look for more clip art on the Web using the Clip Art task pane.

Insert Clip Art

1 Click where you want to add clip art.

You can move the clip art to a different location after you insert the art.

2 Click the **Insert** tab.

3 In the Illustrations group, click **Clip Art**.

The Clip Art task pane opens.

4 To search for a particular category of clip art, type a keyword or phrase in the **Search for** field.

● To specify what type of item you need — illustration, photograph, video, or audio — click the **Results should be** ▼ and click the type of item.

● You can also search for clip art on the Office Web site by clicking to select the **Include Office.com content** check box.

5 Click **Go**.

The Clip Art task pane displays any matches for the keyword or phrase that you typed.

● You can use the scroll bar to move through the list of matches.

⑥ To add a clip art image, click the image.

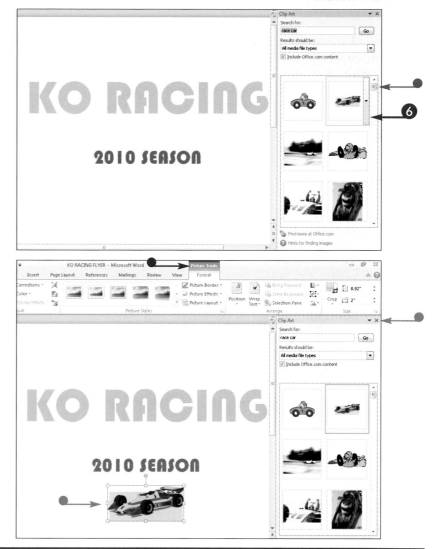

● The clip art is inserted into the file.

● The Picture tools appear on the Format tab.

You can resize or move the clip art.

Note: *See the "Resize and Move Objects" section, later in this chapter, to learn more.*

To deselect the clip art, you can click anywhere else in the work area.

● You can click ☒ to close the pane.

TIPS

How do I search for a particular type of clip art, such as a photo or sound file?

To search for a particular type of media, click the **Results should be** ▾. The drop-down menu displays a list of different media types. You can select or deselect which types to include in your search. If you leave the **All media file types** check box selected, you can search for a match among all of the available media formats.

How do I find details about the clip art?

To find out more about the clip art's properties in the Clip Art task pane, position the ⬚ over the image, click the ▾, and then click **Preview/Properties**. This opens the Preview/Properties dialog box, where you can learn more about the file size, filename, file type, its creation date, and more.

View Clip Art with the Clip Organizer

The Clip Organizer does exactly as its name implies: It organizes clip art images into collections to suit the way you work. For example, you might place all of the clip art related to your company newsletter in one collection. You can insert clip art into your Office file directly from the Clip Organizer.

1 Click **Start**.

2 Click **All Programs**. The All Programs menu option changes to a Back menu option.

3 Click **Microsoft Office**.

4 Click **Microsoft Office 2010 Tools**.

5 Click **Microsoft Clip Organizer**.

The Microsoft Clip Organizer window opens.

6 Click the **Collection List** button if the list is not already shown.

7 Click a collection ⊞ to expand the collection list. The ⊞ changes to a ⊟.

8 Click a category.

If some categories include subcategories, you can click a category ⊞ to expand the list.

● The Clip Organizer displays thumbnails of available clip art in the selected category.

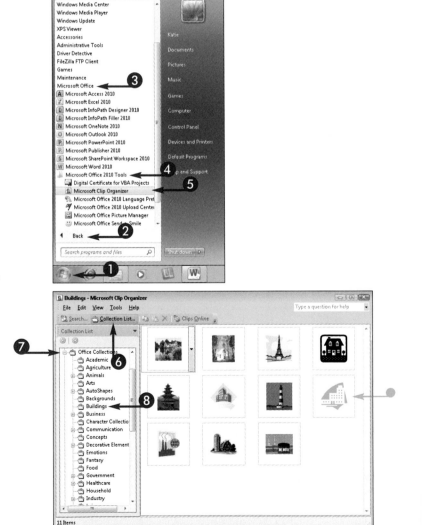

- To view information about a clip art image, you can position the over the image.

To add a clip art image to the current document, you can drag the clip art to your work area.

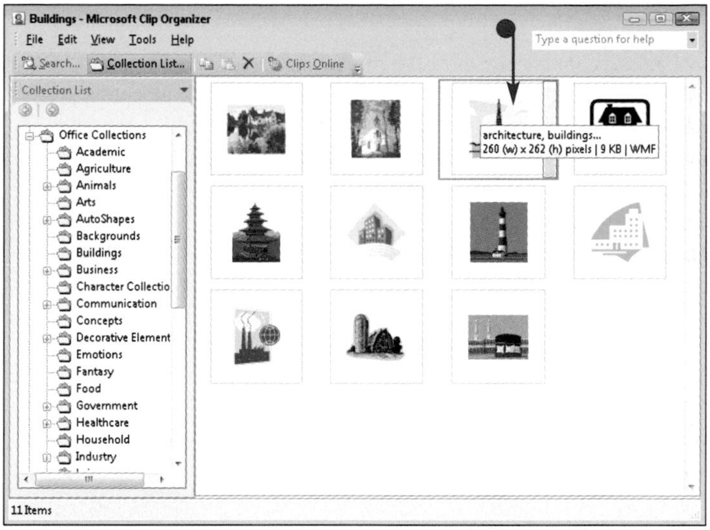

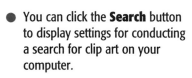

- You can click the **Search** button to display settings for conducting a search for clip art on your computer.

9 When you finish viewing the clip art, click .

The Microsoft Clip Organizer window closes.

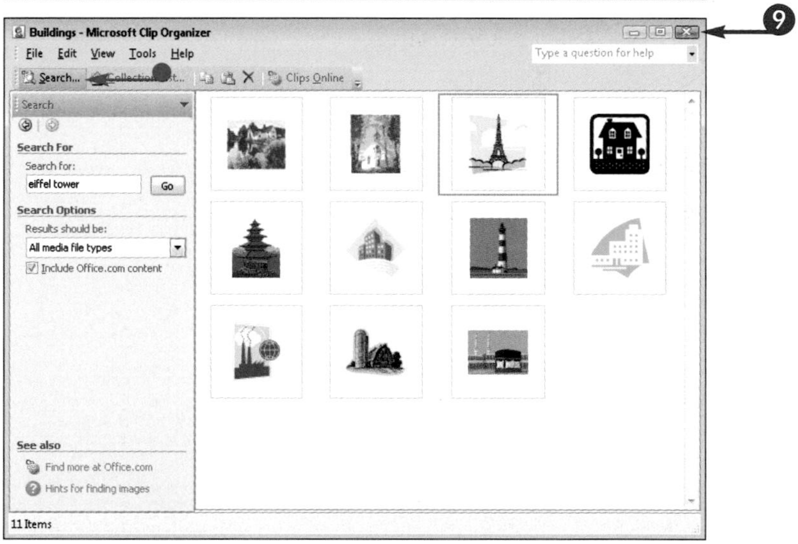

TIPS

How do I create my own clip art collection?

To create your own clip art collection, click the **Collection List** button in the Clip Organizer window, right-click the folder in which you want to create your collection, and choose **New Collection**. In the New Collection dialog box, type a name for your collection; then click **OK**. To add a piece of clip art to the collection, follow the steps in the next section.

Can I copy clip art from one collection to another?

Yes. You can copy clip art from one collection and paste it into another collection using the Microsoft Clip Organizer. Simply click the clip art that you want to copy, and then use the **Copy** ( ) and **Paste** ( ) buttons on the Microsoft Clip Organizer's toolbar to copy and paste the clip art.

Insert a Picture

You can illustrate your Office files with images that you store on your computer. For example, if you have a photo or graphic file that relates to your Excel data, you can insert it onto the worksheet. After you insert an image, you can resize and reposition it, as well as perform other types of edits on the image.

Insert a Picture

① Click the area where you want to add a picture.

You can move the image to a different location after inserting it onto the page.

② Click the **Insert** tab.

③ In the Illustrations group, click **Picture**.

The Insert Picture dialog box appears.

④ Navigate to the folder or drive containing the image file that you want to use.

● To browse for a particular file type, you can click the ⏷ and choose a file format.

⑤ Click the file you want to add.

⑥ Click **Insert**.

Note: Image files, also called objects, come in a variety of file formats, including GIF, JPEG, and PNG.

● The picture is added to the file.

● The Picture tools appear on the Format tab.

You may need to resize or reposition the picture to fit the space.

Note: See the "Resize and Move Objects" section to learn more.

To remove a picture that you no longer want, you can click the picture and press Delete.

 TIPS

If I am sharing my file with others, can I compress the pictures to save space?
Yes. You can compress image files that you add to any file. To do so, click the image, click the **Format** tab on the Ribbon, and click the **Compress Pictures** button (🖼) in the Adjust group. In the Compress Pictures dialog box, fine-tune settings as needed and click **OK** to compress the pictures.

I made changes to my picture, but I do not like the effect. How do I return the picture to the original settings?
You can click the **Reset Picture** button (🖼), located in the Adjust group on the Format tab, to restore a picture to its original state. This command removes any edits that you applied to the image. Activating this command does not restore the original size of the image.

Resize and Move Objects

Clip art and other types of images are also called *objects*. When you select an object in an Office file, handles surround that object; you can use these handles to resize the object. You can also move objects that you place in a file.

Resize an Object

1. Click the object that you want to resize.

2. Click a selection handle.

3. Drag inward or outward to resize the object.

Note: To maintain an object's height-to-width ratio when resizing, drag one of the corner handles.

● When you release the mouse button, the object is resized.

Move an Object

① Click the object that you want to move.

② Drag the object to a new location on the worksheet.

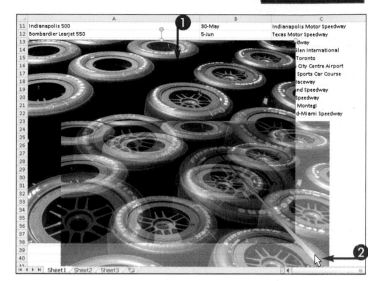

● When you release the mouse button, the object moves to the new location.

Note: *You can also move an object by cutting it from its current location and pasting it in the desired spot. For help, refer to the section "Cut, Copy, and Paste Data" in Chapter 2.*

TIP

How can I wrap text around an object?
If you insert an object into a Word or Publisher file, you can control how text in the file wraps around the object. For example, you may want the text to wrap tightly around a clip art graphic or to make the text appear to overlap an image. To do so, click the object, click the **Text Wrapping** button in the Format tab, and choose a wrap style (●).

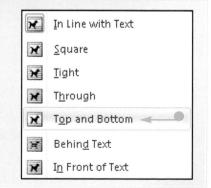

Rotate and Flip Objects

You can rotate and flip objects that you place on your documents, worksheets, slides, or publications to change the appearance of the objects. For example, you might flip a clip art image to face another direction or rotate an arrow object to point elsewhere on the page.

Rotate and Flip Objects

Rotate an Object

1 Click the object that you want to rotate.

● A rotation handle appears on the selected object.

2 Click and drag the handle to rotate the object.

● When you release the mouse, the object rotates.

Note: *You can also use the **Rotate** button (⬜) on the Format tab on the Ribbon to rotate an object 90 degrees left or right.*

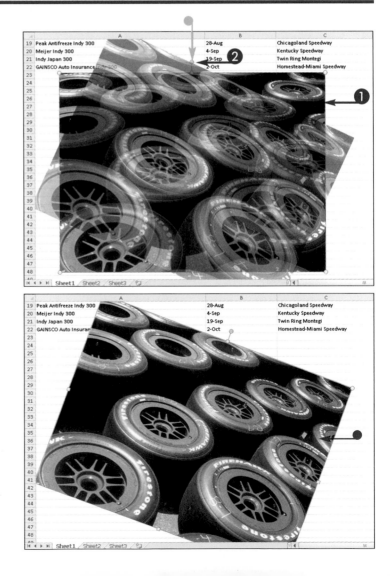

Flip an Object

1 Click the object that you want to flip.

The Format tab opens and displays the Picture tools.

2 Click the **Rotate** button (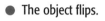) on the Format tab.

3 Click **Flip Vertical** or **Flip Horizontal**.

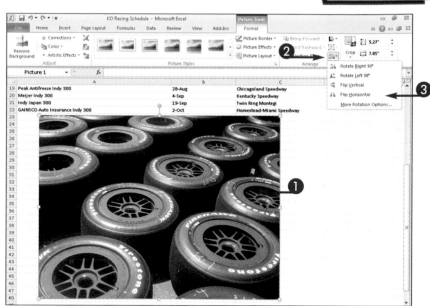

● The object flips.

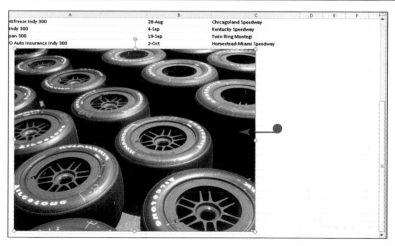

TIPS

How do I rotate text?
The easiest way to rotate text is to first create a WordArt object to rotate. You can learn how to create a WordArt object in the upcoming section "Create a WordArt Object." After you create the WordArt object, you can rotate it using the steps shown in this section. You can also choose from several preset vertical text styles among the WordArt styles.

Is there a way to constrain how much rotation occurs when I drag the rotation handle?
Yes. To constrain the rotation to 15-degree angles, press and hold Shift while rotating the object using the rotation handle. You can also choose to rotate the object in 90-degree increments by clicking the **Rotate** button () on the Format tab and then choosing the **Rotate Right 90°** or **Rotate Left 90°** command.

You can crop a picture that you add to any Office file to create a better fit or to focus on an important area of the image. The Crop tool, located on the Format tab, can help you crop out parts of the image that you do not need. You can also crop clip art pictures.

Crop a Picture

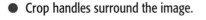

① Click the image that you want to edit.

● The Format tab opens and displays the Picture tools.

② Click the **Crop** button.

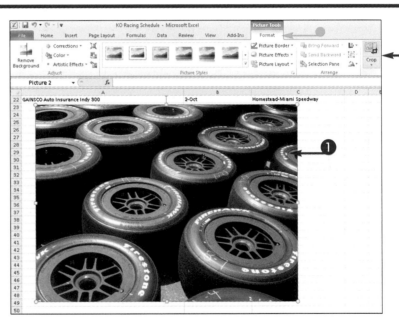

● Crop handles surround the image.

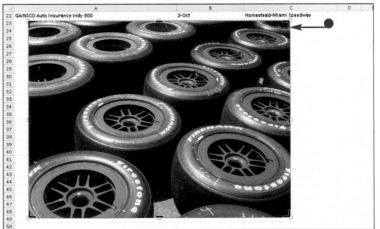

❸ Click and drag a crop handle to crop out an area of the image.

When you release the mouse button, the image is cropped.

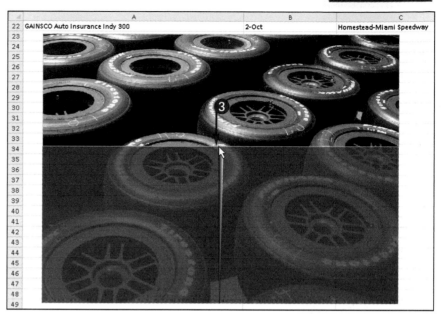

❹ Click outside the image to finalize the crop operation.

Note: See the "Resize and Move Objects" section, earlier in this chapter, to learn how to resize an image.

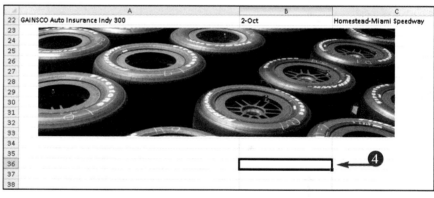

Are there other cropping options?

In addition to cropping your images into square or rectangular shapes, you can use one of any number of predefined shapes, such as an oval, triangle, heart, moon, arrow, and more. To do so, click the down arrow under the Crop button, click **Crop to Shape**, and choose the desired shape from the menu that appears.

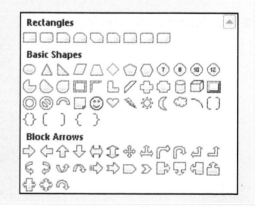

Add a Picture Border

You can quickly add a border to any picture or clip art image using the Office Picture tools. You can choose a border color from among the many theme and standard color selections, or from a palette offering more customized colors. You can also assign a line weight to the border to make thin or thick borders, and apply a dashed border.

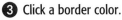

Add a Picture Border

Apply a Border Manually

① Click the picture to which you want to add a border.

The Format tab appears on the Ribbon with the Picture tools shown.

② In the Picture Styles group, click the **Picture Border** button.

③ Click a border color.

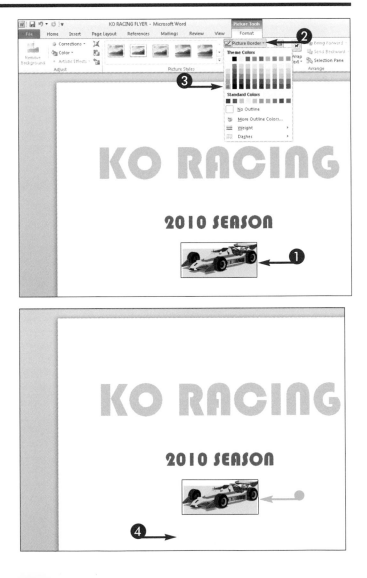

● The border is applied to the picture.

④ Click outside the picture to view the border.

Use a Preset Border

① Click the picture to which you want to add a border.

The Format tab appears on the Ribbon with the Picture tools shown.

② In the Picture Styles group, click the **More** button (▾).

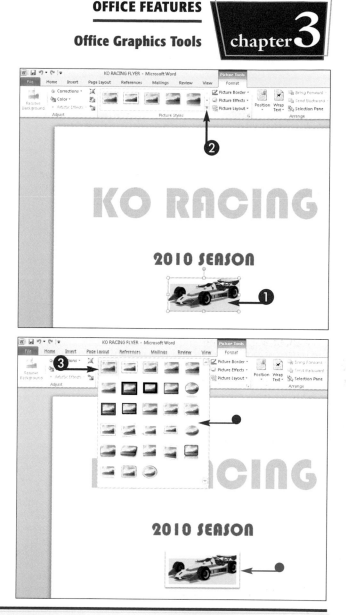

● Office displays various picture styles, including several with preset borders.

③ Click the preset border you want to use.

● The preset border is applied to the picture.

Can I change the border's thickness?
Yes. To change the thickness of a border you have applied, click the image whose border you want to change, click the **Picture Border** button, choose **Weight**, and select a line weight from the Weight submenu that appears. Alternatively, click **More Lines** in the Weight submenu to view additional border options, including settings for dashed borders and more.

Add a Picture Effect

You can use the new Picture Effect tool to assign unique and interesting special effects to your pictures and clip art graphics. For example, you can make the edges of an image seem to glow, or create a mirrored reflection effect. (Note that that the Picture Effects tool is not available in Publisher.)

① Click the picture that you want to edit.

The Format tab appears on the Ribbon with the Picture tools shown.

② In the Picture Styles group, click the **Picture Effects** button.

③ Click an effect category.

④ Click an effect style.

● As you drag over each effect in the menu, the picture displays what the effect looks like when you apply it.

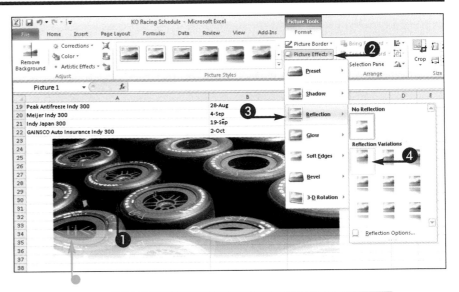

● The new effect is applied to the picture.

Note: To cancel any picture effect, display the Picture Effect menu again and the style that you applied, and then select the **No** option at the top of the category palette to remove the effect.

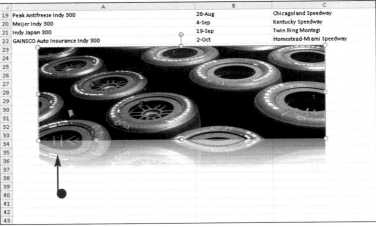

Make Image Corrections

Office 2010 offers tools that enable you to make corrections to clip art and images even after they have been inserted into your file. For example, you can sharpen and soften images, as well as adjust their brightness and contrast.

Make Image Corrections

1 Click the picture that you want to edit.

The Format tab appears on the Ribbon with the Picture tools shown.

2 In the Adjust group, click the **Corrections** button.

● Office highlights the image's current correction settings.

● As you drag over each setting in the menu, the picture displays what the setting looks like when you apply it.

3 Click a correction setting.

● The new setting is applied to the picture.

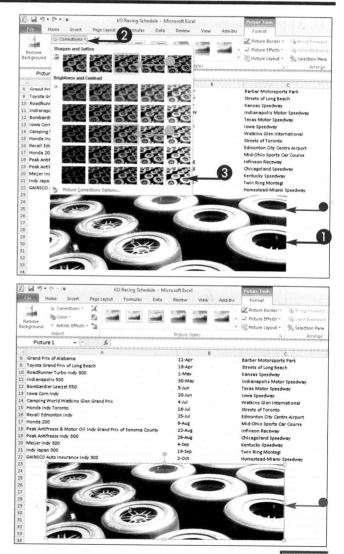

Make Color Adjustments

If you find that the color in an image you insert in an Office 2010 file seems off, you can adjust it using the Office 2010 Color Saturation, Color Tone, or Recolor tool. You can also use these tools to apply artistic effects to an image, such as converting a color image to black and white.

Make Color Adjustments

① Click the picture that you want to edit.

The Format tab appears on the Ribbon with the Picture tools shown.

② In the Adjust group, click the **Color** button.

● Office highlights the image's current color settings.

● As you drag over each setting in the menu, the picture displays what the setting looks like when you apply it.

③ Click a color setting.

● The new setting is applied to the picture.

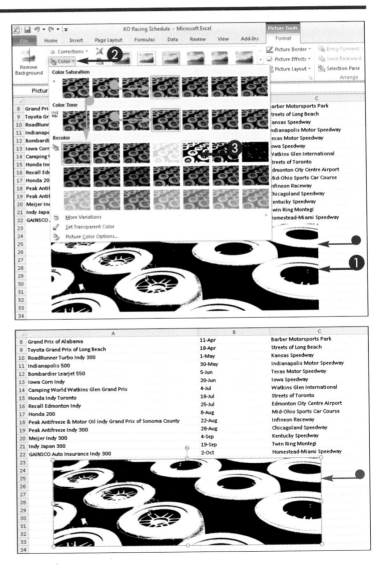

48

Apply Artistic Effects

Office 2010 includes several tools, often called *filters*, for applying artistic effects. For example, you can apply a filter to make an image appear as though it was rendered in marker, pencil, chalk, or paint. Other filters create an effect reminiscent of mosaics, film grain, or glass.

Apply Artistic Effects

① Click the picture that you want to edit.

The Format tab appears on the Ribbon with the Picture tools shown.

② In the Adjust group, click the **Artistic Effects** button.

● Office highlights the image's current effect.

● As you drag over each effect in the menu, the picture displays what the effect looks like when you apply it.

③ Click an artistic effect.

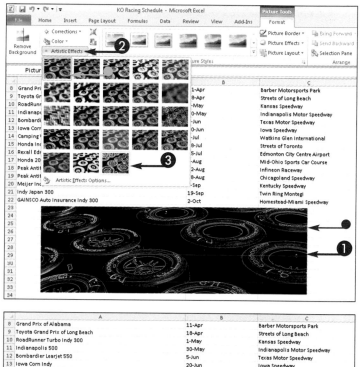

● The new effect is applied to the picture.

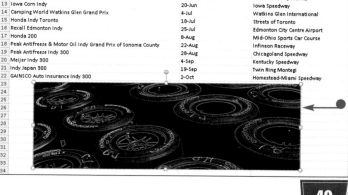

You can use the WordArt feature to turn text into interesting graphic objects to use in your Office files. For example, you can create arched text to appear over a range of data in Excel or vertical text to appear next to a paragraph in Word. You can create text graphics that bend and twist, or display a subtle shading of color.

Create a WordArt Object

① After typing the text you want to convert to a WordArt object, select the text.

② Click the **Insert** tab.

③ In the Text group, click **WordArt**.

④ Click a WordArt option.

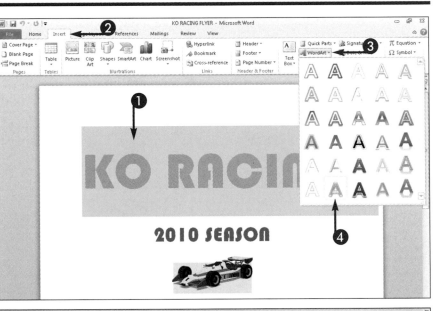

● Office converts the selected text to an object, applies the WordArt option you selected, and opens the Format tab with various Office drawing tools shown.

⑤ Click the **Text Effects** button (🅰).

⑥ Click **Transform**.

⑦ Click a transform style.

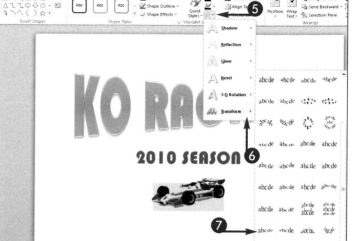

● The WordArt object is transformed.

You can resize or move the image.

Note: *See the section "Resize and Move Objects" to learn more.*

● You can click the **Quick Styles** button to change the text style.

● You can click these buttons to change the text outline color (🅰) and text fill color (🖋).

TIPS

How do I edit my WordArt text?

To edit the WordArt text, simply click the WordArt text box, select the text that you want to change, and type over it. To edit the appearance of the WordArt object, use the WordArt Styles tools, located on the Format menu on the Ribbon.

How do I remove a WordArt object?

To remove the object entirely, click the WordArt text box and then press Delete. Alternatively, click the WordArt text box, click the **Quick Styles** button in the Format tab, and click **Clear Word Art**.

Add SmartArt

You can use the SmartArt feature to create all kinds of diagrams to illustrate concepts and processes. For example, you might insert an organizational diagram in a document to show the hierarchy in your company, or use a cycle diagram to show workflow in your department.

Add SmartArt

1 Click in your file where you want to insert the diagram.

2 Click the **Insert** tab.

3 Click the **SmartArt** button.

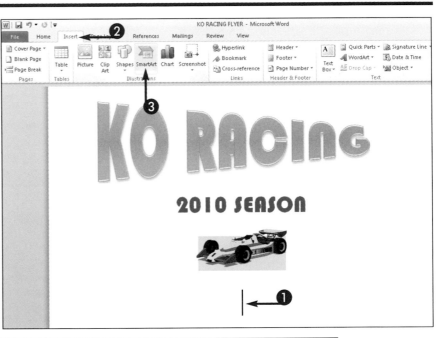

The Choose a SmartArt Graphic dialog box appears.

4 Click a category.

5 Click a chart style.

6 Click **OK**.

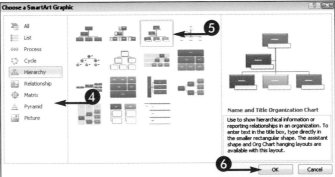

The diagram and placeholder text boxes appear, along with the Text pane.

7 Click in a text box and type the text for the item.

● You can change the layout here.

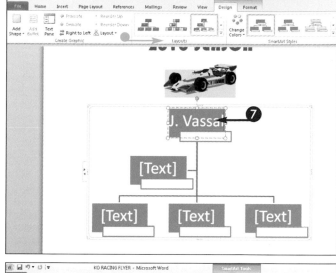

8 Continue typing text in each diagram text box.

● To add another text box and element to the diagram, click the **Add Shape** button.

● To change the shape style, click another shape from the SmartArt Styles group.

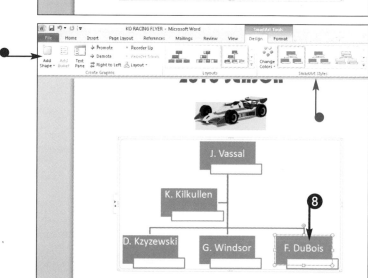

 TIPS

Can I resize my diagram?

Yes. The diagram is an object that you can move and resize just like other objects in the Microsoft Office programs. To move or resize a diagram, see the "Resize and Move Objects" section. You can also use the controls on the Format tab to change the size of the diagram.

Can I change a shape's position or shape in the diagram?

Yes. To change the position, click the shape element in the diagram, and then click the **Promote** or **Demote** button in the Create Graphic group on the Design tab. To change the shape to a new shape, first click the shape to select it; then click the **Format** tab and click the **Change Shape** button in the Shapes group.

You can use Office Live to store and share your Office files. By default, Office Live contains one predefined workspace, called Documents. You can create additional workspaces as needed. For example, you might create a workspace devoted to a particular project. New workspaces can be blank or based on a template. When you create a workspace based on a template, it includes various predefined documents and other items.

Create a New Workspace

① After logging on to Office Live Workspace in your Internet browser, click the **New Workspace** link under My Workspaces.

Note: *For help logging on to Office Live Workspace, see the first tip at the end of this section.*

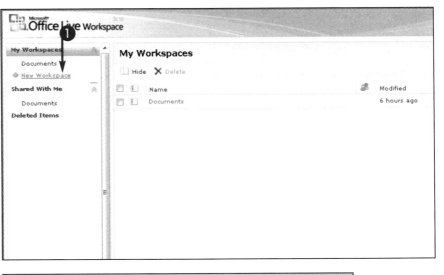

The Create a New Workspace dialog box appears.

② Click the type of workspace you want to create.

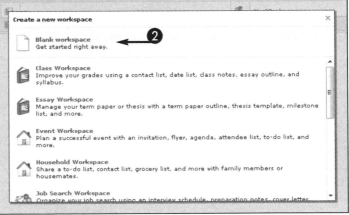

Office Live Workspace creates a new workspace based on the template you chose.

③ Type a name for the new workspace.

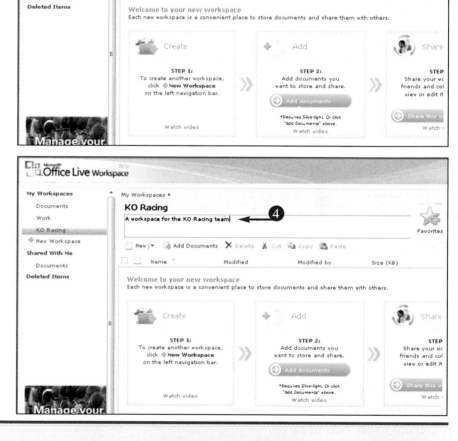

④ Type a description for the new workspace.

How do I log on to Office Live Workspace?

To use Office Live Workspace, you must have a Windows Live account. To create an account, type **home.live.com** in your Web browser's Address bar, click the **Sign Up** link, and enter the requested information. Once you have an account, type **workspace.office.live.com** in your Web browser's Address bar, type your Windows Live ID and password, and click **Sign In**.

What types of workspace templates are available?

Several workspace templates are available — Class, Essay, Event, Household, Job Search, Meeting, Project, School, Sports Team, Study Group, and Travel — each including specific documents and other files. For example, the Household workspace includes an announcement board, an emergency contact list, a grocery list, a household event list, and a household to-do list.

Upload a File to Office Live Workspace

You can upload files on your hard drive to Office Live Workspace. Doing so enables you to access them from any location with an Internet connection, as well as to easily share them with others. You can store as much as 5GB of files on Office Live Workspace.

Upload a File to Office Live Workspace

① Click the workspace in which you want to store the uploaded file.

② Click **Add Documents**.

The Open dialog box appears.

③ Locate and select the file you want to upload.

④ Click **Open**.

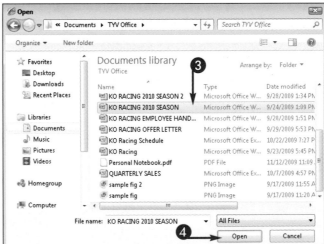

Office Live Workspace uploads the file.

● Office Live Workspace indicates the progress of the upload.

● The uploaded file appears as a clickable link.

Can I upload multiple files at once?

Yes. If you want to upload multiple files to a workspace at once, you can easily do so. Simply click the **Add Documents** button in Office Live Workspace to launch the Open dialog box. There, locate the folder containing the files you want to upload to your workspace; then press `Ctrl` as you click each file you want to include in the upload operation. Once all the desired files are selected, click the **Open** button in the Open dialog box. Office Live Workspace uploads the files.

Create a New File in Office Live Workspace

In addition to uploading files to Office Live Workspace, you can create new Word documents, Excel spreadsheets, and PowerPoint presentations from within a workspace. To do so, you must first install the Office Live Update. (Click the Install Office Live Update button in the Office Live Workspace window to get started.)

Create a New File in Office Live Workspace

① Click the workspace in which you want to create the new file.

② Click **New**.

③ Click the type of file you want to create (in this example, **Word document**).

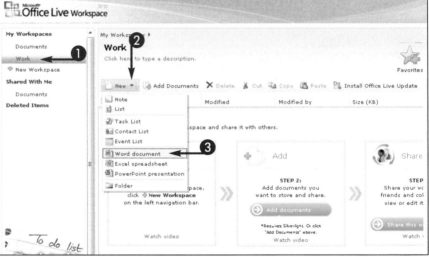

Office Live Workspace creates a new file in the appropriate program.

Note: *You may be warned that the file you have created may be unsafe. Click the **Enable Editing** button to proceed.*

④ Enter your data in the file.

⑤ Click the file's **Close** button (⊠).

Office prompts you to save your changes.

⑥ Click **Save**.

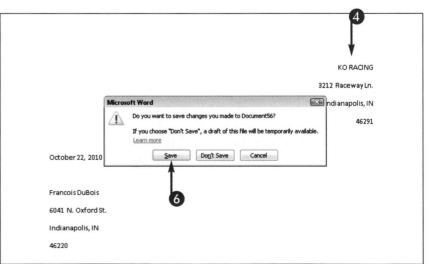

The Save As dialog box appears.

● Your file is saved in your Office Live workspace by default.

⑦ Type a name for your file.

⑧ Click **Save**.

● The file is saved in your Office Live workspace.

What other types of files can I create on Office Live Workspace?

In addition to creating Word documents, Excel spreadsheets, and PowerPoint presentations using Office Live Workspace, you can also create notes and lists (including task lists, contact lists, and event lists). You can also create folders in which to organize your files on Office Live Workspace. To do so, click the **New** button and choose the desired item from the menu that appears.

Is there a faster way to access Office Live Workspace?

Yes. If you use Internet Explorer as your Web browser, you can save any Office Live Workspace as a favorite. Simply click the **Favorites** button in the upper right corner of the Office Live Workspace window and click **Add** in the dialog box that appears. Next time you want to access Office Live Workspace, click the **Favorites** button in the upper left corner of your browser window, click the **Favorites** tab in the pane that appears, and locate and click the **Office Live Workspace** entry.

Edit a File in Office Live Workspace

Suppose you have saved a Word document in an Office Live workspace. You can open that document within Word to edit it. When you save the document, any changes you made to it will be visible in the Office Live workspace. The same is true for Excel and PowerPoint files on an Office Live workspace.

① Click the workspace containing the file you want to edit.

② Click the link for the file to open it.

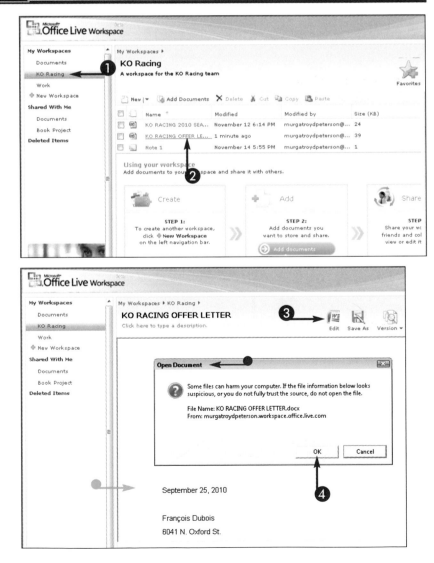

● The file opens in Office Live Workspace.

③ Click the **Edit** button.

● An Open Document dialog box may appear, warning you that you should open the file only if it is from a trusted source.

Note: *Alternatively, you may be warned that the file you have created may be unsafe. Click the* **Enable Editing** *button to proceed.*

④ Click **OK**.

- The file opens in the appropriate Office program (in this example, Microsoft Word).

5 Edit the file as desired.

6 Click the **Save** button () in the Quick Access toolbar.

Note: The Save button in the Quick Access toolbar appears different here because the file you are working on is online.

7 Click the **Close** button (![x]).

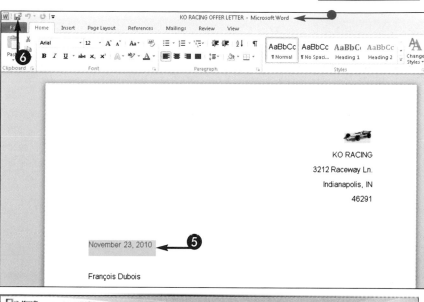

- Your edits appear in the file in your Office Live workspace.

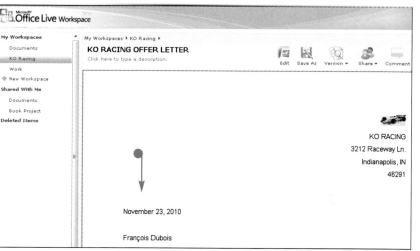

TIPS

How do I view earlier versions of a file?

Office Live Workspace maintains multiple versions of files, creating new versions automatically if more than 12 hours elapse after your last edit or when people with whom you have shared a file make changes to it. To view previous versions of a file, open the file in Office Live Workspace, click the **Version** menu, and click the version you want to view from the list that appears.

What are the Office Live Web apps?

Office Web apps are free, Web-based versions of certain programs in Microsoft Office. They include the Word Web app, the Excel Web app, and the PowerPoint Web app. These free apps are scaled-down versions of the regular Office programs; you access and use them from within your Web browser.

Share a Workspace

After you set up a workspace, you can share it with others. When you do, you can specify what level of permission others may have. Users you designate as Editors can make changes to the document; users you designate as Viewers can only view the document. If you do not want to share an entire workspace, you can share individual files in your Documents workspace instead.

Share an Entire Workspace

① Click the workspace you want to share.

② Click the **Share** button.

Office Live Workspace creates an e-mail invitation.

③ To give someone Editors access, click in the **Editors** field and type his or her e-mail address.

④ To give someone Viewers access, click in the **Viewers** field and type his or her e-mail address.

⑤ Click in the **Message** field and type a message to accompany the invitation.

● Select this check box to enable others to preview your workspace without signing in to Office Live.

● Select this check box to receive a copy of the sharing invitation.

⑥ Click the **Send** button.

Office Live Workspace sends the sharing invitation.

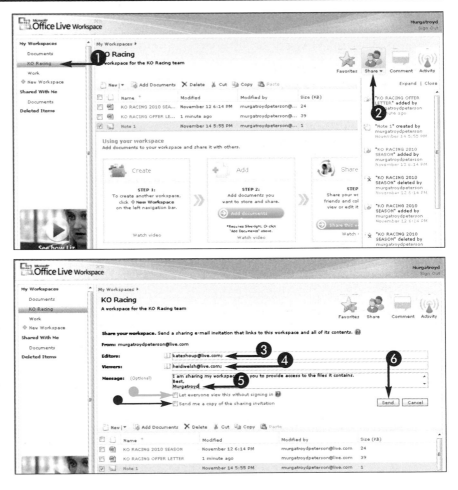

Share a File

1. Click the Documents workspace.

2. Select the check box next to the file you want to share.

3. Click **Share**.

4. Click **Share Document**.

   Office Live Workspace creates an e-mail invitation.

5. To give someone Editors access, click in the **Editors** field and type his or her e-mail address.

6. To give someone Viewers access, click in the **Viewers** field and type his or her e-mail address.

7. Click in the **Message** field and type a message to accompany the invitation.

● Select this check box to enable others to preview your workspace without signing in to Office Live.

● Select this check box to receive a copy of the sharing invitation.

8. Click the **Send** button.

   Office Live Workspace sends the sharing invitation.

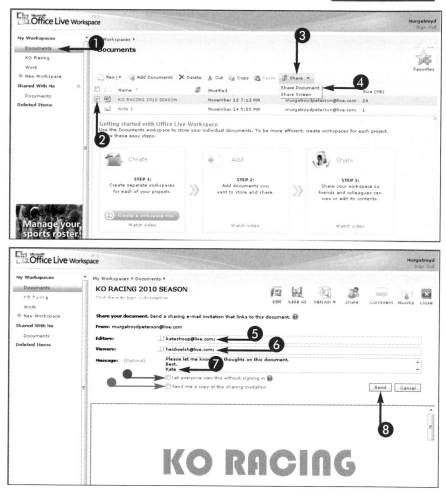

TIPS

How do I change sharing settings?

When you share a workspace with others, a sharing icon (🖾) appears. When the workspace is open in Office Live Workspace, a View Sharing Details link is also shown. Click this link to view users with whom this site is shared and the sharing permissions associated with each user. To share with more users, click the **Share with More** button; to stop sharing, click the **Stop Sharing** button.

What does the Comment feature do?

Clicking the **Comment** button opens a Comments pane. Here, you can type comments, which are visible to anyone who has access to the workspace. To add a comment, simply type your comment text and click **Add Comment**. To close the Comment pane, click the **Close** link.

View Shared Workspaces

Just as you can use Office Live Workspace to share workspaces with other users, others can use the site to share workspaces with you. Shared workspaces appear under Shared With Me in the Office Live Workspace Navigation pane. Depending on what permissions you have been granted, you may be able to simply view files in a shared workspace or you may be able to edit them.

View Shared Workspaces

❶ Under Shared With Me in the Navigation pane, click the shared workspace you want to view.

● Files in the shared workspace appear.

❷ Click a file to view it.

● The file opens in the Office Live Workspace window.

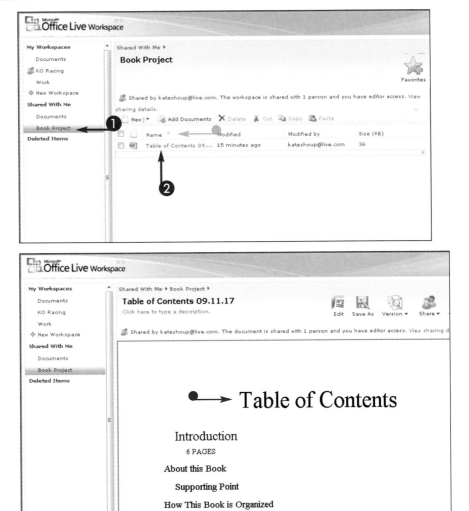

You can delete files you no longer need from Office Live Workspace. Deleted files are moved to the Deleted Items folder. To restore a file deleted in error, click the Deleted Items folder in the Navigation pane, select the check box next to the file, and then click the Restore button. To permanently remove files in the Deleted Items folder from Office Live Workspace, open the Deleted Items folder and click Empty All Items.

Delete a File from Office Live Workspace

1 Click the workspace containing the file you want to delete.

2 Select the check box next to the file you want to delete.

3 Click **Delete**.

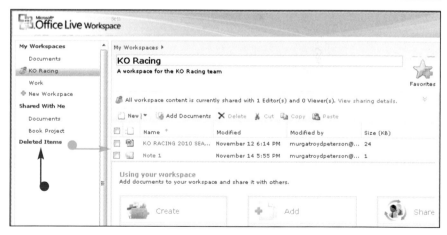

● Office Live Workspace deletes the file.

● The file is moved to the Deleted Items folder.

Word

You can use Word to tackle any project involving text, such as correspondence, reports, and more. Word's versatile formatting features enable you to enhance your text documents with ease and add elements such as tables or headers and footers. Word offers a variety of editing tools to help you make your document look its best. In this part, you learn how to build and format Word documents and tap into Word's many tools to preview, proofread, and print your documents.

Change Word's Views

Word offers you several ways to view your document. For example, the Zoom tool enables you to control the magnification of your document. You can also choose from five different layout views: Print Layout, which displays margins, headers, and footers; Outline, which shows the document's outline levels; Web Layout, which displays a Web page preview of your document; Full Screen Reading, which optimizes your document for easier reading; and Draft, which shows a draft version of your document.

Use the Zoom Tool

① Drag the **Zoom** slider on the Zoom bar.

● You can also click a magnification button to zoom in or out.

● Word applies the magnification to the document.

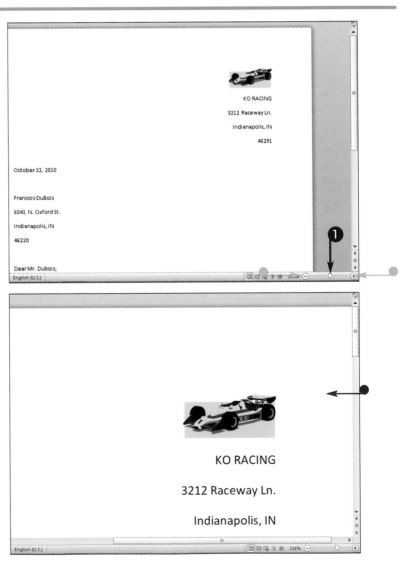

Switch Layout Views

1 Click the **View** tab on the Ribbon.

2 Click a layout view button.

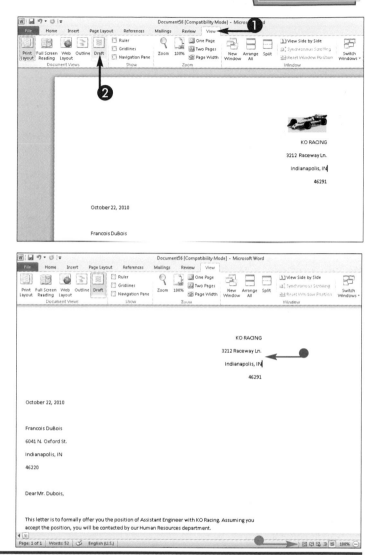

Word immediately displays the new view.

● In this example, Draft view displays the text without graphics or other elements.

● You can also switch views using the View buttons at the bottom of the program window.

TIPS

How do I move through a Word document?

You can use the scroll bars to move up and down a document page, or you can use the keyboard keys. For example, you can press the arrow keys to move up, down, left, and right in the document, or you can press Page Up and Page Down keys to move up and down in the document.

What can I do in the Outline view?

If you create documents built on a structure that incorporates headings, subheadings, and body text, you can use the Outline view to see and make changes to the document structure. When you activate the Outline view, the Outlining tab appears. You can use the buttons on the tab to change heading styles and levels to modify your document's structure.

When you launch Microsoft Word, a blank document appears, ready for you to start typing text. Whether you want to write a letter, a memo, or a report, you can use Word to quickly type and edit text for your project.

Type and Edit Text

Type Text

1 Start typing your text.

● Word automatically wraps the text to the next line for you.

● The insertion point, or cursor, marks the current location where text appears when you start typing.

1 → To enter text, just start typing. Don't worry about what to do when you reach the end of the line. Word automatically wraps the text for you. ◄─●

2 Press **Enter** to start a new paragraph.

● You can press **Enter** twice to add an extra space between paragraphs.

● You can press **Tab** to quickly create an indent for a line of text.

To enter text, just start typing. Don't worry about what to do when you reach the end of the line. Word automatically wraps the text for you.

2 → You can press Enter to start a new line.

● → Or you can press Enter twice to add more space between paragraphs.

● → You can press the Tab key to quickly create an indent.

Edit Text

1 Click in the document where you want to fix a mistake.

2 Press **Backspace** to delete characters to the left of the cursor.

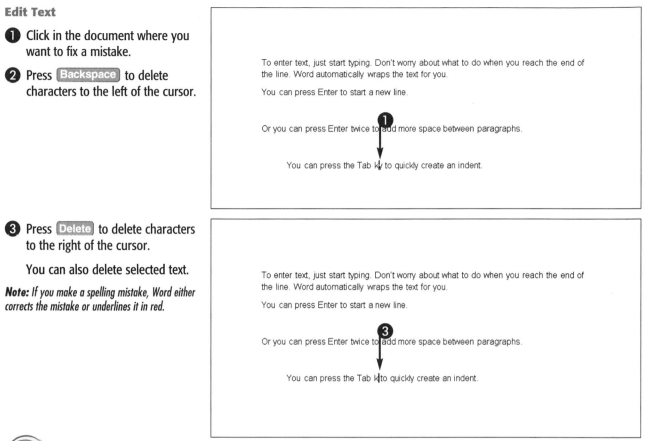

To enter text, just start typing. Don't worry about what to do when you reach the end of the line. Word automatically wraps the text for you.

You can press Enter to start a new line.

Or you can press Enter to add more space between paragraphs.

You can press the Tab key to quickly create an indent.

3 Press **Delete** to delete characters to the right of the cursor.

You can also delete selected text.

***Note:** If you make a spelling mistake, Word either corrects the mistake or underlines it in red.*

To enter text, just start typing. Don't worry about what to do when you reach the end of the line. Word automatically wraps the text for you.

You can press Enter to start a new line.

Or you can press Enter twice to add more space between paragraphs.

You can press the Tab key to quickly create an indent.

TIPS

How do I add lines to my Word documents?

If you type three or more special characters on a new line and press **Enter**, Word replaces the characters with a line of a particular style. For example, if you type three asterisks and press **Enter**, Word displays a dotted line. Use this table for more line styles that you can add:

Character	Line Style
*	Dotted line
=	Double line
~	Wavy line
#	Thick decorative line
_	Thick single line

What is the difference between Insert and Overtype mode?

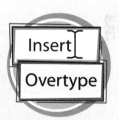

By default, Word is set to Insert mode. That is, when you insert the cursor and start typing, any existing text moves over to accommodate the new text. If you switch to Overtype mode, the new text overwrites the existing text. To toggle between these modes, simply press **Insert**. First, though, you must set up Word to allow this. To do so, click the **File** tab, click **Options**, and click the **Advanced** tab in the window that appears. Under Editing Options, select the **Use the Insert key to control Overtype mode** check box; then click **OK**.

Insert
Quick Parts

Quick Parts are preformatted content that you can add to your documents. Word comes with a wide variety of preset phrases that you can use, or you can create your own. You might use Quick Parts if, for example, you repeatedly type the same company name in your documents; you can add the name to Word's list of Quick Parts entries and select it from the list as needed.

Insert Quick Parts

Add a Quick Parts Entry

1 Select the text that you want to add to the Quick Parts Gallery.

2 Click the **Insert** tab on the Ribbon.

3 Click the **Quick Parts** button.

4 Click **Save Selection to Quick Part Gallery**.

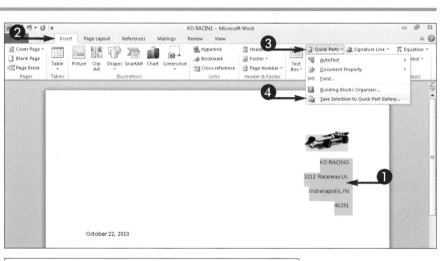

The Create New Building Block dialog box appears.

5 Type a name for the entry, or use the default name.

● You can also assign a gallery, a category, and a description for the entry.

6 Click **OK**.

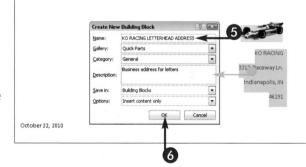

Insert a Quick Part Entry

1. Click in the text where you want to insert a Quick Part.

2. Click the **Insert** tab on the Ribbon.

3. Click the **Quick Parts** button.

4. Click the entry that you want to insert.

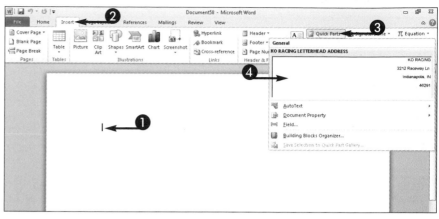

● Word inserts the entry into the document.

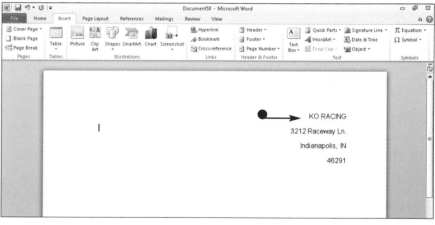

Where can I find Word's preset Quick Parts?

The Building Blocks Organizer keeps a full list of entries, including watermarks, pull quotes, and more. To display this dialog box, click the **Quick Parts** button on the Insert tab, and then click **Building Blocks Organizer**. Building Blocks, including Quick Parts, are organized into galleries and categories. To insert an entry in the dialog box into your text, simply click it in the Organizer and click the **Insert** button.

How do I remove a Quick Parts entry?

You can remove a Quick Parts entry that you no longer need. To do so, open the Building Blocks Organizer (click the **Insert** tab, click **Quick Parts**, and then click **Building Blocks Organizer**). Next, scroll through the list and select the entry that you want to remove. Click **Delete** to remove the entry, and then click **Yes** to close the confirmation dialog box that appears.

Insert Symbols

From time to time, you might need to insert a special symbol or character into your Word document, such as a trademark symbol or an em-dash character. You can use the Symbol palette to access a wide range of special characters and symbols, including mathematical and Greek symbols, architectural symbols, and more. For yet more symbols, open the Symbol dialog box.

1 Click where you want to insert a symbol.

2 Click the **Insert** tab.

3 Click the **Symbol** button.

4 If the symbol you want to insert appears in the Symbol palette, click it. Otherwise, click **More Symbols**.

The Symbol dialog box appears.

⑤ Click the character that you want to insert.

Note: You can click the **Font** ▼ and click another font to change which symbols appear in the Symbols tab. For example, the Wingdings font includes a library of character icons, such as clocks and smiley faces, whereas the Symbols font lists basic symbols.

⑥ Click **Insert**.

● Word adds the character to the current cursor location in the document.

The dialog box remains open so that you can add more characters to your text.

⑦ When finished, click **Close**.

TIP

How do I add a special character?
To add a special character, such as an em dash, a copyright symbol, an ellipsis, or similar characters, open the Symbol dialog box and click the **Special Characters** tab. Locate and click the character you want to add, and then click **Insert**. Click **Close** to close the dialog box.

Create a Blog Post

If you keep an online blog, you can use Word to create a document to post on it. This enables you to take advantage of Word's many proofing and formatting tools. To post your blog entry, you must first set up Word to communicate with the Internet server that hosts your online blog; you are prompted to facilitate this communication the first time you post a blog entry from Word.

Create a Blog Post

Note: You must be connected to the Internet to complete this section.

1. Click the **File** tab.

2. Click **New**.

3. Click **Blog post**.

4. Click **Create**.

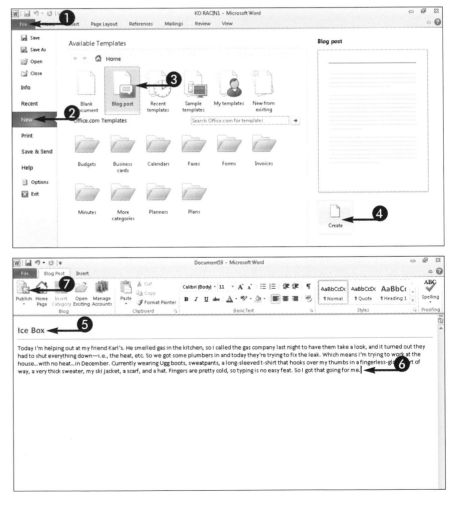

Word opens the blog post document.

Note: The first time you use the blog feature, Word prompts you to register your blog account. Click **Register Now**, choose your blog provider in the dialog box that appears, and follow the on-screen prompts.

5. Click in the title area and type a title for your post.

6. Click in the body of the post and type your blog entry.

7. When you are ready to post your blog, click the **Publish** button.

Word connects to the server that hosts your online blog.

8 Type the user name you have set up with your blog host.

9 Type your blog password.

10 Click **OK**.

● Word posts your blog entry online.

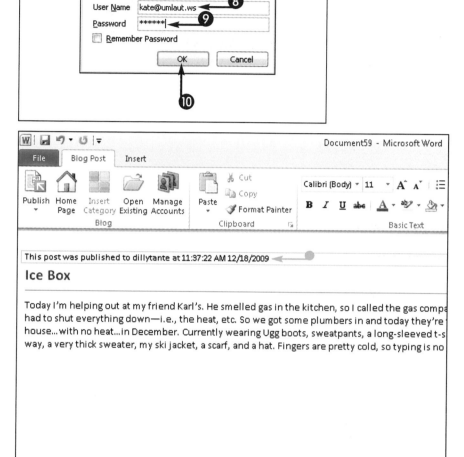

Can I edit my blog accounts from within Word?

Yes. You can click the **Manage Accounts** button on the Blog Post tab when viewing a blog page in Word. This opens the Blog Accounts dialog box where you can edit an existing account, add a new account, or delete an account that you no longer use.

Can I turn an existing Word document into a blog post?

Yes. If you create a text document first and then decide to use it as your blog post document, you can easily turn it into a blog page for publishing on the Web. To do so, click the **File** tab, click **Share**, click **Publish as Blog Post**, and then click **Publish as Blog Post** again. Word immediately turns it into a blog file, and you can publish it to your online blog account.

Change the Font, Size, and Color

By default, Word 2010 applies an 11-point Calibri font to every new document that you create. You can change the text font, size, and color to alter the appearance of text in a document. For example, you might change the text font, size, and color of the title of your document to emphasize it.

Change the Font

1. Select the text that you want to format.

2. Click the **Home** tab on the Ribbon.

3. Click the **Font** ⏷.

4. Click a font.

Note: With Word's Live Preview feature on, you can immediately preview any font in the list by positioning your mouse pointer over it in the Font list.

● Word applies the font to the text.

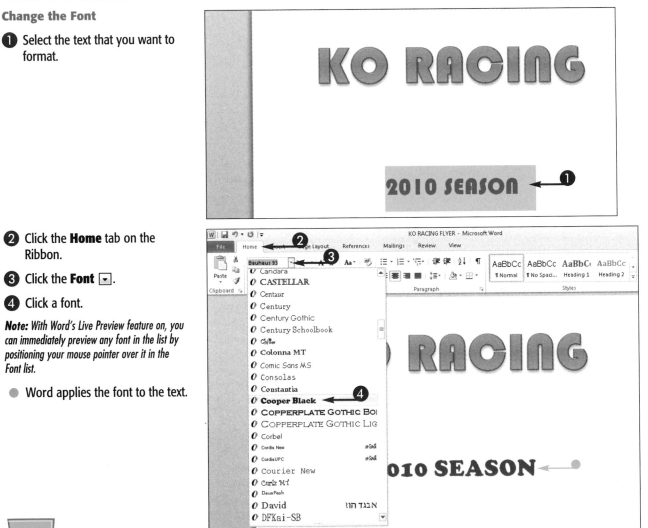

Change the Size

① Select the text that you want to format.

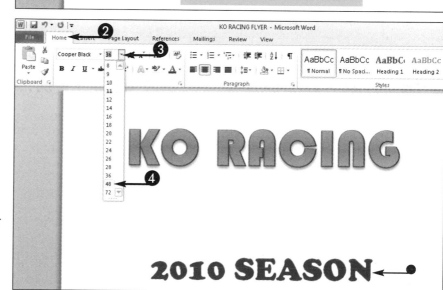

② Click the **Home** tab on the Ribbon.

③ Click the **Font Size** ▾.

④ Click a size.

● Word applies the font size to the text.

This example applies a 36-point font size to the text.

*Note: Another way to change the font size is to click the **Grow Font** and **Shrink Font** buttons (A⌃ and A⌄) on the Home tab. Word increases or decreases the font size with each click of the button.*

 TIPS

How do I apply formatting to my text?

You can use Word's basic formatting commands — Bold, Italic, Underline, Strikethrough, Subscript, and Superscript — to quickly add formatting to your text. To do so, select the text you want to format, click the **Home** tab, and click the **Bold** (**B**), **Italic** (*I*), **Underline** (U̲), **Strikethrough** (a̶b̶c̶), **Subscript** (x₂), or **Superscript** (x²) button. To undo the formatting, simply select the text and click the appropriate button again.

What is the toolbar that appears when I select text?

When you select text, Word's mini toolbar appears, giving you quick access to common formatting commands. You can also right-click selected text to display the toolbar. If you want to use any of the tools on the toolbar, simply click the desired tool; otherwise, continue working, and the toolbar disappears.

Changing the text color can go a long way toward emphasizing it on the page. For example, if you are creating an invitation, you might make the description of the event a different color to stand out from the other details. Obviously, when selecting text colors, you should avoid choosing colors that make your text difficult to read.

Change the Font, Size, and Color *(continued)*

Change the Color

1 Select the text that you want to format.

2 Click the **Home** tab on the Ribbon.

3 Click the ▾ next to the **Font Color** button (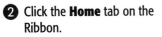).

4 Click a color.

● Word applies the color to the text.

This example applies a gold color to the text.

Use the Font Dialog Box

1 Select the text that you want to format.

2 Click the **Home** tab on the Ribbon.

3 Click the corner group button (⬒) in the Font group.

The Font dialog box appears.

4 Click the font, style, size, color, underline style, or effect that you want to apply.

5 Click **OK**.

● Word applies the font change.

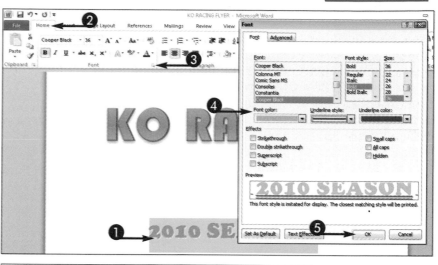

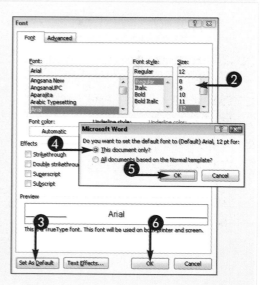

TIP

Can I change the default font and size that Word always applies to new documents?

Yes. To change the default font and size, follow these steps:

1 Display the Font dialog box.

2 Click the font and font size that you want to set as defaults.

3 Click **Set As Default**.

4 Specify whether the change should apply to this document only or to all documents created with the current template.

5 Click **OK**.

6 Click **OK**.

The next time you create a new document, Word applies the default font and size that you specified.

Align Text

You can use Word's alignment commands to change how text is positioned horizontally on a page. By default, Word assigns the Left Align command. You can also choose to center your text on a page, align it to the right side of the page, or justify it so that it lines up at both the left and right margins of the page.

① Select the text that you want to format.

② Click the **Home** tab on the Ribbon.

③ Click an alignment button.

  Click the **Align Left** button (▤) to left-align text.

  Click the **Center** button (▤) to center text.

  Click the **Align Right** button (▤) to right-align text.

  Click the **Justify** button (▤) to justify text between the left and right margins.

● Word applies the alignment to the text.

  This example centers the text on the document page.

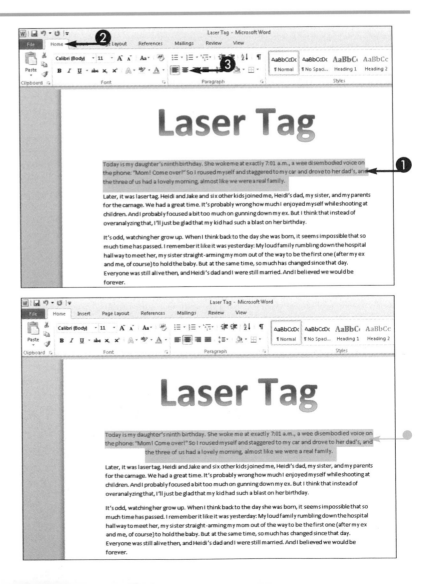

Set Line Spacing

You can adjust the amount of spacing that appears between lines of text in your paragraphs. For example, you may need to set 2.5 spacing to allow for handwritten edits in your printed document, or set 1.5 spacing to make the paragraphs easier to read. By default, Word assigns 1.15 spacing for all new documents that you create.

Set Line Spacing

1 Select the text that you want to format.

2 Click the **Home** tab on the Ribbon.

3 Click the **Line Spacing** button (📇).

4 Click a line spacing option.

● Word immediately applies the new spacing.

This example applies 2.0 line spacing.

5 To control the spacing that surrounds a paragraph, click the corner group button (◻) in the Paragraph group.

The Paragraph dialog box opens.

6 Use the **Before** spin box to specify how much space should appear before the paragraph.

7 Use the **After** spin box to specify how much space should appear after the paragraph.

8 Click **OK**.

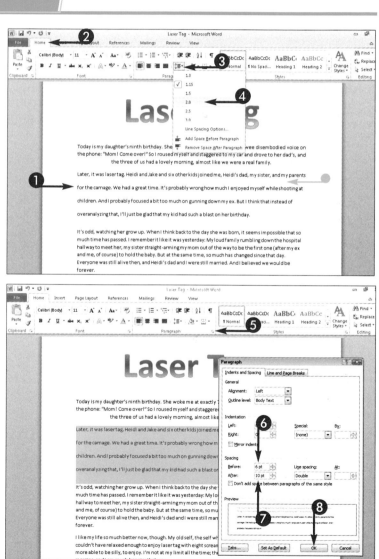

Indent Text

You can use indents as another way to control the horizontal positioning of text in a document. Indents are simply margins that affect individual lines or paragraphs. You might use an indent to distinguish a particular paragraph on a page — for example, a long quote.

Set Quick Indents

1 Click anywhere in the paragraph you want to indent.

2 Click the **Home** tab on the Ribbon.

3 Click an indent button.

You can click the **Decrease Indent** button (📑) to decrease the indentation.

You can click the **Increase Indent** button (📑) to increase the indentation.

● Word applies the indent change.

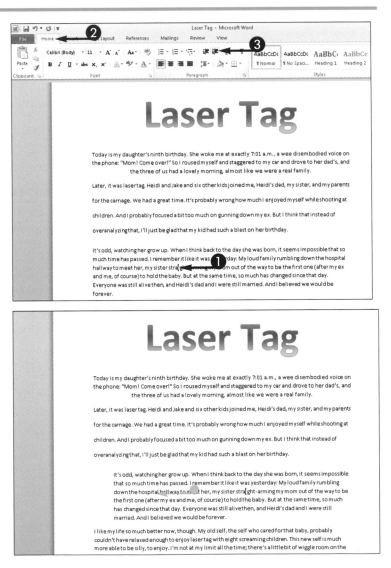

Set Precise Indents

① Click anywhere in the paragraph you want to indent.

② Click the **Home** tab on the Ribbon.

③ Click the corner group button (▣) in the Paragraph group.

The Paragraph dialog box appears.

④ Type a specific indentation in the **Left** or **Right** indent text boxes.

● You can also click ⬧ to set an indent measurement.

● To set a specific kind of indent, you can click the **Special** ⬧ and then click an indent.

● The Preview area shows a sample of the indent.

⑤ Click **OK**.

Word applies the indent to the text.

What is the difference between an indent and a tab?

You use tabs to create columnar text across a page, whereas indents control where a paragraph or line of text starts in relation to the margins. However, you can press `Tab` to quickly create an indent for a line of text or for the first line of a paragraph. By default, pressing `Tab` indents the text by 0.5 inches.

Can I set indents using the Word ruler?

Yes. You can drag the indent marker (▣) on the ruler bar to quickly set an indent. If the ruler is not shown, position your mouse pointer over the top of the work area and pause. The ruler opens and displays markers for changing the left indent, right indent, first-line indent, and hanging indent. You can position your mouse pointer over each marker to identify the correct one.

Set Tabs

You can use tabs to create vertically aligned columns of text in your Word document. By default, Word creates tab stops every 0.5 inches across the page, and left-aligns the text on each tab stop. You can set your own tab stops using the ruler or the Tabs dialog box. You can also change the tab alignment and specify an exact measurement between tab stops.

Set Tabs

Set Quick Tabs

1. Position your mouse pointer over the top edge of the work area and pause to display the ruler.

● You can also click the **View** tab and click **Ruler** to turn on the ruler.

2. Click the **Tab marker** area to cycle through to the type of tab marker that you want to set.

   ⌊ sets a left-aligned tab.

   ⌐ sets a center-aligned tab.

   ⌐ sets a right-aligned tab.

   ⌐ sets a decimal tab (for lining up columns of numbers on decimal points).

   ⌐ sets a bar tab (for setting a vertical bar between columns).

3. Click in the ruler where you want to insert the tab.

4. Click at the end of the text after which you want to add a tab.

5. Press `Tab`.

6. Type the text that should appear in the next column.

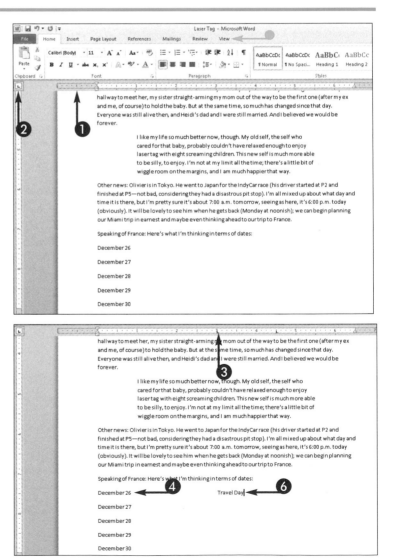

Set Precise Tabs

① Click the **Home** tab on the Ribbon.

② Click the corner group button (▫) in the Paragraph group.

The Paragraph dialog box appears.

③ Click **Tabs** on the Indents and Spacing tab.

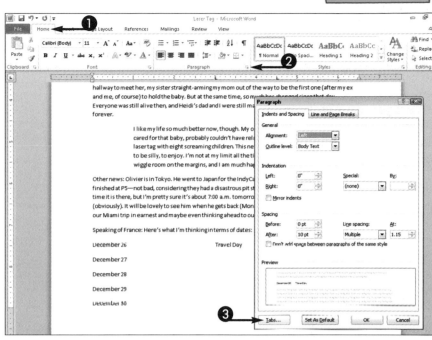

The Tabs dialog box appears.

④ Click in the **Tab stop position** text box and type a new tab stop measurement.

⑤ Click to select a tab alignment.

● You can also select a tab leader character.

⑥ Click **Set**.

Word saves the new tab stop.

⑦ Click **OK**.

Word exits the dialog box, and you can use the new tab stops.

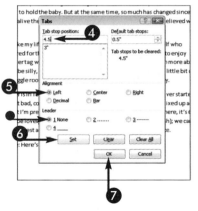

 TIPS

How do I remove tab stops that I no longer need?

To remove a tab stop from the ruler, simply drag the tab stop off of the ruler. To remove a tab stop in the Tabs dialog box, you can select it, and then click **Clear**. To clear every tab stop that you saved in the Tabs dialog box, click **Clear All**.

What are leader tabs?

You can use leader tabs to separate tab columns with dots, dashes, or lines. Leader tabs can help readers follow the information across tab columns. You can set leader tabs using the Tabs dialog box, as shown in this section.

You can control the margins of your document pages. By default, Word assigns a 1-inch margin all the way around the page in every new document that you create. You can set wider margins to fit more text on a page, or set smaller margins to fit less text on a page.

Set Margins

Set Margins Using Page Layout Tools

1. Click the **Page Layout** tab on the Ribbon.

2. Click the **Margins** button.

3. Click a margin setting.

● Word applies the new settings.

Set a Custom Margin

1 Click the **Page Layout** tab on the Ribbon.

2 Click the **Margins** button.

3 Click **Custom Margins**.

The Page Setup dialog box opens, with the Margins tab shown.

4 Type a specific margin in the **Top**, **Bottom**, **Left**, and **Right** boxes.

● You can also click 🔼 to set a margin measurement.

5 Choose a page orientation.

6 Preview the margin settings in the Preview section.

7 Click the **Apply To** 🔽 and specify whether the margin should apply to the whole document or from this point in the document forward.

8 Click **OK**.

Word immediately adjusts the margin in the document.

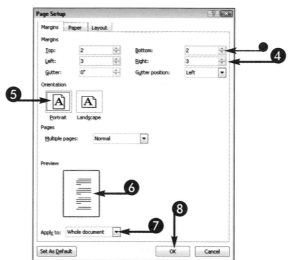

 TIPS

How do I set new default margins for all of my Word documents?

If your company or organization consistently uses the same margins, you can choose those settings as the default for every new document that you open in Word. To do so, make the desired changes to the Margins tab of the Page Setup dialog box, and then click **Set As Default**.

I set new margins, but my printer did not follow them. Why not?

Use caution when setting margins that are too wide. Some printers have a minimum margin in which nothing can be printed. For example, with many printers, anything less than 0.25 inches is outside the printable area. Be sure to test the margins, or check your printer documentation for more information.

Create Lists

You can set off lists of information in your documents by using bullets or numbers. A bulleted list adds dots in front of each list item, whereas a numbered list adds sequential numbers in front of each list item. Bulleted and numbered lists can help you keep your information better organized.

Create Lists

Set Quick Lists

1 Select the text that you want to format.

2 Click the **Home** tab on the Ribbon.

3 Click a list button.

You can click the **Bullets** button (▤) to create a bulleted list.

You can click the **Numbering** button (▤) to create a numbered list.

You can click the **Multilevel List** button (▤) to create a multi-level list.

Word applies the formatting to the list.

● This example shows a bulleted list.

To add more text to the list, you can click at the end of the line and press **Enter**; Word immediately starts a new line in the list with a bullet or number.

● To turn off a bulleted or numbered list, you can press **Enter** twice after the last item in the list, or click the **Bullets** (▤), **Numbering** (▤), or **Multilevel List** (▤) button.

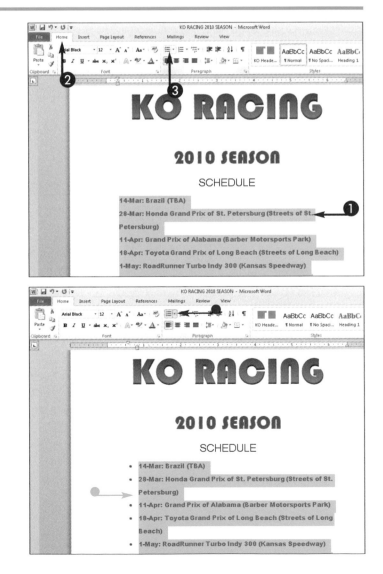

Change Bullet or Number Styles

① Select the text that you want to format.

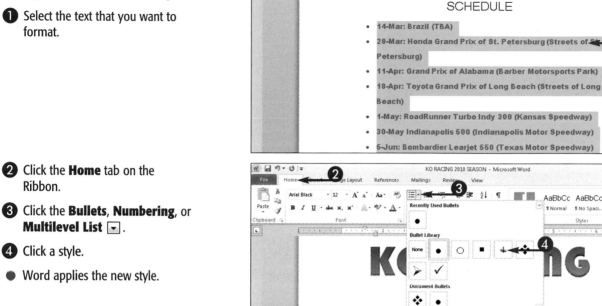

② Click the **Home** tab on the Ribbon.

③ Click the **Bullets**, **Numbering**, or **Multilevel List** ▾.

④ Click a style.

● Word applies the new style.

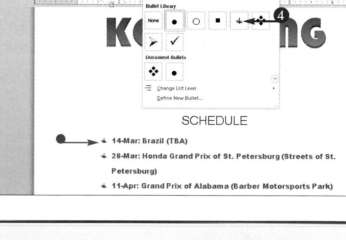

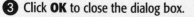

TIP

Can I customize a style?

Yes. You can create a customized style or control the positioning of bullets and numbers. Follow these steps:

① Click the **Bullets** or **Numbering** ▾ and then click **Define New Bullet** or **Define New Number Format**.

The Define New Bullet or Define New Number Format dialog box appears.

② Set any options for the format and position of the bullets or numbers.

③ Click **OK** to close the dialog box.

Word applies the customized style.

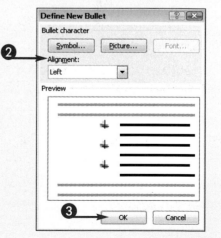

Copy Formatting

Suppose you have applied a variety of formatting options to a paragraph to create a certain look. If you want to re-create the same look elsewhere in the document, you do not have to repeat the same steps as when you applied the original formatting. Instead, you can use Word's Format Painter feature to "paint" the formatting to the other text in one swift action.

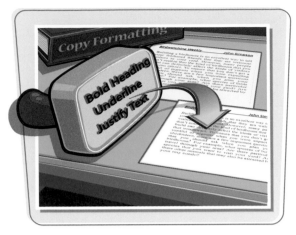

Copy Formatting

① Select the text that contains the formatting that you want to copy.

② Click the **Home** tab on the Ribbon.

③ Click the **Format Painter** button (🖌).

④ Click and drag over the text to which you want to apply the same formatting.

● Word immediately copies the formatting to the new text.

● To copy the same formatting multiple times, you can double-click the **Format Painter** button (🖌).

You can press Esc to cancel the Format Painter feature at any time.

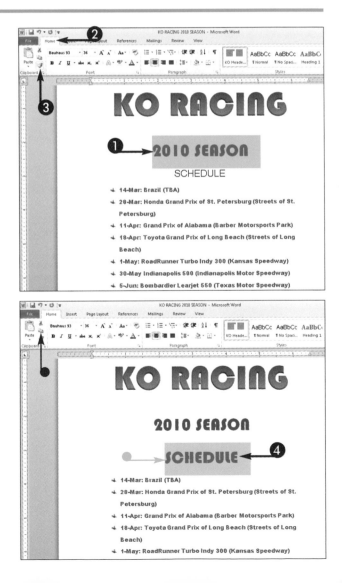

Clear Formatting

You can use Word's Clear Formatting command to remove any formatting applied to the document text. When you apply the Clear Formatting command, Word removes any formatting applied to the text, and restores the default settings.

Clear Formatting

① Select the text containing the formatting that you want to remove.

② Click the **Home** tab on the Ribbon.

③ Click the **Clear Formatting** button ().

● Word immediately removes the formatting and restores the default settings.

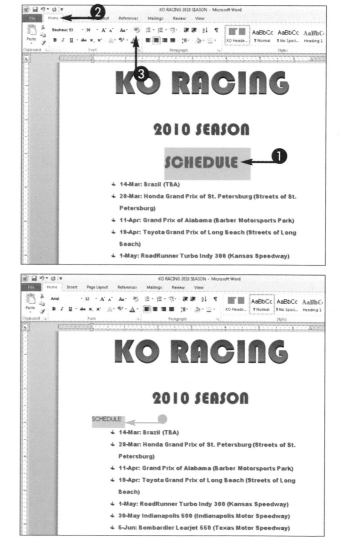

Format with Styles

Suppose a corporate report requires specific formatting for every heading. Instead of assigning multiple formatting settings over and over again, you can create a style with the required formatting settings and apply it whenever you need it. In addition to creating your own styles, you can apply any of Word's preset styles.

Create a New Quick Style

1 Format the text as desired and then select the text.

2 Click the **Home** tab on the Ribbon.

3 Click the **More** button (⧉) in the Styles group.

4 Click **Save Selection as a New Quick Style**.

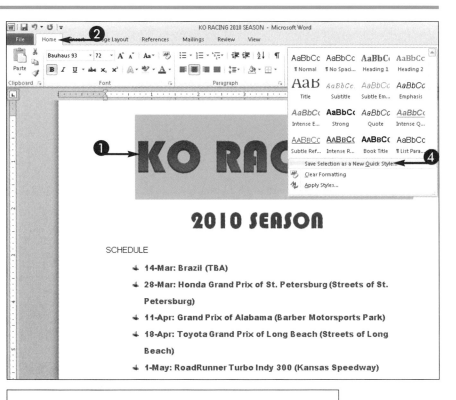

The Create New Style from Formatting dialog box appears.

5 Type a name for the style.

6 Click **OK**.

Word adds the style to the list of Quick Styles.

Apply a Quick Style

1 Select the text that you want to format.

2 Click the **Home** tab on the Ribbon.

3 Click a style from the Styles list.

● You can click the **More** button (⊡) to see the full palette of available styles.

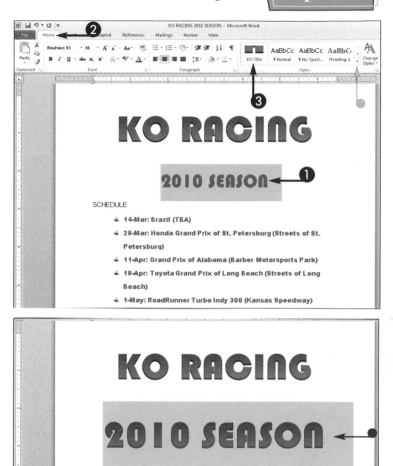

● Word applies the style.

How do I remove a style that I no longer need?

From the Home tab, display the full Quick Styles palette, right-click the style that you want to remove, and click the **Remove from Quick Style Gallery** command. Word immediately removes the style from the Quick Styles list.

How do I customize an existing style?

Apply a style to your text and then leave the text selected. Click the **Change Styles** button on the Home tab, and then click the type of change that you want to make in the menu that appears. For example, if you want to switch fonts, click the **Fonts** option and then select another font. If you want to change style colors, click the **Colors** option and then select another color set.

Apply a Template

A *template* is a special file that stores styles and other Word formatting tools. When you apply a template to a Word document, the styles and tools in that template become available for your use. Alternatively, you can attach a template to an existing document, as outlined here.

① With the document to which you want to apply a template open in Word, click the **File** tab.

② Click **Options**.

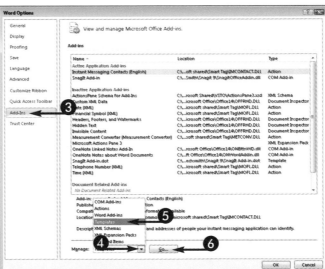

The Word Options window opens.

③ Click **Add-Ins**.

④ Click the **Manage** ▾.

⑤ Click **Templates**.

⑥ Click **Go**.

The Templates and Add-ins dialog box opens.

⑦ Click to select the **Automatically update document styles** check box.

⑧ Click **Attach**.

The Attach Template dialog box opens.

⑨ Locate and select the template you want to apply.

⑩ Click **Open**.

Word applies the template.

● The styles used in the document are updated to reflect those appearing in the template.

TIP

Can I create my own templates?
Yes. The easiest way to create a template is to base it on an existing Word document. With the document on which you want to base your template open in Word, click the **File** tab. Click **Save As**. The Save As dialog box opens. Open the folder in which you want to save the template. Type a name for the template in the **File Name** field. Click the **Save as Type** ⊡ and choose **Word Template**. Click **Save**. Word saves the template in the folder you chose. Simply follow the steps outlined in this section to attach it to any Word document.

Assign a Theme

Assigning a theme — a predesigned set of color schemes and fonts — quickly adds polish to your document. Because themes are shared among the Office programs, you can use a theme in your Word document to match the same theme in worksheets that you create with Excel or slides that you create in PowerPoint.

Apply a Theme

1 Click the **Page Layout** tab on the Ribbon.

2 Click the **Themes** button.

3 Click a theme.

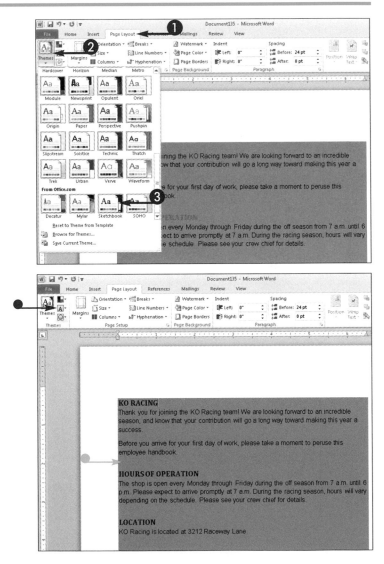

● Word immediately applies the theme to the current document.

● You can use these tools to change the formatting of the theme's colors (■), fonts (A), and effects (○).

Create a Custom Theme

① Apply a theme and edit the formatting to create the theme that you want to save.

② Click the **Page Layout** tab on the Ribbon.

③ Click the **Themes** button.

④ Click **Save Current Theme**.

The Save Current Theme dialog box appears.

⑤ Type a unique name for the theme.

● By default, Word saves the theme to the Document Themes folder so that it is accessible in the Themes Gallery.

⑥ Click **Save**.

Word saves the theme and adds it to the list of available themes.

TIP

I applied a theme, but my document did not change. Why?
If you assign styles such as headings to your document, you will better see the difference that an applied theme can make. Themes are even more pronounced when you assign a background color to a page. To add a background color, click the **Page Layout** tab on the Ribbon and then click the **Page Color** button in the Page Background group of controls. When you click a color from the palette, Word immediately assigns it to the page. To apply a heading style, select the text to which you want to apply the style, click the **Home** tab on the Ribbon, and then click a style in the Styles list. If the style you want to apply is not shown, click the **More** button (▾) to see the full palette of available styles.

Add Borders

You can add borders to your document text to add emphasis or make the document aesthetically appealing. For example, you can add a border to a paragraph to bring attention to the text. You can also add a border to the entire document page. (Be aware that you should not add too many effects, such as borders, to your document because it will become difficult to read.)

Add a Border

1 Select the text to which you want to add a border.

2 Click the **Home** tab on the Ribbon.

3 Click the **Borders** button (▦).

4 Click a border.

● Word applies the border to the text.

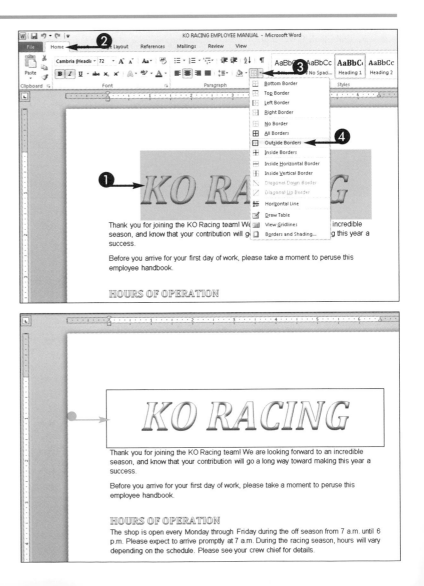

Add a Page Border

1 Click the **Page Layout** tab on the Ribbon.

2 Click the **Page Borders** button.

The Borders and Shading dialog box appears, and displays the Page Border tab.

3 Click the type of border that you want to add.

● You can use these settings to select a different border line style, color, and width.

● You can set a graphical border using this option.

● The Preview area displays a sample of the selections.

4 Click **OK**.

● Word applies the border to the page.

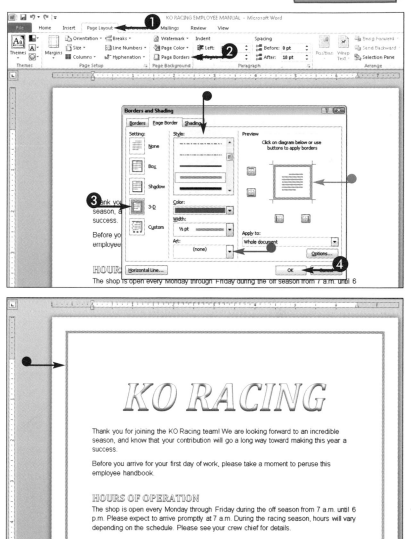

TIPS

How do I add shading to my text instead of a border?

To add shading behind a block of text, you can use the **Shading** tool, which is located on the Home tab in the Paragraph group. Simply select the text you want to shade; then click the **Shading** button (⬚) and click a color to apply. Word immediately applies the shading to the selected text.

How do I create a custom border?

You can create a custom border — for example, making each border line a different color or thickness. To do so, select the text you want to border. Then open the Borders and Shading dialog box, click the **Borders** tab, and choose **Custom**. Choose the settings that you want to apply to the first line; then click in the **Preview** area where you want the line to appear. Repeat this process for each line that you want to add, and then click **OK**.

Create Columns

You can create columns in Word to present your text in a format similar to a newspaper or magazine. For example, if you are creating a brochure or newsletter, you can use columns to make text flow from one block to the next.

Create Columns

Create Quick Columns

1 Select the text that you want to place into columns.

2 Click the **Page Layout** tab on the Ribbon.

3 Click the **Columns** button.

4 Click the number of columns that you want to assign.

● Word places the selected text into the number of columns that you specify.

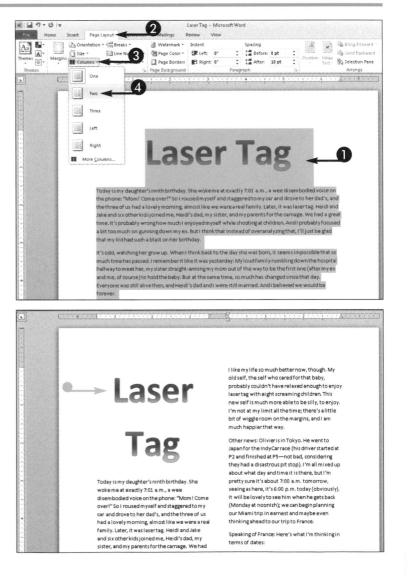

102

Create Custom Columns

1 Select the text that you want to place into columns.

2 Click the **Page Layout** tab on the Ribbon.

3 Click the **Columns** button.

4 Click **More Columns**.

The Columns dialog box appears.

5 Click a preset for the type of column style that you want to apply.

● You can also specify the number of columns here.

● You can set an exact column width and spacing here.

● You can specify whether the columns apply to the selected text or the entire document.

● You can include a vertical line separating the columns.

6 Click **OK**.

● Word applies the column format to the selected text.

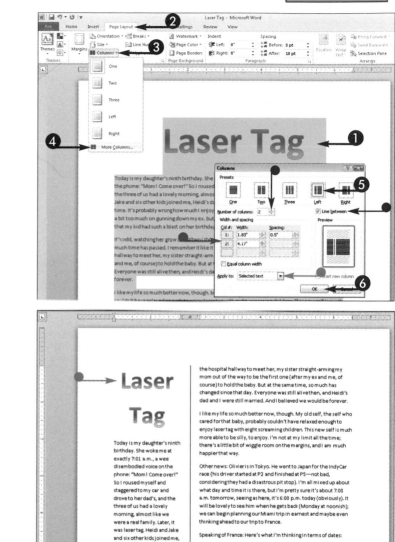

TIPS

How do I wrap column text around a picture?

Click the picture or other object that you want to wrap, click the **Format** tab, click the **Wrap Text** button, and then click the type of wrapping that you want to apply. For example, select **Tight** to allow column text to flow neatly around the image, regardless of where you move the image in the column area.

How do I create a break within a column?

You can add a column break by first clicking where you want the break to occur and then pressing Ctrl + Shift + Enter. To remove a break, select it and press Delete. To return to a one-column format, click the **Columns** button on the Page Layout tab, and then select the single-column format.

Insert a Table

You can use tables to present data in an organized fashion. For example, you can add a table to your document to display a list of items or a roster of classes. Tables have columns and rows that intersect to form *cells*. You can insert all types of data in cells, including text and graphics. You can insert a table manually or use one of Word's preset tables, called Quick Tables.

Insert a Table

Insert a Table

1 Click in the document where you want to insert a table.

2 Click the **Insert** tab on the Ribbon.

3 Click the **Table** button.

4 Drag across the number of columns and rows that you want to set for your table.

● Word previews the table as you drag over cells.

● Word adds the table to the document.

5 Click inside a cell and type your data.

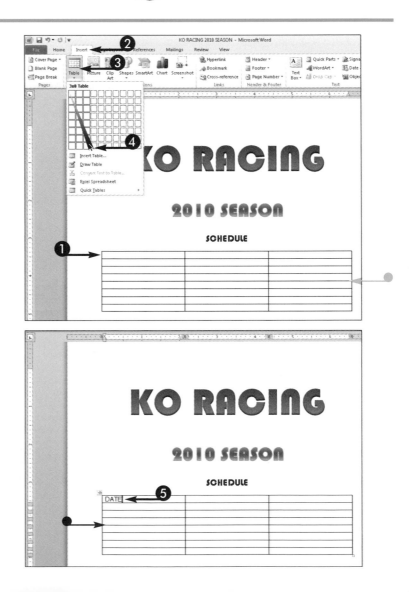

Insert a Quick Table

1 Click in the document where you want to insert a table.

2 Click the **Insert** tab on the Ribbon.

3 Click the **Table** button.

4 Click **Quick Tables**.

● You can use the scroll bar to scroll through the available tables.

5 Click the table that you want to insert.

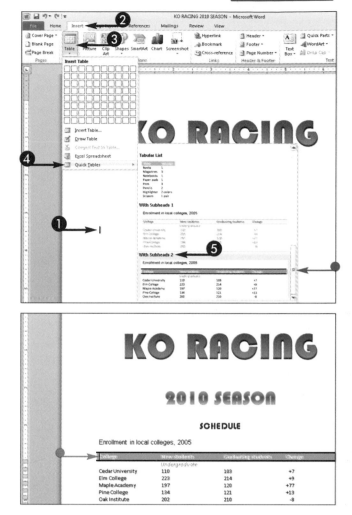

● Word adds the table to the document.

You can click inside a cell and replace the "dummy" data with your own text.

TIPS

Can I create a customized table?
Yes. You can create a customized table by drawing the table. When you do, you control the table's size and how the rows and columns appear. To draw a table, click the **Table** button in the Insert tab and choose **Draw Table**. Then drag across the document to draw an outside border for your table. Drag an internal line to delineate a row or column in your table; continue adding inner lines to build your table cells.

How do I enter and edit data in my table?
After you create a table, you can press Tab to move from one cell to another, or you can click in the cell in which you want to add or edit data. As you type data, Word wraps the text to fit the current cell size. You can select cells, rows, and columns in a table to perform editing tasks and apply formatting.

Apply Table Styles

You can add instant formatting to your Word tables by assigning one of the many formatting styles designed specifically for tables. Table styles offer a variety of designs that include shading and color, borders, and fonts.

Apply Table Styles

1. Click anywhere in the table that you want to format.

2. Click the **Design** tab on the Ribbon.

3. Click a style from the Table Styles list.

● You can click the **More** button (⊡) to display the entire palette of available styles.

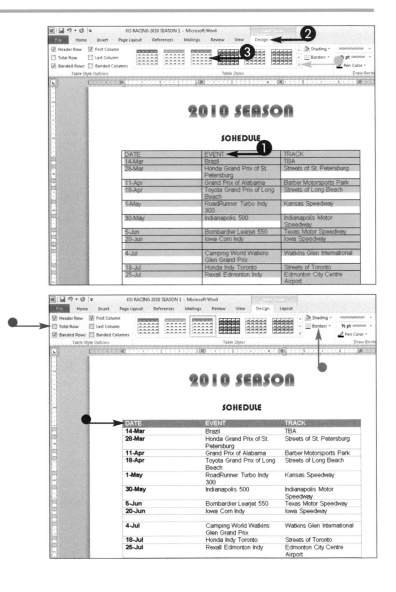

● Word applies the style.

● You can toggle table parts on or off using the Table Style Options check boxes.

● You can click these options to change the shading and borders.

Insert an Excel Spreadsheet

If Excel is installed on your computer, you can insert an Excel spreadsheet into your Word document. When adding an Excel spreadsheet, you can use Excel's features to add table data, including formulas and cell formatting controls.

Insert an Excel Spreadsheet

1 Click in the document where you want to insert a table.

2 Click the **Insert** tab on the Ribbon.

3 Click the **Table** button.

4 Click **Excel Spreadsheet**.

● An Excel spreadsheet appears, along with tools associated with the Excel program.

5 Click in a cell and type the data that you want to add.

● The Home tab displays tools for formatting your cells and data.

● The Formulas tab offers tools for building Excel formulas.

● You can click anywhere outside of the table to return to Word's tools and features.

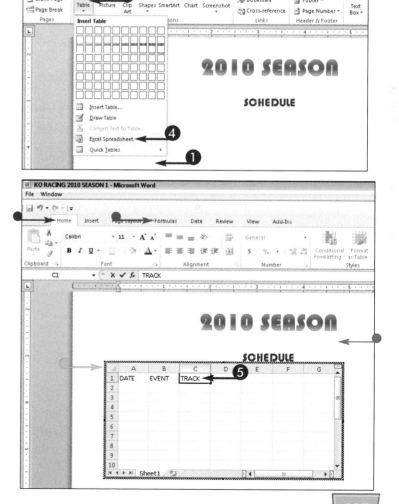

Add Headers and Footers

To add text that you want to appear at the top or bottom of every page — such as the title of your document, the author name, or the date — you can use headers and footers. Header text appears at the very top of the page outside the text margin; footer text appears at the very bottom.

Add a Header or Footer

1. Click the **Insert** tab on the Ribbon.

2. Click the **Header** button to add a header, or click the **Footer** button to add a footer.

3. Click the type of header or footer that you want to add.

   This example adds a header.

   Word adds the header and displays the Header & Footer Tools tab.

4. To create header text, click the field in the header area and type your text.

5. If the header style you chose includes a date, click the **Date** field and choose a date from the calendar that appears.

   ● You can click the **Quick Parts** button to insert additional fields.

   ● You can insert more headers and footers using these controls.

6. Click the **Close Header and Footer** button.

   Word closes the Header & Footer Tools tab.

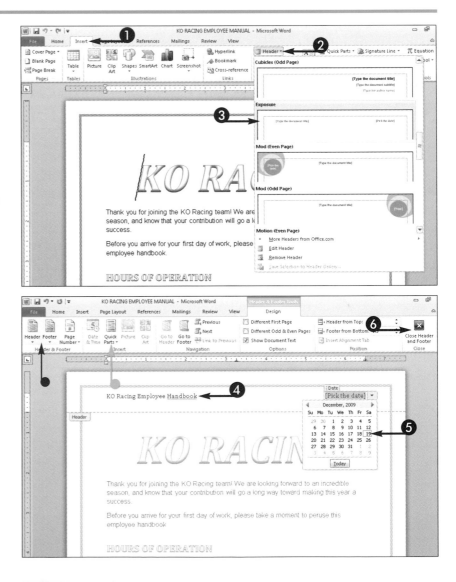

● Word displays the header or footer on the document page.

*Note: If the header or footer is not visible, click the **View** tab and click the **Print Layout** button. Then double-click the top or bottom of the page, respectively, to view the header or footer.*

KO Racing Employee Handbook ← ●   December 19, 2009

KO RACING

Thank you for joining the KO Racing team! We are looking forward to an incredible season, and know that your contribution will go a long way toward making this year a success.

Before you arrive for your first day of work, please take a moment to peruse this employee handbook.

HOURS OF OPERATION

Edit a Header or Footer

① Click the **Insert** tab on the Ribbon.

② Click the **Header** or **Footer** button.

③ Click **Edit Header** or **Edit Footer**.

Word displays the Header & Footer Tools tab; you can now edit the header or footer text.

KO RACING EMPLOYEE MANUAL - Microsoft Word

File Home Insert References Mailings Review View

Cover Page Blank Page Page Break | Table | Picture Clip Art Shapes SmartArt Chart Screenshot | Hyperlink Bookmark Cross-reference | Header Quick Parts Signature Line Equation

Built-In

Blank

[Type text]

Blank (Three Columns)

[Type text]   [Type text]   [Type text]

Alphabet

[Type the document title]

Annual

[Type the document title] [Year]

More Headers from Office.com
Edit Header ← ③
Remove Header
Save Selection to Header Gallery...

KO Racing Employee Handbook

KO RA

Thank you for joining the KO Racing team! We are season, and know that your contribution will go a l success.

Before you arrive for your first day of work, please employee handbook.

HOURS OF OPERATION

Can I remove a header or footer from the first page and keep it for the remaining pages?

Yes. To do so, click the **Header** or **Footer** button on the Insert tab, and then click **Edit Header** or **Edit Footer**. Next, click the **Different First Page** check box in the Options group. If you want to remove the header or footer for odd or even pages, click to select the **Different Odd & Even Pages** check box.

How do I remove a header or footer that I no longer want?

Click the **Insert** tab on the Ribbon and click either the **Header** or **Footer** button. Then click the **Remove Header** or **Remove Footer** command at the bottom of the menu. Word immediately removes the header or footer from your document.

HEADER

FOOTER

Insert Footnotes and Endnotes

You can add footnotes and endnotes to your document to identify sources or references to other materials or add explanatory information. Footnotes appear at the bottom of a page, and endnotes appear at the end of the document. When you insert footnotes or endnotes in a document, Word automatically numbers them. As you add, delete, and move text in your document, any associated footnotes or endnotes are likewise added, deleted, or moved, as well as renumbered.

Insert Footnotes and Endnotes

Insert a Footnote

① Click where you want to insert the footnote reference.

② Click the **References** tab on the Ribbon.

③ Click the **Insert Footnote** button.

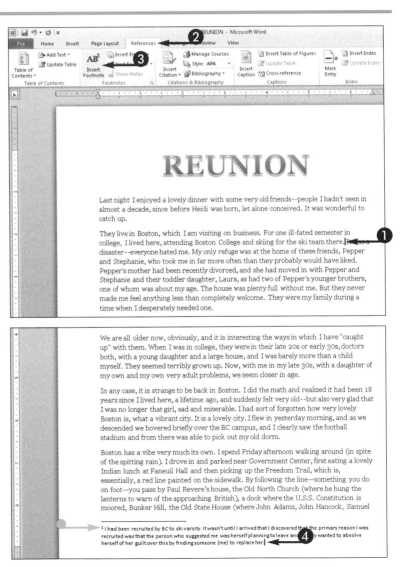

④ Type the note text.

● To return to the reference mark in the document, you can double-click the footnote number.

You can repeat these steps to add more footnotes.

Insert an Endnote

1. Click where you want to insert the footnote reference.

2. Click the **References** tab on the Ribbon.

3. Click the **Insert Endnote** button.

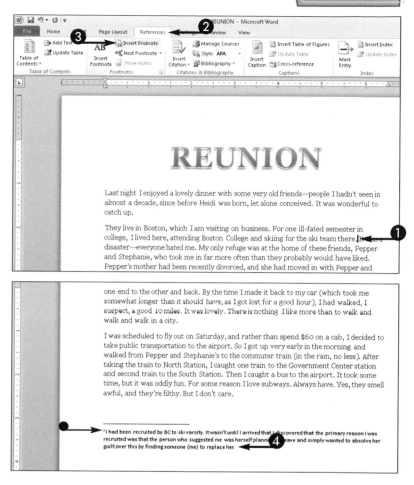

4. Type your note text at the bottom of the last page of the document.

● The endnote number appears automatically.

To return to the reference mark in the document, you can double-click the endnote number.

TIP

How can I reset the footnote number in my document?

If you need to reset the footnote number, perhaps for a new chapter in the document, click the **References** tab on the Ribbon and click the corner group button (▣) in Footnotes group. The Footnote and Endnote dialog box appears. Next, click inside the **Start at** text box and type a number, or use the spin arrow (⬘) to set a new number (●). Click **Apply** to apply the changes to the document.

Insert Page Numbers and Page Breaks

You can add page numbers and page breaks to your documents to make the pages more manageable. For example, adding page numbers to longer documents can help you keep the pages in order after printing. Adding page breaks can help you control what text appears on what page of the document. Page numbers are added to the header or footer area of the document.

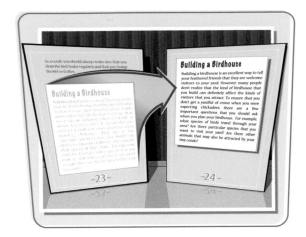

Insert Page Numbers and Page Breaks

Insert Page Numbers

1 Click the **Insert** tab on the Ribbon.

2 Click the **Page Number** button.

3 Click a location for the page numbers.

4 Click a page number style.

● Word assigns page numbers to your document.

5 Click **Close Header and Footer** to exit the header or footer area.

Note: *See the "Add Headers and Footers" section to learn more.*

Insert Page Breaks

① Click in the document where you want to insert a page break.

② Click the **Insert** tab on the Ribbon.

③ Click the **Page Break** button.

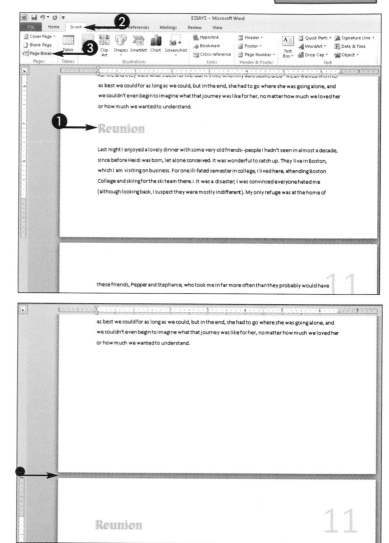

● Word assigns the page break.

TIPS

Is there a faster way to insert a page break?

Yes. You can use keyboard shortcuts to quickly insert a page break as you type in your document. You can insert a manual page break by pressing Ctrl + Enter. You can also insert a line break by pressing Shift + Enter.

Can I change the number style used in my document's page numbers?

Yes. Click the **Page Number** button on the Insert tab, and then click **Format Page Numbers**. This opens the Page Number Format dialog box. You can change the number style to Roman numerals, alphabetical, and more. You can also include chapter numbers with your page numbers.

Mark Index Entries

If your document requires an index, you can use Word to build one. First, however, you must mark any words or phrases in your document that should appear in the index. When you do, Word adds a special index field, called an XE field, to the document that includes the marked word or phrase, as well as any cross-reference information you might have added.

Building a Birdhouse

Building a birdhouse is an excellent way to tell your feathered friends that they are welcome visitors to your yard. However, many people don't realize that the kind of birdhouse that you build can definitely affect the kinds of visitors that you attract. To ensure that you don't get a yardful of crows when you were hoping for chickadees, there are a few important questions that you should ask when you build your birdhouse. For example, what types of birds travel through your area? Are there particular species that you want to visit your yard? Are there other animals that may be attracted by your tiny condo?

Mark Index Entries

Mark a Word or Phrase

① Select the text for which you want to create an index entry.

② Click the **References** tab.

③ Click the **Mark Entry** button.

The Mark Index Entry dialog box opens.

● The text you selected appears in the Main Entry field.

Note: To create an entry for a person's name, type the name in the **Main Entry** field in this format: Last Name, First Name.

● The Current Page radio button is selected.

● If you want the index to include an entry for the word or phrase on this page only, click **Mark**.

● To mark all occurrences of the word or phrase in the document, click **Mark All**.

● Word adds an index entry field to your document.

Note: To view the field, click the Home tab's **Show/Hide** button (¶).

④ Click **Close**.

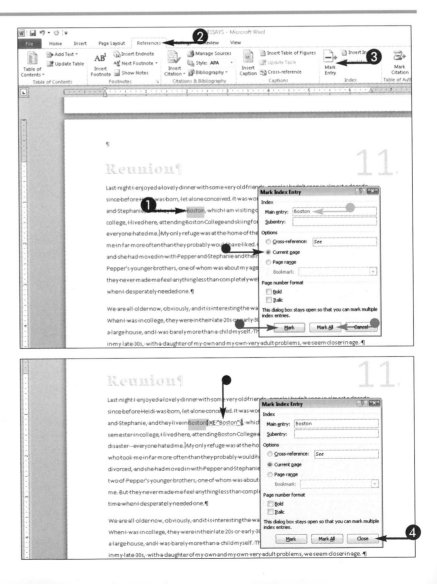

Mark a Word or Phrase that Spans a Range of Pages

1. Select the range of text to which the index entry should refer.

2. Click the **Insert** tab.

3. In the Links group, click **Bookmark**.

   The Bookmark dialog box opens.

4. Type a name for the bookmark.

Note: Do not include spaces in the bookmark name.

5. Click **Add**.

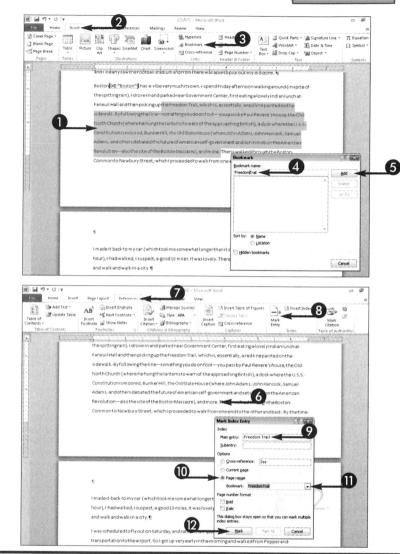

6. Click at the end of the text you selected.

7. Click the **References** tab.

8. Click the **Mark Entry** button.

   The Mark Index Entry dialog box opens.

9. Type the word or phrase that should appear in the index for this entry.

10. Click the **Page range** radio button.

11. Click the **Bookmark** and choose the bookmark you just created.

12. Click **Mark**.

    Word adds an XE field to your document.

13. Click **Close**.

TIPS

Can I add a subentry?

To format the selected text as a subentry rather than a main entry, type the entry under which the selected text should appear in the Mark Index Entry dialog box's **Main entry** field, and then type the selected text in the **Subentry** field. If the text should appear as a subentry *and* a main entry, add two XE fields — one for the main entry and one for the subentry.

•Entry
   •Subentry
   •Subentry
   •Subentry

Can I add cross-references?

To create index entries that refer to other entries, click **Cross-reference** in the Mark Index Entry dialog box and type the word or phrase to which the entry should refer.

Generate an Index

After you mark the words and phrases in your document that you want to appear as index entries, you can generate the index. When you do, Word searches for marked words and phrases, sorts them alphabetically, adds page-number references, and removes duplicate entries that cite the same page number. If, after generating the index, you make a change to your document, you can update the index to reflect it.

Generate an Index

① Click the spot in your document where you want to insert the index.

② Click the **References** tab.

③ Click the **Insert Index** button.

The Index dialog box opens.

④ Click the **Formats** ▾ and select an index design.

● Preview the selected index design here.

⑤ Click the **Indented** radio button.

⑥ Click the **Columns** ⬍ to change the number of columns per page the index will contain.

⑦ Click **OK**.

● Word generates the index.

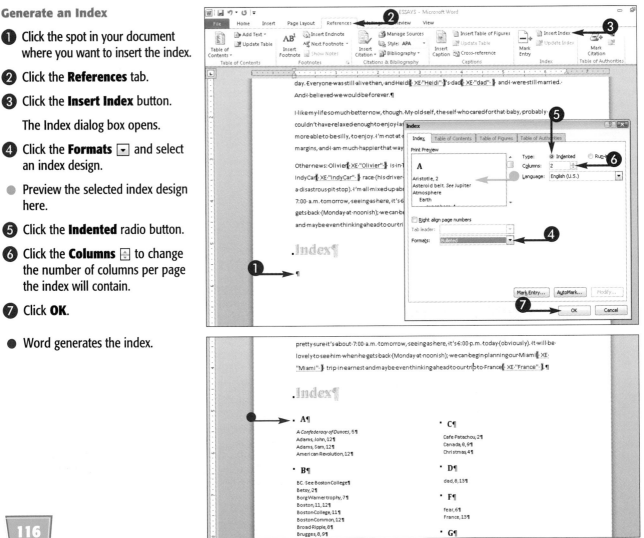

Update the Index

1. After making changes to your document, click in the index.

2. Click the **References** tab.

3. Click the **Update Index** button.

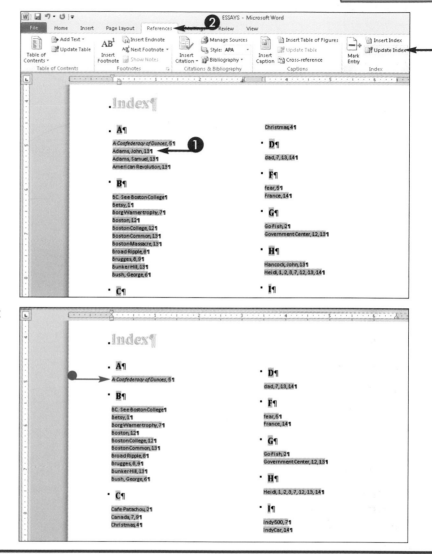

● Word updates the index to reflect changes to the document that have occurred since the original index was generated.

Can I customize the layout of my index?

Yes. To use a custom layout, click the **Formats** ▼ in the Index dialog box, choose **From Template**, and click **Modify**. The Style dialog box opens; click the index style you want to change, and again click **Modify**. Finally, select the desired options in the Formatting section. If you want all documents you create with the template to use this new index style, choose **All Documents Based on the Template**.

How do I edit index entries?

To edit an index entry, click the **Replace** button in the Home tab, type the contents of the XE field that you need to replace in the **Find What** field (for example, **XE "John Adams"**), type the replacement text in the **Replace With** field (for example, **XE "Adams, John"**), and click **Replace All**. To delete an index entry, select the XE field (including the braces that surround it) and press Delete.

Generate a Table of Contents

If your document requires a table of contents (TOC), you can use Word to generate one. By default, Word generates a TOC by searching for any text in your document that was formatted in one of Word's predefined heading styles. It then copies this text and pastes it into the TOC. You can choose from Word's gallery of TOC styles to establish its look and feel.

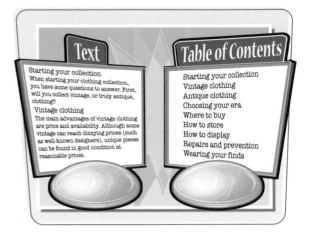

Generate a Table of Contents

Style Text as Headers

1 Select text in your document that you want to style as a header.

2 Click the **Home** tab.

● If the style you want to apply appears in the Styles group, click it to select it.

● If the style you want to apply does not appear in the Styles group, click the **More** button (▾) and choose the desired style from the Quick Style gallery.

● If the style you want to apply does not appear in the Quick Style gallery, click the corner group button (▣) and choose the desired style from the Styles pane, as shown here.

● Word applies the style you chose to the selected text.

Generate a Table of Contents

1 Click the spot in your document where you want to insert a TOC.

2 Click the **References** tab.

3 Click the **Table of Contents** button.

4 Choose the desired TOC style.

● Word generates a TOC.

Note: To delete a TOC, click the **Table of Contents** button and choose **Remove Table of Contents**.

Note: If you edit your document, you can update your TOC to reflect the changes. To do so, click the **Update Table** button in the References tab's Table of Contents group and specify whether you want to update page numbers only or the entire table.

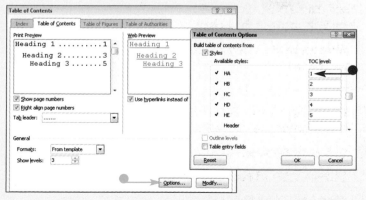

TIP

Can I create a TOC from custom styles?

To generate a TOC from custom styles instead of Word's predefined header styles, click the **References** tab, click **Table of Contents**, and choose **Insert Table of Contents**. In the Table of Contents dialog box, click **Options** (●). The Table of Contents Options dialog box opens; under **Available Styles**, locate the top-level heading style you applied to your document; then type **1** (●) in the corresponding field to indicate that it should appear in the TOC as a level-1 heading. Repeat for additional heading styles, typing **2**, **3**, **4**, and so on to indicate their levels. Click **OK** to close the Table of Contents Options dialog box, and click **OK** again to close the Table of Contents dialog box.

Create a Bibliography

You can use Word to generate a bibliography for your document, formatting the entries using the style of your choice — APA, MLA, The Chicago Manual of Style, and more. For Word to determine what entries should appear in the bibliography, you must cite sources in your document as you work. Word then collects the information from these citations to generate the bibliography.

Add a Citation

1 Click at the end of the sentence or phrase that contains information you want to cite.

2 Click the **References** tab.

3 Click the **Insert Citation** button.

4 Click **Add New Source**.

The Create Source dialog box opens.

5 Click the **Type of Source** and select the type of source you want to cite (here, **Document From Web site**).

The fields in the Create Source dialog box change depending on what you select in the Type of Source drop-down list.

6 Enter the requested information.

7 Click **OK**.

Word adds a citation to your document, and adds the source to the Insert Citation menu.

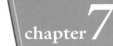

Generate the Bibliography

1. Click the spot in the document where you want the bibliography to appear (typically at the end).

2. Click the **References** tab.

3. Click the **Bibliography** button.

4. Choose one of the gallery options to insert a predesigned bibliography into your document.

● Word inserts the bibliography.

Note: To specify which style guide you want to use, click the **References** tab, click the **Style** ▼ in the Citations & Bibliography group, and choose a style guide from the list that appears.

TIPS

Can I reuse a source?
When you add a source to a document, Word saves it for use in subsequent documents. To reuse a source from another document, click the **References** tab and click **Manage Sources** in the Citations & Bibliography group. The Manage Sources dialog box opens; under Master List, click the citation you want to add to your current document, click **Copy**, and click **Close**.

What do I do if I do not have all the information I need about a citation?
If you want to add a citation to your document but you are missing some of the required information, you can create a placeholder. To do so, click the **References** tab, click **Insert Citation**, and choose **Add New Placeholder**. The Placeholder Name dialog box opens; type a name for the placeholder. Later, add citation information by opening the Manage Sources dialog box, clicking the placeholder under Current List, clicking **Edit**, and entering the necessary information.

Find and Replace Text

You can use Word's Find tool to search your document for a particular word or phrase. In addition, you can use the Replace tool to replace instances of a word or phrase with other text. For example, suppose you complete a long report, only to discover that you have misspelled the name of a product you are reviewing; you can use the Replace tool to locate and correct the misspellings.

Find Text

1 Click at the beginning of your document.

2 Click the **Home** tab on the Ribbon.

3 Click the **Find** button.

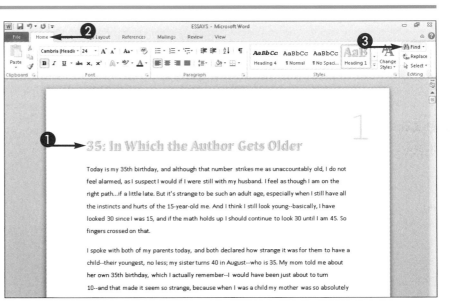

● The Navigation pane appears.

4 Type the text that you want to find and press <kbd>Enter</kbd>.

● Word searches the document and highlights occurrences of the text.

● Word also lists occurrences of the text in the Navigation pane.

5 Click an entry in the Navigation pane.

● Word selects the corresponding text in the document.

When finished, click the Navigation pane's ☒ button.

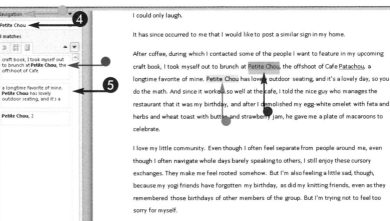

Replace Text

1. Click at the beginning of your document.

2. Click the **Home** tab on the Ribbon.

3. Click the **Replace** button.

The Find and Replace dialog box opens with the Replace tab shown.

4. In the **Find what** field, type the text that you want to find.

5. Type the replacement text in the **Replace with** field.

6. Click **Find Next**.

● Word locates the first occurrence.

7. Click **Replace** to replace the occurrence.

● To replace every occurrence in the document, you can click **Replace All**.

8. When finished, click **Cancel**.

Note: *If Word displays a prompt box when the last occurrence is found, click* ***OK.***

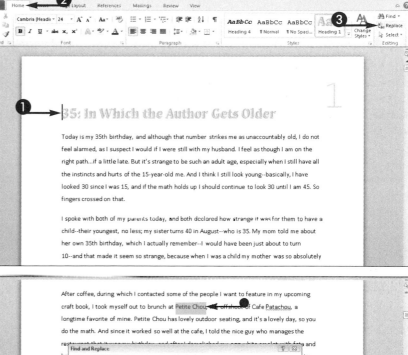

Where can I find detailed search options?

You can click **More** in the Find and Replace dialog box to reveal additional search options that you can apply. For example, you can search for matching text case, whole words, and more. You can also search for specific formatting or special characters by clicking **Format** and **Special**. To hide the additional search options, click **Less**.

How can I search for and delete text?

You can search for a particular word or phrase using the Find and Replace dialog box, and remove the text completely from the document. Start by typing the text in the **Find What** field; then leave the **Replace With** field empty. When you activate the search, Word looks for the text and deletes it without adding new text to the document.

Scan Document Content

If you are working with a very long document, locating a particular page in that document can be time-consuming. To rectify this, Word 2010 includes the Navigation pane. Depending on which option you choose, this pane can display all the headings in your document or a thumbnail image of each page in your document. You can then click a heading or a thumbnail image in the Navigation pane to view the corresponding page.

① Click the **View** tab on the Ribbon.

② Click to select the **Navigation Pane** check box in the Show group.

● Word displays the Navigation pane with the headings in your document listed.

● The page currently shown in the main Word window is highlighted in orange.

● You can click a heading in the Navigation pane to view the page that contains that heading.

③ Click the **Browse the Pages in Your Document** tab.

● The Navigation pane displays thumbnail images of each page in the open document.

④ Click an image in the Navigation pane to switch to a different page.

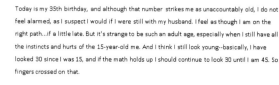

35: In Which the Author Gets Older

Today is my 35th birthday, and although that number strikes me as unaccountably old, I do not feel alarmed, as I suspect I would if I were still with my husband. I feel as though I am on the right path...if a little late. But it's strange to be such an adult age, especially when I still have all the instincts and hurts of the 15-year-old me. And I think I still look young--basically, I have looked 30 since I was 15, and if the math holds up I should continue to look 30 until I am 45. So fingers crossed on that.

I spoke with both of my parents today, and both declared how strange it was for them to have a child--their youngest, no less; my sister turns 40 in August--who is 35. My mom told me about her own 35th birthday, which I actually remember--I would have been just about to turn 10--and that made it seem so strange, because when I was a child my mother was so absolutely an adult in my mind, so absolutely the authority in my world, and chances are she was just as

● Word displays the page you clicked.

birthday latte, complete with a milk-foam heart, and it was so lovely that I took a picture of it. It reminded me of a trip we took to L.A., when we visited a cafe near our hotel, and they made lattes that featured the most amazing foamy designs, which I also felt compelled to photograph. Later in our trip, we were kicked out of said cafe for playing Go Fish with our daughter. We hadn't noticed the "No Game Playing" sign. And the whole thing was so ridiculous I could only laugh.

It has since occurred to me that I would like to post a similar sign in my home.

After coffee, during which I contacted some of the people I want to feature in my upcoming craft book, I took myself out to brunch at Petite Chou, the offshoot of Cafe Patachou, a longtime favorite of mine. Petite Chou has lovely outdoor seating, and it's a lovely day, so you do the math. And since it worked so well at the cafe, I told the nice guy who manages the restaurant that it was my birthday, and after I demolished my egg-white omelet with feta and herbs and wheat toast with butter and strawberry jam, he gave me a plate of macaroons to celebrate.

I love my little community. Even though I often feel separate from people around me, even though I often navigate whole days barely speaking to others, I still enjoy these cursory

---

TIPS

Can I view multiple heading levels in the Navigation pane?

If your document contains multiple levels of headings, you can opt to display them in the Navigation pane. Alternatively, you can display top-level headings only. If you decide to display top-level headings, you can choose to expand the outline to view subheadings beneath a top-level heading by clicking the right arrow to the left of the heading.

How do I view entries in the Navigation pane?

If your document contains too many headings or pages for the Navigation pane to handle, you can use the scroll bar on the right side of the pane to move up and down through the entries in the pane. Alternatively, click ⬆ and ⬇ located near the top of the pane to move up and down through the entries.

Check Spelling and Grammar

Word automatically checks for spelling and grammar errors. Misspellings appear underlined with a red wavy line, and grammar errors are underlined with a green wavy line. In addition, you can use Word's Spelling and Grammar check features to review your document for spelling and grammatical errors. (Of course, these features are no substitute for good proofreading with your own eyes. They can catch some errors, but not all!)

Check Spelling and Grammar

Correct a Mistake

① When you encounter a spelling or grammar problem, right-click the underlined text.

The menu that appears shows possible corrections.

② Click a correction from the menu.

● To ignore the error, you can click **Ignore** or click **Ignore All** for all instances of the error.

● To add the word to the built-in dictionary, you can click **Add to Dictionary**.

Run the Spell Checker

① Click the **Review** tab on the Ribbon.

② Click the **Spelling & Grammar** button.

To check only a section of your document, you can select the section before activating the spell check.

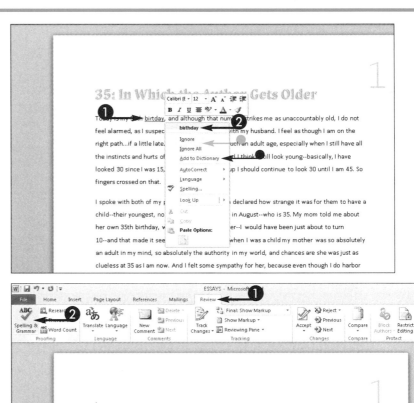

- Word searches the document for any mistakes. If it finds an error, it flags it in the document and displays the Spelling and Grammar dialog box.

3 Click **Change** to make a correction.

- To correct all of the misspellings of the same word, you can click **Change All**.

- To ignore the error one time, you can click **Ignore Once**.

- To ignore every occurrence, you can click **Ignore All** or **Ignore Rule**.

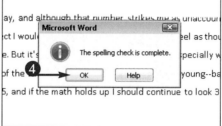

When the spell check is complete, a prompt box appears.

4 Click **OK**.

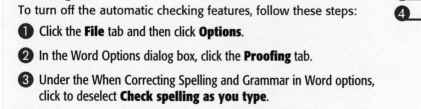

TIP

How do I turn the automatic spelling and grammar checking off?

To turn off the automatic checking features, follow these steps:

1 Click the **File** tab and then click **Options**.

2 In the Word Options dialog box, click the **Proofing** tab.

3 Under the When Correcting Spelling and Grammar in Word options, click to deselect **Check spelling as you type**.

4 Click to deselect **Mark grammar errors as you type**.

5 Click **OK** to exit the Word Options dialog box.

Word turns off the automatic checking features.

Work with AutoCorrect

As you may have noticed, Word automatically corrects your text as you type. It does this using its AutoCorrect feature, which works from a preset list of misspellings. To speed up your text-entry tasks, you can add your own problem words — ones you commonly misspell — to the list. The next time you mistype the word, AutoCorrect fixes your mistake for you.

1 Click the **File** tab.

2 Click **Options**.

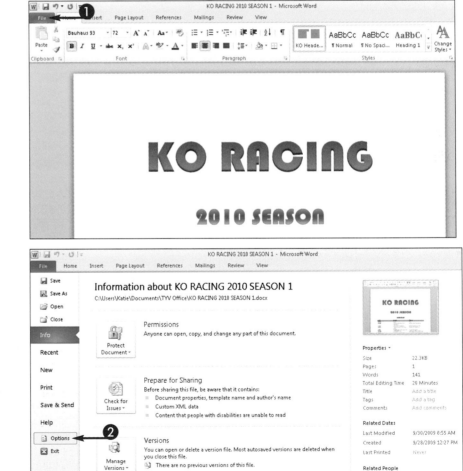

The Word Options dialog box appears.

3 Click **Proofing**.

4 Click **AutoCorrect Options**.

The AutoCorrect dialog box appears, displaying the AutoCorrect tab.

5 Type a common misspelling in the **Replace** text field.

6 Type the correct spelling in the **With** text field.

7 Click **Add**.

AutoCorrect adds the word to the list.

8 Click **OK** to exit the AutoCorrect dialog box.

9 Click **OK** to exit the Word Options dialog box.

The next time you misspell the word, AutoCorrect corrects it for you.

Note: If AutoCorrect corrects text that you do not want to be changed, press Ctrl + Z to undo the change.

How do I remove or edit a word from the AutoCorrect list?

Open the AutoCorrect dialog box as shown in this section with the AutoCorrect tab shown; then click the word you want to remove and click **Delete**. To edit a word, click it in the list and make your change in the **Replace** or **With** text field. Click **OK** to close the dialog box and apply your changes.

Can I customize how the AutoCorrect feature works?

Yes. Open the AutoCorrect dialog box, display the AutoCorrect tab, and select or deselect the check boxes as needed. To prevent AutoCorrect from replacing text as you type, deselect the **Replace text as you type** check box. Click **OK** to close the dialog box and apply your changes.

Use Word's Thesaurus and Dictionary

If you are having trouble finding just the right word or phrase, you use Word's thesaurus to find synonyms as well as antonyms. Word also includes a dictionary, which you can use to look up unfamiliar words in a document. You access these tools from within Word's Research pane; this pane also offers access to Word's translation tools and other reference-based features.

Use Word's Thesaurus

1. Select the word for which you want to find a synonym.

2. Click the **Review** tab on the Ribbon.

3. Click the **Thesaurus** button.

The Research task pane opens, displaying suggested replacements for the selected word.

4. In the Research pane, position your mouse pointer over the word you want to use as a replacement.

5. Click the ▾ that appears.

6. Click **Insert**.

Word replaces the word you selected in your document with the one you chose in the Research pane.

● Click the **Close** button (⊠) to close the pane.

Note: Another way to replace text with a synonym is to right-click the word you want to replace; Word displays a context menu from which you can choose the desired replacement text.

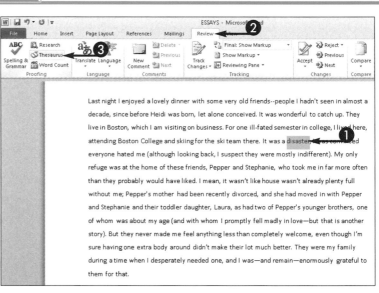

Use Word's Dictionary

1 Right-click the word you want to look up.

2 Click the right arrow (▸) next to **Look Up**.

A list of research resources appears.

3 Click **Encarta Dictionary: English (North America)**.

Word launches the Research pane.

● Word displays definitions of the word.

TIP

What other research tools are available?
Word's Research pane offers easy access to several research tools, including Factiva iWorks (for news and business information), HighBeam Research (a repository of millions of newspaper, magazine, and journal articles), MSN Money, and the Thomson Gale Company Profiles site. To use these tools, open the Research pane, type the topic you want to research in the pane's **Search for** field (●), click the ▾ near the top of the pane (●), and choose the desired resource from the menu that appears. The pane displays a list of links to research resources that relate to the word you typed; click one to launch your Web browser and access the resource you chose with the related article shown.

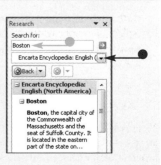

Translate Text

Word contains translation tools, including bilingual dictionaries and machine-translation functions, that enable you to quickly and easily translate words or phrases that you write in your native tongue into one of several other languages (and vice versa). Note that your ability to translate text to and from a language may be limited by your computer's operating system.

Translate a Word or Phrase

1 Select the word or phrase that you want to translate.

2 Click the **Review** tab.

3 Click the **Translate** button.

4 Click **Translate Selected Text**.

Note: *If you are using Word's Translate function for the first time, you may be prompted to install the necessary bilingual dictionaries. Click* **OK.**

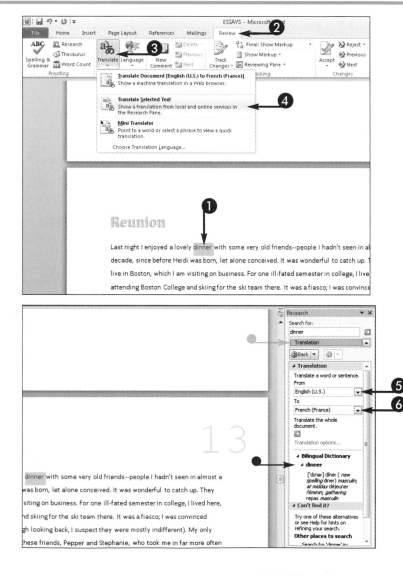

● Word launches the Research pane, with the Translation options displayed.

5 Click the **From** ▼ and choose the language from which you want to translate.

6 Click the **To** ▼ and select the language to which you want to translate.

● Word translates the selected text.

Translate a Document

1 With the document you want to translate open in Word, click the **Review** tab.

2 Click the **Translate** button.

3 Click **Translate Document**.

The Translate Whole Document dialog box opens, notifying you that your document will be sent over the Internet for translation.

4 Click the **Send** button.

● Word displays the translated text alongside the original text.

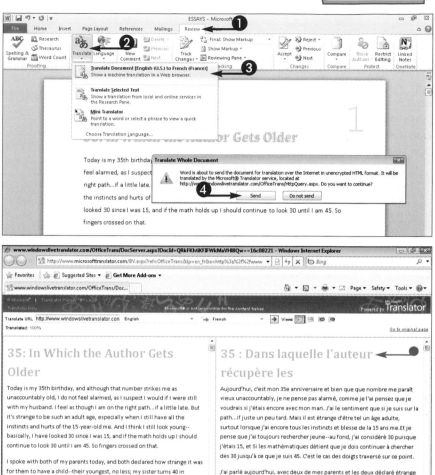

How do I choose a different language?

To choose a different language when translating a document, click the **Translate** button and select **Choose Translation Language**. The Translation Language Options dialog box opens; click the **Translate Document** tab, click the **From** ⏷ and choose the language you are translating from, click the **To** ⏷ and choose the language you are translating to, and click **OK**.

Is there a faster way to translate text?

If you only need to translate the occasional word, you can use Word's Mini Translator feature. To enable this feature, click the **Translate** button and select **Mini Translator**. Word displays the Translation Language Options dialog box with the Mini Translator tab displayed; click the **Translate To** ⏷ and choose the language into which you need to translate. Then, simply position your mouse pointer over the word in question (●); Word displays a translation for the word.

Bilingual Dictionary

lovely
['lʌvlɪ] *adjective* beau; *house, wife* ravissant; *character* charmant; *meal* délicieux; *we had a lovely time* nous nous sommes bien amusés; *it's lovely to be here again* c'est formidable d'être à nouveau ici

lovely dinner with some very old friends--people

Track and Review Document Changes

If you share your Word documents with others, you can use the program's Track Changes feature to keep track of what edits others have made, including formatting changes and text additions or deletions. The Track Changes feature uses different colors for each person's edits, making it easy to see who changed what in the document. When you review the document, you can choose to accept or reject the changes.

Track and Review Document Changes

Turn On Tracking

1 Click the **Review** tab on the Ribbon.

2 Click the **Track Changes** button.

Word activates the Track Changes feature.

3 Edit the document.

● Any additions to the text appear underlined and in color.

● Word marks the deleted text with a strikethrough.

Review Changes

1. Click the **Review** tab on the Ribbon.

2. Click the **Reviewing Pane** button.

● The Reviewing pane opens.

   The Reviewing pane shows each person's edits, including the user's name.

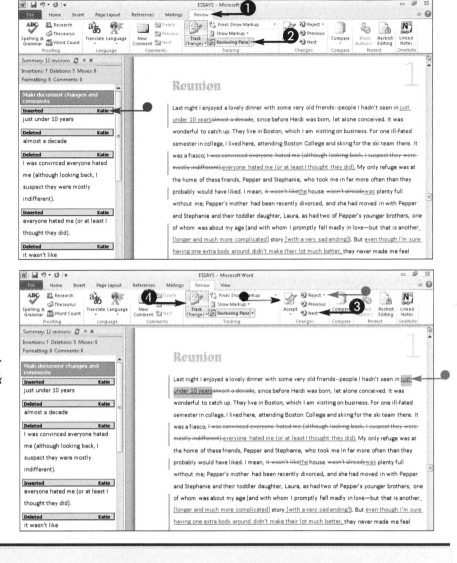

3. Click the **Next** button.

● Word highlights the next edit in the document.

● Click the **Accept** button to add the change to the final document.

*Note: To accept all changes in the document, click the down arrow under the **Accept** button and choose **Accept All Changes in Document**.*

● Click the **Reject** button to reject the change.

4. When you complete the review, click the **Track Changes** button to turn the feature off.

Can I customize the markup options?

Yes. You can change the color used for your edits. To do so, click the **Review** tab, click the **Track Changes** button, and then click **Change Tracking Options**. The Track Changes dialog box opens; here, you can make changes to the tracking color, formatting, and more.

Can I control which markup elements appear in a document?

Yes. You can click the **Show Markup** button on the Review tab to select which elements you want to include in the review. For example, you may want to hide comments or review marks for a particular user.

135

Compare Documents

Suppose someone edits a document without first enabling the Track Changes feature. To determine what edits were made, you can compare the edited document with the original version; the result is a third file that flags any discrepancies such that they appear exactly like edits made with Track Changes enabled. You can then choose to accept or reject each change.

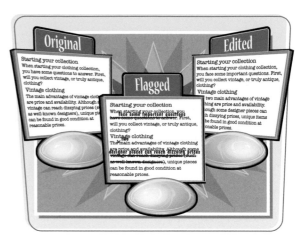

Compare Documents

1. Click the **Review** tab on the Ribbon.

2. Click the **Compare** button.

3. Click **Compare**.

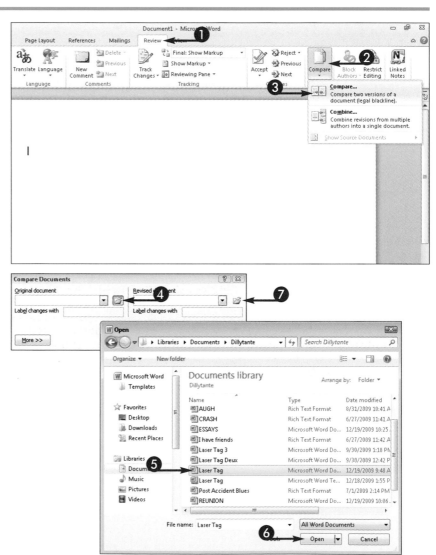

The Compare Documents dialog box opens.

4. Click 🖼 next to the Original Document field.

Word launches the Open dialog box.

5. Locate and select the original document.

6. Click **Open**.

7. Repeat Steps **4** to **6**, this time clicking 🖼 next to the Revised Document field.

Note: *A faster way to specify which documents to compare is to click* ▼ *next to the Original Document and Revised Document fields and choose the desired document from the list that appears.*

8. Click **OK** in the Compare Documents dialog box.

● Word compares the document, flagging discrepancies such as text additions and deletions as well as formatting changes.

● The original document appears here.

● The revised document appears here.

● Use the Reviewing pane, as well as the Next, Accept, and Reject buttons on the Review tab, to review and accept or reject the changes.

TIP

Can I customize the Compare operation?

Yes. You can specify what aspects of the original and revised documents should be compared, including formatting, case changes, and more. You can also specify that changes be shown in the original document or the revised document instead of in a new, third document. To do so, click the **More** button in the Compare Documents dialog box (after you click the More button, it changes to a Less button), select or deselect the appropriate check boxes and radio buttons, and click **OK**.

Insert Comments

You can add comments to your documents to make a note to yourself about a particular section or task, or as a note for other users to see. For example, if you share your documents with other users, you can use comments to leave feedback about the text without typing directly in the document. Word displays comments in a balloon (assuming you are using Print Layout view) or in the Reviewing pane.

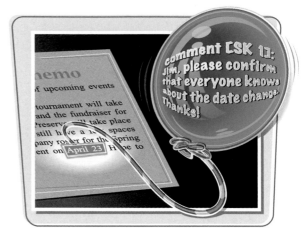

Add a Comment

① Click or select the text where you want to insert a comment.

② Click the **Review** tab on the Ribbon.

③ Click the **New Comment** button.

● A comment balloon appears.

④ Type your comment.

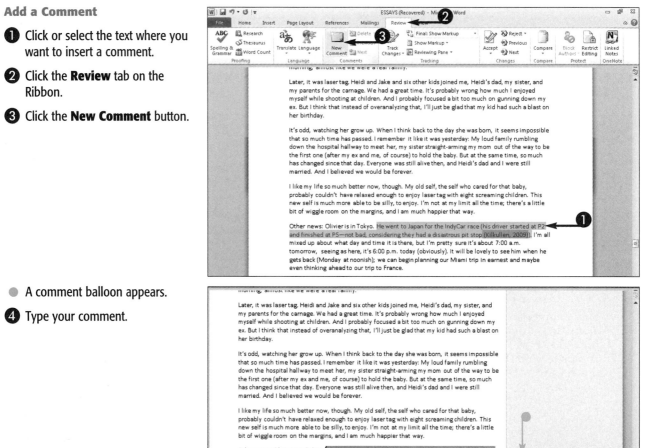

View Comments in the Reviewing Pane

1 Click the **Review** tab on the Ribbon.

2 Click the **Reviewing Pane** button.

● Word displays the Reviewing pane, and lists all of the comments associated with the document.

You can click the **Reviewing Pane** button again to hide the pane.

Delete a Comment

1 Click the comment that you want to remove.

2 Click the **Delete** button on the Review tab.

You can also right-click over a comment and click **Delete**.

Word deletes the comment.

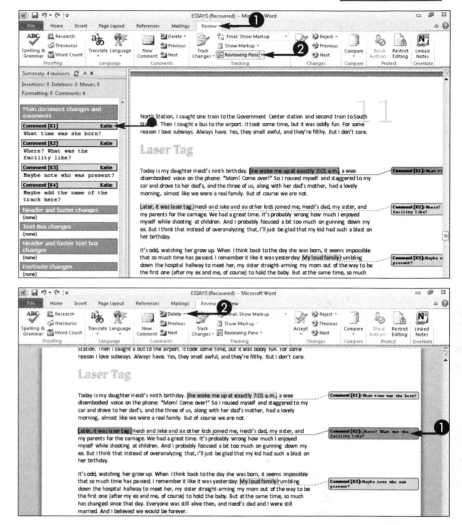

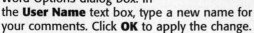

TIPS

How do I change the name used in my comments?

Click the **Review** tab on the Ribbon, click the **Track Changes** button, and click the **Change User Name** command to display the Word Options dialog box. In the **User Name** text box, type a new name for your comments. Click **OK** to apply the change.

How do I respond to a comment?

You can respond to a comment by adding a new comment adjacent to the existing comment. To do so, simply click the existing comment to select it, and then click the **New Comment** button. Word inserts a new comment; add your text as you normally would.

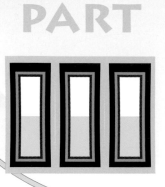

PART

Excel

Excel is a powerful spreadsheet program you can use to enter and organize data and to perform a wide variety of number-crunching tasks. You can use Excel strictly as a program for manipulating numerical data, or you can use it as a database program to organize and track large quantities of data. In this part, you learn how to enter data into worksheets and tap into the power of Excel's formulas and functions to perform mathematical calculations and analysis.

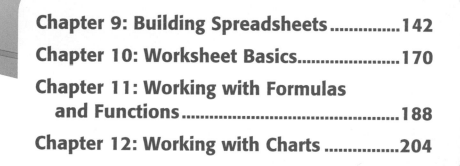

Enter Cell Data

You can enter data into any cell in an Excel worksheet. You can type data directly into the cell, or you can enter data using the Formula bar. Data can be text, such as row or column labels, or numbers, which are called *values*. Values also include formulas. Excel automatically left-aligns text data in a cell and right-aligns values.

Enter Cell Data

Type into a Cell

1 Click the cell into which you want to enter data.

The cell you clicked becomes the active cell. It appears highlighted, with a thicker border than the other cells.

● To add data to another worksheet in your workbook, click the worksheet tab to display the worksheet.

● To magnify your view of the worksheet, click and drag the **Zoom** slider.

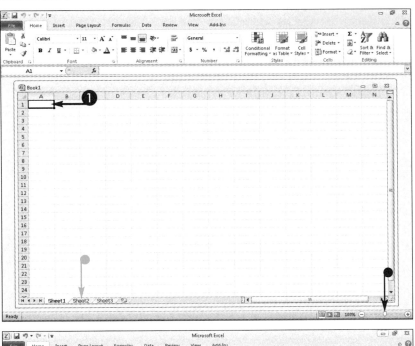

2 Type your data.

● The data appears both in the cell and in the Formula bar.

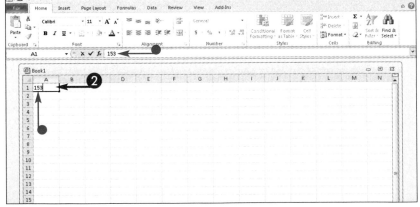

Type Data in the Formula Bar

1 Click the cell into which you want to enter data.

2 Click in the Formula bar.

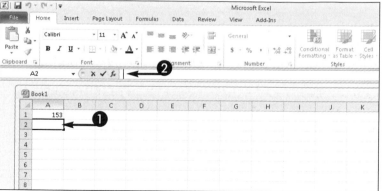

3 Type your data.

● The data appears both in the Formula bar and in the cell.

4 Click **Enter** (☑) or press Enter to enter the data.

● To cancel an entry, you can click **Cancel** (☒) or press Esc.

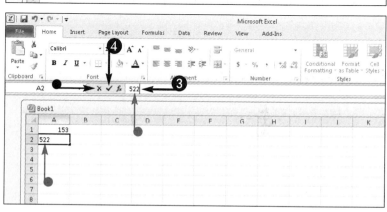

TIPS

What if the data that I type is too long to fit in my cell?

Long text entries appear truncated if you type additional data into adjoining cells. You can remedy this by resizing the column to fit the data, or by turning on the cell's text wrap feature, which wraps the text to fit in the cell and remain visible. Text wrapping causes the cell depth to increase. To learn how to resize columns, see the "Resize Columns and Rows" section. To learn how to turn on the text wrap feature, see the "Turn On Text Wrapping" section.

When I start typing in a cell, Excel tries to fill in the text for me. Why?

Excel's AutoComplete feature is automatic. If you repeat an entry from anywhere in the same column, AutoComplete attempts to complete the entry for you, based on the first few letters that you type. If the AutoComplete entry is correct, press Enter, and Excel fills in the text for you. If not, just keep typing the text that you want to insert into the cell. The AutoComplete feature is just one of many Excel tools that help you speed up your data-entry tasks.

Select Cells

You can select cells in Excel to perform editing, mathematical, and formatting tasks. Selecting a single cell is easy: You just click the cell. To select a group of cells, called a *range*, you can use your mouse or keyboard. For example, you might apply formatting to a range of cells rather than format each cell individually.

Select a Range of Cells

① Click the first cell in the range of cells that you want to select.

② Click and drag across the cells that you want to include in the range.

	A	B	C	D	E	F
1	**2010 Quarterly Sales**					
2	**1st Quarter**					
3		**January**	**February**	**March**		
4						
5	w York Office	26500	31420	21050		
6	**London Office**	15600	19505	2075		
7	**Paris Office**	29750	34650	22760		
8						
9						
10						
11						
12						
13						
14						
15						

③ Release the mouse button.

● Excel selects the cells.

● To select all of the cells in the worksheet, you can click here (▱).

You can select multiple noncontiguous cells by pressing and holding **Ctrl** while clicking cells.

	A	B	C	D	E	F
1	**2010 Quarterly Sales**					
2	**1st Quarter**					
3		**January**	**February**	**March**		
4						
5	New York Office	26500	31420	36340		
6	**London Office**	15600	19505	23410		
7	**Paris Office**	29750	34650	22760		
8						
9						
10						
11						
12						
13						
14						
15						

Select a Column or Row

1 Position the mouse pointer over the header of the column or row that you want to select.

The ⟁ changes to ↓.

Book1						
	A	B	C	D	E	F
1	2010 Quarterly Sales					
2	1st Quarter					
3		January	February	March		
4						
5	New York Office	26500	31420	36340		
6	London Office	15600	19505	23410		
7	Paris Office	29750	34650	22760		
8						
9						
10						
11						
12						
13						
14						
15						

2 Click the column or row.

● Excel selects the entire column or row.

To select multiple columns or rows, you can click and drag across the column or row headings.

You can select multiple noncontiguous columns or rows by pressing and holding **Ctrl** while clicking column or row headings.

Book1						
	A	B	C	D	E	F
1	2010 Quarterly Sales					
2	1st Quarter					
3		January	February	March		
4						
5	New York Office	26500	31420	36340		
6	London Office	15600	19505	23410		
7	Paris Office	29750	34650	22760		
8						
9						
10						
11						
12						
13						
14						
15						

TIPS

How do I select data inside a cell?

To select a word or number inside a cell, first click the cell. Then, click in front of the data in the Formula bar and drag over the characters or numbers that you want to select. You can also select data directly in a cell; click the cell to select it, and then double-click the data you want to select.

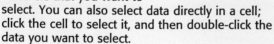

How do I use my keyboard to select cells?

You can use the arrow keys to navigate to the first cell in the range. Next, press and hold **Shift** while using an arrow key to select the range, such as ← or ↓. Excel selects any cells that you move over using the keyboard navigation keys.

Faster Data Entry with AutoFill

You can use Excel's AutoFill feature to add duplicate entries or a data series to your worksheet. In addition to creating your own custom data lists, you can use Excel's built-in lists of common entries such as days of the week, months, and number series. When you click a cell, a small fill handle appears in the lower right corner of the selector; you use this to create an AutoFill series.

Faster Data Entry with AutoFill

AutoFill a Text Series

1 Type the first entry in the text series.

2 Click and drag the cell's fill handle across or down the number of cells that you want to fill.

The ⊕ changes to +.

You can also use AutoFill to copy the same text to every cell that you drag over.

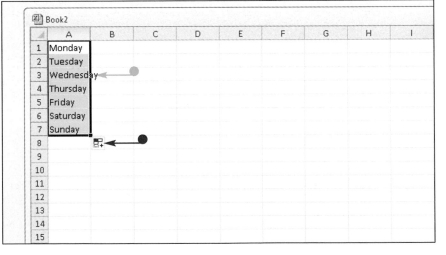

3 Release the mouse button.

● AutoFill fills in the text series.

● An AutoFill smart tag (📋) may appear, offering additional options that you can assign to the data.

AutoFill a Number Series

1 Type the first entry in the number series.

2 In an adjacent cell, type the next entry in the number series.

3 Select both cells.

Note: *See the "Select Cells" section to learn more.*

4 Click and drag the fill handle across or down the number of cells that you want to fill.

The ✥ changes to +.

5 Release the mouse button.

● AutoFill fills in the number series.

● An AutoFill smart tag (▦) may appear, offering additional options that you can assign to the data.

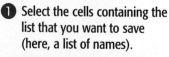

TIP

How do I create a custom list?

To add your own custom list to AutoFill's list library, first create the custom list in your worksheet cells. Then follow these steps:

1 Select the cells containing the list that you want to save (here, a list of names).

2 Click the **File** tab and then click the **Options** button.

3 In the Options dialog box, click the **Advanced** tab.

4 Click the **Edit Custom Lists** button.

● The Custom Lists dialog box opens with the list you selected highlighted.

5 Click **Import**.

Excel adds the series to the custom lists.

6 Click **OK**.

7 Click **OK** again to close the Options dialog box.

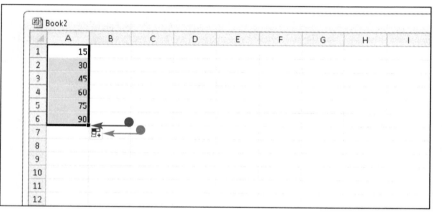

Turn On Text Wrapping

By default, long lines of data that you type into a cell remain on one line. You can turn on the cell's text-wrapping option to make data wrap to the next line and fit into the cell without truncating the data. Text wrapping makes the row size taller to fit the number of lines that wrap.

Turn On Text Wrapping

① Click the cell that you want to edit.

Note: *You can also apply text wrapping to multiple cells. See the "Select Cells" section, earlier in this chapter, to learn how to select multiple cells for a task.*

② Click the **Home** tab on the Ribbon.

③ Click the **Wrap Text** button (⊞).

● Excel applies text wrapping to the cell.

Note: *See the section "Resize Columns and Rows" to learn how to adjust cell depth and width to accommodate your data.*

Center Data Across Columns

EXCEL

Building Spreadsheets — chapter 9

You can center a title or heading across a range of cells in your worksheet. For example, you may want to include a title across multiple columns of labels. You can use the Merge and Center command to quickly create a merged cell to hold the title text.

Center Data Across Columns

1 Select the cell containing the data that you want to center, and the cells that you want to center the data across.

Note: Refer to the "Select Cells" section to learn how to select columns and rows.

2 Click the **Home** tab on the Ribbon.

3 Click the **Merge and Center** button ().

You can also click the **Merge and Center** to select from several different merge commands.

● Excel merges the cells and centers the data.

149

Adjust Cell Alignment

You can control the alignment of data within your worksheet cells. By default, Excel automatically aligns text data to the left and number data to the right. Data is also aligned vertically to sit at the bottom of the cell. You can change horizontal and vertical alignments to improve the appearance of your worksheet data.

Set Horizontal Alignment

① Select the cells that you want to format.

② Click the **Home** tab on the Ribbon.

③ Click an alignment button from the Alignment group.

Click the **Align Left** button (▤) to align data to the left.

Click the **Center** button (▤) to center-align the data.

Click the **Align Right** button (▤) to align data to the right.

Note: To justify cell data, click the corner group button (▣) in the Alignment group. In the Format Cells dialog box that appears, click the **Horizontal** ▾ and click **Justify**.

Excel applies the alignment to your cells.

● This example centers the data.

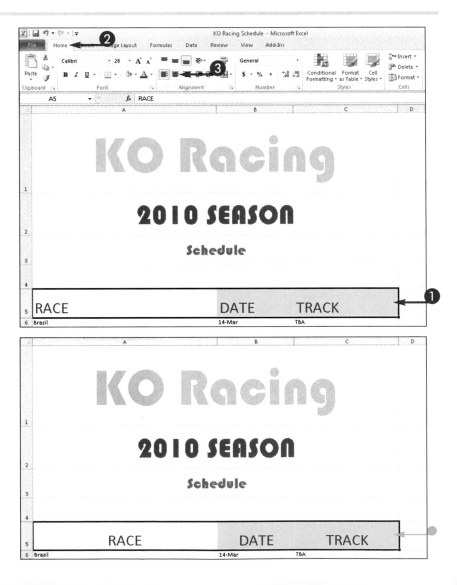

Set Vertical Alignment

1. Select the cells that you want to format.

2. Click the **Home** tab on the Ribbon.

3. Click an alignment button from the Alignment group.

   Click the **Top Align** button (▤) to align data to the top.

   Click the **Middle Align** button (▤) to align the data in the middle.

   Click the **Bottom Align** button (▤) to align data to the bottom.

   Excel applies the alignment to your cells.

● This example aligns the data to the middle of the cell.

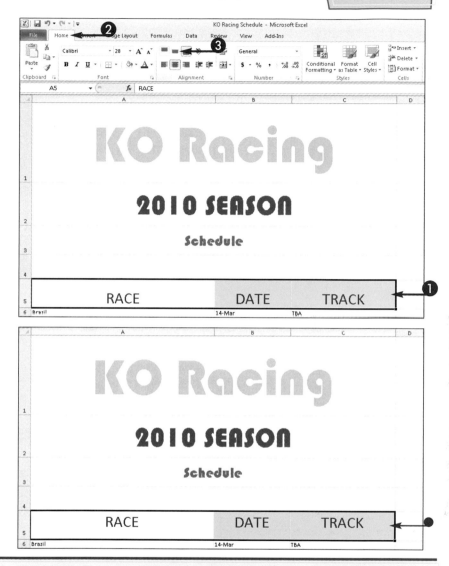

TIPS

How do I indent cell data?

You can use the Increase Indent and Decrease Indent buttons to add indents to lines of data in your worksheet. To indent data, click the **Increase Indent** button (▤) on the Home tab. To decrease an indent, click the **Decrease Indent** button (▤).

Can I change the orientation of data in a cell?

Yes. For example, you might angle column labels to make them easier to distinguish from one another. To do so, select the cells you want to change, click the **Home** tab on the Ribbon, click the ▾ next to the **Orientation** button (▨), and click an orientation. Excel applies the orientation to the data in the selected cell or cells.

151

Change the Font and Size

You can change the font that you use for your worksheet data, along with the size of the data text. For example, you may want to make the worksheet title larger than the rest of the data, or you may want to resize the font for the entire worksheet to a more legible size to make the data easier to read.

Change the Font

1. Select the cell or data that you want to format.

2. Click the **Home** tab on the Ribbon.

3. Click the **Font** 🔽.

● You can use the scroll arrows or scroll bar to scroll through all of the available fonts.

You can also begin typing a font name to choose a font.

4. Click a font.

● Excel applies the font.

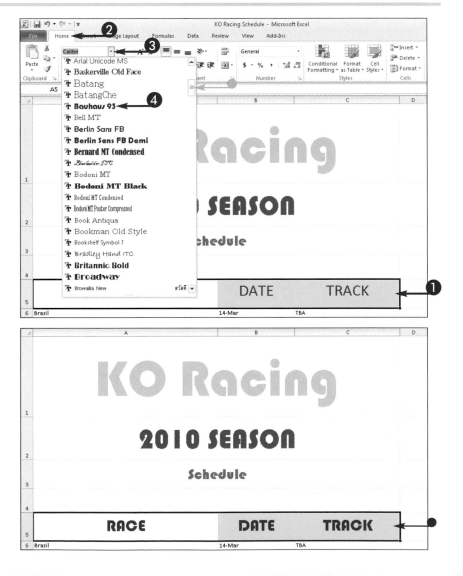

Change the Font Size

1. Select the cell or data that you want to format.

2. Click the **Home** tab on the Ribbon.

3. Click the **Font Size** ⏷.

4. Click a size.

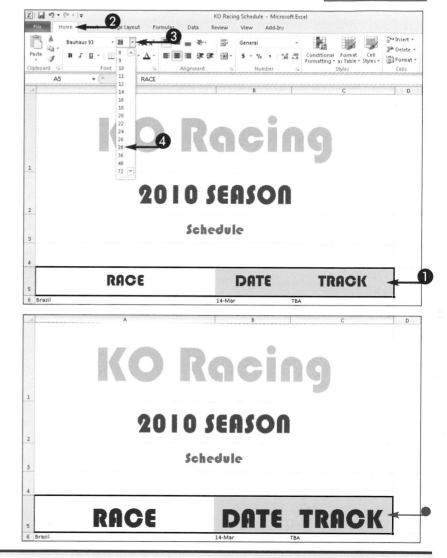

● Excel applies the new size to the selected cell or data.

TIPS

Is there a way to apply multiple formatting options at the same time?
Yes. You can use the Format Cells dialog box to apply a new font, size, or any of the basic formatting, such as bold, italics, and underlining. To open this dialog box, click the **Home** tab on the Ribbon and click the corner group button (⏷) in the Font group.

Can I copy cell formatting?
Yes. If you have applied a variety of formatting options to a range of cells to create a certain look, you can re-create that look elsewhere by "painting" the formatting rather than reapplying all the formatting step-by-step. Simply select the cell or range containing the formatting you want to copy, click the **Home** tab, and click the **Format Painter** button (🖌). Then click and drag over the cells to which you want to copy the formatting.

153

Change Number Formats

You can use number formatting to control the appearance of numerical data in your worksheet. For example, if you have a column of prices, you format the data as numbers with dollar signs and decimal points. Excel offers several different number categories, or styles, to choose from. You can apply number formatting to single cells, ranges, columns, rows, or an entire worksheet.

① Select the cell, range, or data that you want to format.

② Click the **Home** tab on the Ribbon.

③ Click the **Number Format** ▼.

④ Click a number format.

Excel applies the number format to the data.

● Click the **Accounting Number Format** button (\$) to quickly apply dollar signs to your data. Click the button's down arrow to specify a different currency, such as Euro.

● To quickly apply percent signs to your data, click the **Percent Style** button (%).

● To quickly apply commas to your number data, click the **Comma Style** button.

● Click the corner group button to open the Format Cells dialog box, with more number-formatting options.

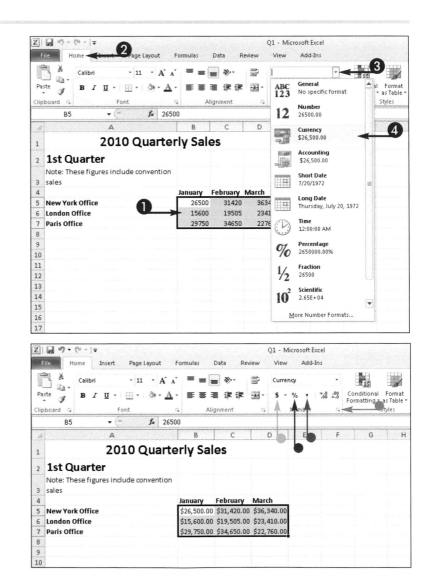

Increase or Decrease Decimals

You can control the number of decimals that appear with numeric data using the Increase Decimal and Decrease Decimal buttons. For example, you may want to increase the number of decimals shown in a cell, or reduce the number of decimals in a formula result.

Increase or Decrease Decimals

① Select the cell or range that you want to format.

② Click the **Home** tab on the Ribbon.

③ Click a decimal button.

You can click **Increase Decimal** (🔢) to increase the number of decimals.

You can click **Decrease Decimal** (🔢) to decrease the number of decimals.

	January	February	March
New York Office	$26,500.00	$31,420.00	$36,340.00
London Office	$15,600.00	$19,505.00	$23,410.00
Paris Office	$29,750.00	$34,650.00	$22,760.00

Excel adjusts the number of decimals that appear in the cell or cells.

● This example removes one decimal.

● You can click **Decrease Decimal** (🔢) again to remove another decimal.

	January	February	March
New York Office	$26,500.0	$31,420.0	$36,340.0
London Office	$15,600.0	$19,505.0	$23,410.0
Paris Office	$29,750.0	$34,650.0	$22,760.0

Add Borders

By default, Excel displays a grid format to help you enter data, but the lines defining the borders of the grid do not print. You can add printable borders to your worksheet cells to help define the contents or more clearly separate the data from surrounding cells. Borders can be added to all four sides of a cell or to just one, two, or three sides.

Add Quick Borders

1. Select the cells that you want to format.

2. Click the **Home** tab on the Ribbon.

3. Click the ▾ next to the **Borders** button (▦).

Note: To apply the current border selection shown, simply click the **Borders** button (▦).

4. Click a border style.

- Excel assigns the borders to the cell or cells.

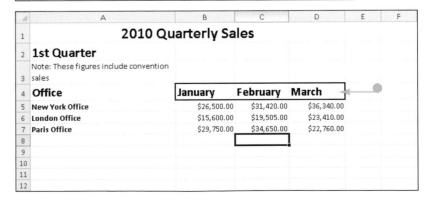

156

Create Custom Borders

1 Select the cells that you want to format.

2 Click the **Home** tab on the Ribbon.

3 Click the ▾ next to the **Borders** button (▦).

4 Click **More Borders**.

The Format Cells dialog box appears with the Border tab displayed.

5 Click the type of border that you want to add.

● Click here to assign a preset style.

● You can use these settings to select a different border line style and color.

● You can click multiple border buttons to create a custom border.

● The Preview area displays a sample of the selections.

6 Click **OK**.

● Excel applies the border.

A	B	C	D	E	F	G	H
1	**2010 Quarterly Sales**						
2	**1st Quarter**						
3	Note: These figures include convention sales						
4	**Office**	**January**	**February**	**March**			
5	New York Office	$26,500.00	$31,420.00	$36,340.00			
6	London Office	$15,600.00	$19,505.00	$23,410.00			
7	Paris Office	$29,750.00	$34,650.00	$22,760.00			

TIPS

How do I turn worksheet gridlines on and off?

The Excel work area contains a grid, but this grid does not print. To see how your data will look when printed, you can hide the grid. Click the **Page Layout** tab and, in the Sheet Options group, deselect the **View** check box under **Gridlines**. Note that you can also turn the gridlines on or off for printing via the **Print** check box under **Gridlines**.

How do I add color inside my worksheet cells?

You can click the ▾ next to the Home tab's **Fill Color** button (▦) to display a palette of fill colors. When you select a color from the palette, the cell's background changes to the color you chose. Avoid picking a color that makes it difficult to read your cell data.

Format Data with Styles

You can use Excel's styles to apply preset formatting designs to your worksheet data. You can apply table styles to a group of worksheet data, or you can apply cell styles to individual cells or ranges of cells. When you apply a table style, Excel converts the data into a table.

Format as a Table

1. Select the cells that you want to format.

2. Click the **Home** tab on the Ribbon.

3. Click the **Format as Table** button.

4. Click a table style.

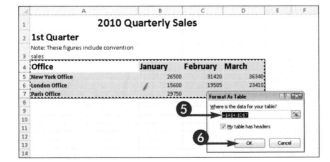

The Format As Table dialog box appears.

5. Verify the selected cells.

6. Click **OK**.

● Excel applies the formatting style.

Apply a Cell Style

1 Select the cell or cells that you want to format.

2 Click the **Home** tab on the Ribbon.

3 Click the **Cell Styles** button.

4 Click a style.

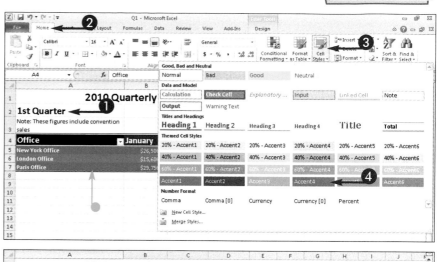

● Excel applies the formatting to the selected cell.

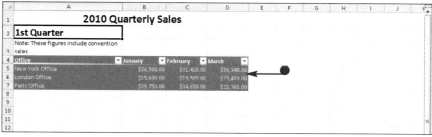

Can I add a background to my spreadsheet?

Yes. You can add a background picture to any sheet. To do so, click the **Page Layout** tab on the Ribbon and click the **Background** button. The Sheet Background dialog box opens; locate and select the picture you want to use. Be careful when applying background images to your worksheet; make sure the image does not distract from the legibility of your cell data.

How do I apply a theme?

You can use themes to create a similar appearance among all the Office documents that you create. Themes are shared through Word, PowerPoint, and Excel. To apply a theme to your spreadsheet, simply click the **Page Layout** tab on the Ribbon, click the **Themes** button, and select a theme from the list. You can use the Colors, Fonts, and Effects tools to fine-tune a theme.

Apply Conditional Formatting

You can use conditional formatting to apply certain formatting when the value of a cell meets the required condition. For example, if your worksheet tracks weekly sales, you might set up conditional formatting to alert you if a sales figure falls below what is required for you to break even. You can also use color scales and data bars to help you distinguish the degree to which various cells meet your conditional rules.

Apply Conditional Formatting

Apply a Conditional Rule

① Select the cell or range to which you want to apply conditional formatting.

② Click the **Home** tab on the Ribbon.

③ Click the **Conditional Formatting** button.

④ Click **Highlight Cells Rules**.

⑤ Click the type of rule that you want to create.

A rule dialog box appears.

⑥ Specify the values that you want to assign for the condition.

⑦ Click **OK**.

- If the value of a selected cell meets the condition, Excel applies the conditional formatting.

Apply a Color Scale

1. Select the cell or range that contains the conditional formatting.

2. Click the **Home** tab on the Ribbon.

3. Click the **Conditional Formatting** button.

4. Click **Color Scales**.

5. Click a color scale.

- You can apply color bars instead by clicking **Data Bars**.

- Excel applies the color scale to the conditional formatting.

2010 Quarterly Sales

1st Quarter

Note: These figures include convention sales

Office	January	February	March
New York Office	$26,500.00	$31,420.00	$36,340.00
London Office	$15,600.00	$19,505.00	$23,410.00
Paris Office	$29,750.00	$34,650.00	$22,760.00

2010 Quarterly Sales

1st Quarter

Note: These figures include convention sales

Office	January	February	March
New York Office	$26,500.00	$31,420.00	$36,340.00
London Office	$15,600.00	$19,505.00	$23,410.00
Paris Office	$29,750.00	$34,650.00	$22,760.00

 TIPS

How do I create a new rule for conditional formatting?

You use the New Formatting Rule dialog box to set a new rule and formatting for the condition that you set. To open this dialog box, click the **Conditional Formatting** button on the Home tab, and then click **New Rule**. Use the dialog box to define the condition of the rule, as well as what formatting you want to apply when the condition is met.

How do I remove conditional formatting from a cell?

To remove conditional formatting, select the data that contains the formatting you want to remove, click the **Conditional Formatting** button on the Home tab, and then click **Manage Rules**. Next, click the rule that you want to remove, and click **Delete Rule**. Click **OK** to close the dialog box.

Add Columns and Rows

You can add columns and rows to your worksheets to include more data. For example, you may need to add a column in the middle of several existing columns to add data that you left out the first time you created the workbook.

Add a Column

1 Click the heading of the column to the right of where you want to insert a new column.

2 Click the **Home** tab on the Ribbon.

3 Click the **Insert** ⏷.

4 Click **Insert Sheet Columns**.

You can also right-click a column heading and click **Insert**.

● Excel adds a column.

● A smart tag icon (🗇) may appear when you insert a column; click it to view a list of options that you can apply.

Add a Row

1. Click the heading of the row below where you want to insert a new row.

2. Click the **Home** tab on the Ribbon.

3. Click the **Insert** ⏷.

4. Click **Insert Sheet Rows**.

   You can also right-click a row heading and click **Insert**.

- Excel adds a row.

- A smart tag icon (⬦) may appear, and you can click the icon to view a list of options that you can assign.

Can I insert multiple columns and rows?
Yes. First, select two or more columns and rows in the worksheet and then activate the **Insert** command as shown in this section. Excel adds the same number of new columns and rows as the number you originally selected. You can also right-click the selected columns or rows, and then click **Insert** to insert multiple columns or rows into your worksheet.

Can I insert columns or rows using the Insert dialog box?
Yes. Click a cell, click the **Insert** ⏷ on the Home tab, and click **Insert Cells** to open the Insert dialog box. You can then click the **Entire Row** or **Entire Column** options. When you click **OK** to exit the dialog box, Excel adds a single row or column above or to the left of the active cell.

Resize Columns and Rows

You can resize your worksheet's columns and rows to accommodate text or make the worksheet more aesthetically appealing.

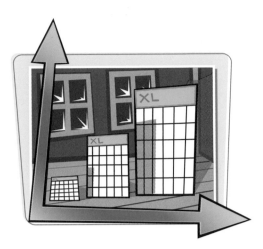

① Position the mouse pointer over the border of the heading of the column or row that you want to resize.

The pointer changes to ✛.

② Click and drag the border to the desired size.

● A dotted line marks the new border of the column or row as you drag.

③ Release the mouse button.

Excel resizes the column or row.

● You can also click the **Format** button on the Home tab, and then click **AutoFit Selection** to quickly resize a highlighted column to fit existing text.

Freeze a Column or Row

You can freeze a column or row to keep the labels in view as you scroll through larger worksheets. You cannot scroll the area that you freeze, but you can scroll the unfrozen areas of the worksheet.

Freeze a Column or Row

1 Click the cell to the right of the column or below the row that you want to freeze.

2 Click the **View** tab on the Ribbon.

3 Click the **Freeze Panes** ⏷.

4 Click **Freeze Panes**.

You can also choose to freeze a row of column headings or a column of row titles.

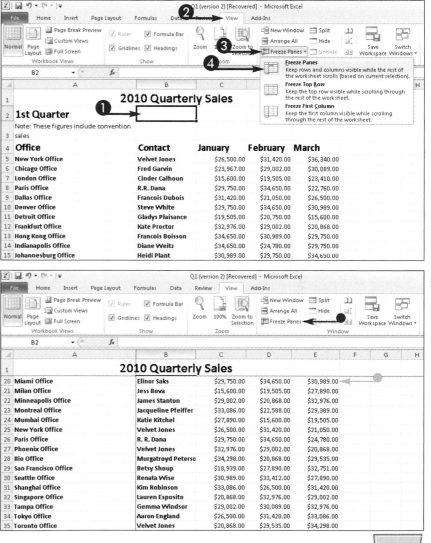

● Excel freezes the areas above or to the left of the selected cell (depending on whether you are scrolling up and down or left and right).

● To unlock the columns and rows, click the **Freeze Panes** ⏷, and then click **Unfreeze Panes**.

Name a Range

You can assign distinctive names to the cells and ranges of cells that you work with in a worksheet, making it easier to identify its contents. A *range* is simply a rectangular group of related cells; a range can also consist of a single cell. Naming ranges can also help you when deciphering formulas. (Formulas are discussed later in this book.)

Name a Range

Assign a Range Name

1. Select the cells comprising the range that you want to name.

2. Click the **Formulas** tab on the Ribbon.

3. Click the **Define Name** button.

   The New Name dialog box opens.

4. Type a name for the selected range in the **Name** field.

● You can add a comment or note about the range here. For example, you might indicate what data the range contains.

5. Click **OK**.

Note: *Another way to name a range is to select the cells in the range, click in the **Name** field to the left of the Formula bar, type the desired name, and press* **Enter**.

● Excel assigns the name to the cells.

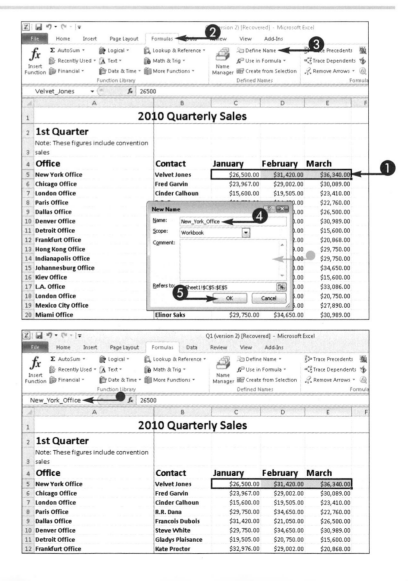

Go to a Range

1 Click the **Name** ▾.

2 Click the name of the range of cells to which you want to move.

● Excel selects the cells in the range.

Are there any rules for naming ranges?

Yes. Range names must start with a letter or an underscore (_) or backslash (\). After that, you can use any character, uppercase or lowercase, or any punctuation or keyboard symbols, with the exception of a hyphen or space. Because neither hyphens nor spaces are allowed in range names, you can substitute them with a period or underscore.

How do I edit a range name?

You can use the Name Manager feature to make changes to your range names. To display the Name Manager, click the **Name Manager** button on the Formulas tab. You can edit existing range names, change the cells referenced by a range, or remove ranges to which you no longer need names assigned in the worksheet.

Delete Data or Cells

You can delete Excel data that you no longer need. When you decide to delete data, you can choose whether you want to remove the data and keep the cells or delete the cells entirely. When you delete a cell's contents, Excel removes only the data. When you delete a cell, Excel removes the cell as well as its contents. The existing cells in your worksheet shift over to fill any gap in the worksheet structure.

Delete Data or Cells

Delete Data

① Select the cell or cells containing the data that you want to remove.

② Press **Delete**.

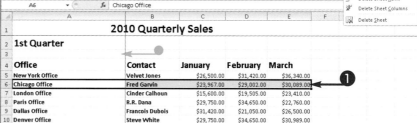

● Excel deletes the data from the cell, but the cell remains.

Delete Cells

① Select the cell or cells that you want to remove.

② Click the **Home** tab.

③ Click the **Delete** ⏷.

④ Click **Delete Cells**.

You can also right-click the selected cells and then click the **Delete** command.

The Delete dialog box appears.

5 Click a deletion option.

6 Click **OK**.

▲	A	B	C	D	E	F
1			2010 Quarterly Sales			
2	1st Quarter					
3						
4	Office	Contact	January	February	March	
5	New York Office	Velvet Jones	$26,500.00	$31,420.00	$36,340.00	
6	Chicago Office	Fred Garvin	$23,967.00	$29,002.00	$30,089.00	
7	London Office	Cinder Calhoun	$15,600.00	$19,505.00	$23,410.00	
8	Paris Office	R.R. Dana	$29,750.00	$34,650.00	$22,760.00	
9	Dallas Office	Francois Dubo	21,050.00	$26,500.00		
10	Denver Office	Steve White	34,650.00	$30,989.00		
11	Detroit Office	Glad..Plaisar	20,750.00	$15,600.00		
12	Frankfurt Office	Kate..ctor	29,002.00	$20,868.00		
13	Hong Kong Office	Francois Boiss	30,989.00	$29,750.00		
14	Indianapolis Office	Diane Weitz	24,780.00	$29,750.00		
15	Johannesburg Office	Hei..ant	29,750.00	$34,650.00		
16	Kiev Office	Velvet Jones	27,890.00	$15,600.00		
17	L.A. Office	Velvet Jones	$26,500.00	$31,420.00	$33,086.00	

Delete dialog box:
Delete
- ○ Shift cells left
- ⦿ Shift cells up ← **5**
- ○ Entire row
- ○ Entire column

6 → OK Cancel

● Excel removes the cells and their content from the worksheet.

Other cells shift over or up to fill the void of any cells that you remove from your worksheet.

▲	A	B	C	D	E	F
1			2010 Quarterly Sales			
2	1st Quarter					
3						
4	Office	Contact	January	February	March	
5	New York Office	Velvet Jones	$26,500.00	$31,420.00	$36,340.00	
6	London Office	Cinder Calhoun	$15,600.00	$19,505.00	$23,410.00	
7	Paris Office	R.R. Dana	$29,750.00	$34,650.00	$22,760.00	
8	Dallas Office	Francois Dubois	$31,420.00	$21,050.00	$26,500.00	
9	Denver Office	Steve White	$29,750.00	$34,650.00	$30,989.00	
10	Detroit Office	Gladys Plaisance	$19,505.00	$20,750.00	$15,600.00	
11	Frankfurt Office	Kate Proctor	$32,976.00	$29,002.00	$20,868.00	
12	Hong Kong Office	Francois Boisson	$34,650.00	$30,989.00	$29,750.00	
13	Indianapolis Office	Diane Weitz	$34,650.00	$24,780.00	$29,750.00	
14	Johannesburg Office	Heidi Plant	$30,989.00	$29,750.00	$34,650.00	
15	Kiev Office	Velvet Jones	$19,505.00	$27,890.00	$15,600.00	

TIPS

How do I delete a whole column or row?

If you no longer need a column or row in your worksheet, you can delete it. When you do, Excel deletes any existing data within the selected column or row, as well as moving subsequent columns or rows to fill the space left by the deletion. To delete a column or row, click its heading to select it; then click the **Delete** button in the Home tab.

Can I remove a cell's formatting without removing the content?

Yes. To do so, select the cell or cells that you want to edit and click the **Home** tab on the Ribbon. Click the **Clear** button (⬚). A submenu appears; click **Clear Formats** to remove all of the formatting in the cell. Click **Clear Contents** to remove all of the cell's data. Click **Clear Comments** to remove any comments assigned to the cell. Click **Clear Hyperlinks** to remove any hyperlinks from the cell. To remove all formatting, contents, and comments at the same time, click **Clear All**.

CLEAR

Add a Worksheet

You can add a worksheet to your workbook in which to enter more data. By default, every Excel workbook opens with three worksheets. You can add more worksheets as you need them.

1 Click the **Insert Worksheet** button (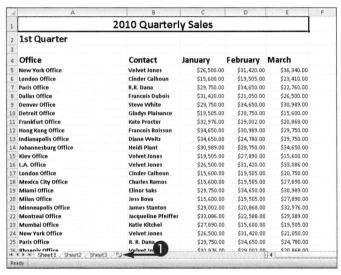).

You can also right-click a worksheet tab and click **Insert** to open the Insert dialog box, where you can choose to insert a worksheet.

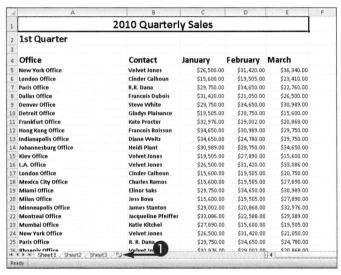

● Excel adds a new worksheet and gives it a default worksheet name.

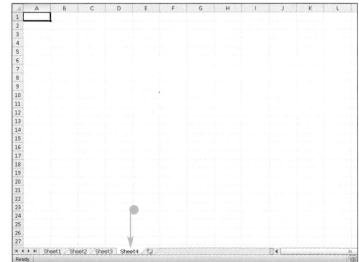

Name a Worksheet

You can name your Excel worksheets to help identify
their content. For example, if your workbook contains
four worksheets, each detailing a different sales quarter,
then you can give each worksheet a unique name, such as
Quarter 1, Quarter 2, and so on.

Name a Worksheet

① Double-click the worksheet tab
that you want to rename.

Excel highlights the current name.

You can also right-click the
worksheet name and click
Rename.

	A	B	C	D	E
1		**2010 Quarterly Sales**			
2	**1st Quarter**				
3					
4	**Office**	**Contact**	**January**	**February**	**March**
5	New York Office	Velvet Jones	$26,500.00	$31,420.00	$36,340.00
6	London Office	Cinder Calhoun	$15,600.00	$19,505.00	$23,410.00
7	Paris Office	R.R. Dana	$29,750.00	$34,650.00	$22,760.00
8	Dallas Office	Francois Dubois	$31,420.00	$21,050.00	$26,500.00
9	Denver Office	Steve White	$29,750.00	$34,650.00	$30,989.00
10	Detroit Office	Gladys Plaisance	$19,505.00	$20,750.00	$15,600.00
11	Frankfurt Office	Kate Proctor	$32,976.00	$29,002.00	$20,868.00
12	Hong Kong Office	Francois Boisson	$34,650.00	$30,989.00	$29,750.00
13	Indianapolis Office	Diane Weitz	$34,650.00	$24,780.00	$29,750.00
14	Johannesburg Office	Heidi Plant	$30,989.00	$29,750.00	$34,650.00
15	Kiev Office	Velvet Jones	$19,505.00	$27,890.00	$15,600.00
16	L.A. Office	Velvet Jones	$26,500.00	$31,420.00	$33,086.00
17	London Office	Cinder Calhoun	$15,600.00	$19,505.00	$20,750.00
18	Mexico City Office	Charles Ramos	$15,600.00	$19,505.00	$27,890.00
19	Miami Office	Elinor Saks	$29,750.00	$34,650.00	$30,989.00
20	Milan Office	Jess Bova	$15,600.00	$19,505.00	$27,890.00
21	Minneapolis Office	James Stanton	$29,002.00	$20,868.00	$32,976.00
22	Montreal Office	Jacqueline Pfeiffer	$33,086.00	$22,588.00	$29,389.00
23	Mumbai Office	Katie Kitchel	$27,890.00	$15,600.00	$19,505.00
24	New York Office	Velvet Jones	$26,500.00	$31,420.00	$21,050.00
25	Paris Office	R. R. Dana	$29,750.00	$34,650.00	$24,780.00
26	Phoenix Office	Velvet Jones	$32,976.00	$29,002.00	$20,868.00

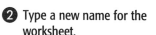

Sheet1 Sheet2 Sheet3 Sheet4

Ready

② Type a new name for the
worksheet.

③ Press **Enter**.

Excel assigns the new worksheet
name.

	A	B	C	D	E
1		**2010 Quarterly Sales**			
2	**1st Quarter**				
3					
4	**Office**	**Contact**	**January**	**February**	**March**
5	New York Office	Velvet Jones	$26,500.00	$31,420.00	$36,340.00
6	London Office	Cinder Calhoun	$15,600.00	$19,505.00	$23,410.00
7	Paris Office	R.R. Dana	$29,750.00	$34,650.00	$22,760.00
8	Dallas Office	Francois Dubois	$31,420.00	$21,050.00	$26,500.00
9	Denver Office	Steve White	$29,750.00	$34,650.00	$30,989.00
10	Detroit Office	Gladys Plaisance	$19,505.00	$20,750.00	$15,600.00
11	Frankfurt Office	Kate Proctor	$32,976.00	$29,002.00	$20,868.00
12	Hong Kong Office	Francois Boisson	$34,650.00	$30,989.00	$29,750.00
13	Indianapolis Office	Diane Weitz	$34,650.00	$24,780.00	$29,750.00
14	Johannesburg Office	Heidi Plant	$30,989.00	$29,750.00	$34,650.00
15	Kiev Office	Velvet Jones	$19,505.00	$27,890.00	$15,600.00
16	L.A. Office	Velvet Jones	$26,500.00	$31,420.00	$33,086.00
17	London Office	Cinder Calhoun	$15,600.00	$19,505.00	$20,750.00
18	Mexico City Office	Charles Ramos	$15,600.00	$19,505.00	$27,890.00
19	Miami Office	Elinor Saks	$29,750.00	$34,650.00	$30,989.00
20	Milan Office	Jess Bova	$15,600.00	$19,505.00	$27,890.00
21	Minneapolis Office	James Stanton	$29,002.00	$20,868.00	$32,976.00
22	Montreal Office	Jacqueline Pfeiffer	$33,086.00	$22,588.00	$29,389.00
23	Mumbai Office	Katie Kitchel	$27,890.00	$15,600.00	$19,505.00
24	New York Office	Velvet Jones	$26,500.00	$31,420.00	$21,050.00
25	Paris Office	R. R. Dana	$29,750.00	$34,650.00	$24,780.00
26	Phoenix Office	Velvet Jones	$32,976.00	$29,002.00	$20,868.00

1st Quarter Sheet2 Sheet3 Sheet4

Ready

Change Page Setup Options

You can assign page setup options, such as orientation, margins, paper size, and more. For example, if your workbook data is too wide to fit on a standard sheet of paper, you can change the page orientation to Landscape to fit more data on the page horizontally. You can also insert your own page breaks to control the placement of data on a printed page.

Change the Page Orientation

① Click the **Page Layout** tab on the Ribbon.

② Click the **Orientation** button.

③ Click **Portrait** or **Landscape**.

Note: Portrait is the default orientation.

Excel applies the new orientation. This example applies Landscape.

● Excel marks the edge of the page with a dotted line.

● You can click the **Margins** button to set up page margins.

Insert a Page Break

1 Select the row above which you want to insert a page break.

2 Click the **Page Layout** tab on the Ribbon.

3 Click the **Breaks** button.

4 Click **Insert Page Break**.

	A		B	C	D	E	F	G	H
1			**2010 Quarterly Sales**						
2	**1st Quarter**								
3									
4	**Office**		**Contact**	**January**	**February**	**March**			
5	New York Office		Velvet Jones	$26,500.00	$31,420.00	$36,340.00			
6	London Office		Cinder Calhoun	$15,600.00	$19,505.00	$23,410.00			
7	Paris Office		R.R. Dana	$29,750.00	$34,650.00	$22,760.00			
8	Dallas Office		Francois Dubois	$31,420.00	$21,050.00	$26,500.00			
9	Denver Office		Steve White	$29,750.00	$34,650.00	$30,989.00			
10	Detroit Office		Gladys Plaisance	$19,505.00	$20,750.00	$15,600.00			
11	Frankfurt Office		Kate Proctor	$32,976.00	$29,002.00	$20,868.00			
12	Hong Kong Office		Francois Boisson	$34,650.00	$30,989.00	$29,750.00			
13	Indianapolis Office		Diane Weitz	$34,650.00	$24,780.00	$29,750.00			
14	Johannesburg Office		Heidi Plant	$30,989.00	$29,750.00	$34,650.00			
15	Kiev Office		Velvet Jones	$19,505.00	$27,890.00	$15,600.00			
16	L.A. Office		Velvet Jones	$26,500.00	$31,420.00	$33,086.00			
17	London Office		Cinder Calhoun	$15,600.00	$19,505.00	$20,750.00			
18	Mexico City Office		Charles Ramos	$15,600.00	$19,505.00	$27,890.00			
19	Miami Office		Elinor Saks	$29,750.00	$34,650.00	$30,989.00			
20	Milan Office		Jess Bova	$15,600.00	$19,505.00	$27,890.00			
21	Minneapolis Office		James Stanton	$29,002.00	$20,868.00	$32,976.00			
22	Montreal Office		Jacqueline Pfeiffer	$33,086.00	$22,588.00	$29,389.00			

Excel inserts a page break.

● Excel marks the edge of the page with a dotted line.

	A	B	C	D	E	F	G
1			**2010 Quarterly Sales**				
2	**1st Quarter**						
3							
4	**Office**		**Contact**	**January**	**February**	**March**	
5	New York Office		Velvet Jones	$26,500.00	$31,420.00	$36,340.00	
6	London Office		Cinder Calhoun	$15,600.00	$19,505.00	$23,410.00	
7	Paris Office		R.R. Dana	$29,750.00	$34,650.00	$22,760.00	
8	Dallas Office		Francois Dubois	$31,420.00	$21,050.00	$26,500.00	
9	Denver Office		Steve White	$29,750.00	$34,650.00	$30,989.00	
10	Detroit Office		Gladys Plaisance	$19,505.00	$20,750.00	$15,600.00	
11	Frankfurt Office		Kate Proctor	$32,976.00	$29,002.00	$20,868.00	
12	Hong Kong Office		Francois Boisson	$34,650.00	$30,989.00	$29,750.00	
13	Indianapolis Office		Diane Weitz	$34,650.00	$24,780.00	$29,750.00	
14	Johannesburg Office		Heidi Plant	$30,989.00	$29,750.00	$34,650.00	
15	Kiev Office		Velvet Jones	$19,505.00	$27,890.00	$15,600.00	
16	L.A. Office		Velvet Jones	$26,500.00	$31,420.00	$33,086.00	
17	London Office		Cinder Calhoun	$15,600.00	$19,505.00	$20,750.00	
18	Mexico City Office		Charles Ramos	$15,600.00	$19,505.00	$27,890.00	
19	Miami Office		Elinor Saks	$29,750.00	$34,650.00	$30,989.00	
20	Milan Office		Jess Bova	$15,600.00	$19,505.00	$27,890.00	
21	Minneapolis Office		James Stanton	$29,002.00	$20,868.00	$32,976.00	
22	Montreal Office		Jacqueline Pfeiffer	$33,086.00	$22,588.00	$29,389.00	

TIPS

How do I define a print area?

If you want to print only a portion of a worksheet, you can define a print area. This prevents Excel from printing the entire worksheet every time you print. To do so, select the cells that you want to define as the print area, click the **Page Layout** tab on the Ribbon, click the **Print Area** button, and click **Set Print Area**. Excel defines the print area.

How do I print a spreadsheet with gridlines?

By default, the gridlines that you see on a worksheet do not print with the cell data. To turn on gridlines for printing purposes, simply select the **Print** check box under **Gridlines** on the Page Layout tab. A check mark in the check box indicates that the feature is on.

Move and Copy Worksheets

You can move a worksheet within a workbook to rearrange the worksheet order. For example, you may want to position the worksheet that you use most often as the first worksheet in the workbook. In addition to moving worksheets within a workbook, you can copy them. You might copy a worksheet to use it as a starting point for data that is new, yet similar.

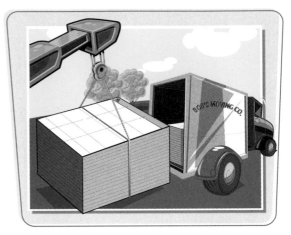

❶ Click the tab of the worksheet that you want to move or copy.

❷ Move or copy the worksheet to the desired spot.

To move the worksheet, drag it to a new position in the list of worksheets. (The ⍉ changes to ⍉.)

To copy the worksheet, press and hold **Ctrl** and drag the worksheet copy to a new position in the list of worksheets. (The ⍉ changes to ⍉.)

● A small black triangle icon keeps track of the worksheet's location in the group while you drag.

❸ Release the mouse button.

● Excel moves or copies the worksheet. (Here, the worksheet was moved.)

17	London Office		Cinder Calhoun	$15,600.00	$19,505.00
18	Mexico City Office		Charles Ramos	$15,600.00	$19,505.00
19	Miami Office		Elinor Saks	$29,750.00	$34,650.00
20	Milan Office		Jess Bova	$15,600.00	$19,505.00
21	Minneapolis Office		James Stanton	$29,002.00	$20,868.00
22	Montreal Office		Jacqueline Pfeiffer	$33,086.00	$22,588.00
23	Mumbai Office		Katie Kitchel	$27,890.00	$15,600.00
24	Phoenix Office		Velvet Jones	$32,976.00	$29,002.00
25	Rio Office		Murgatroyd Peterso	$34,298.00	$20,868.00
26	San Francisco Office		Betsy Shoun	$18,939.00	$27,890.00

|◀ ◀ ▶ ▶| **1st Quarter** / 2nd Quarter / 3rd Quarter / 4th Quarter / 🗐 /

Ready

17	London Office		Cinder Calhoun	$15,600.00	$19,505.00
18	Mexico City Office		Charles Ramos	$15,600.00	$19,505.00
19	Miami Office		Elinor Saks	$29,750.00	$34,650.00
20	Milan Office		Jess Bova	$15,600.00	$19,505.00
21	Minneapolis Office		James Stanton	$29,002.00	$20,868.00
22	Montreal Office		Jacqueline Pfeiffer	$33,086.00	$22,588.00
23	Mumbai Office		Katie Kitchel	$27,890.00	$15,600.00
24	Phoenix Office		Velvet Jones	$32,976.00	$29,002.00
25	Rio Office		Murgatroyd Peterso	$34,298.00	$20,868.00
26	San Francisco Office		Betsy Shoun	$18,939.00	$27,890.00

|◀ ◀ ▶ ▶| 2nd Quarter / **1st Quarter** / 3rd Quarter / 4th Quarter / 🗐 /

Ready

Note: Excel names worksheet copies sequentially with a number, starting with (2), after the worksheet name.

You can delete a worksheet that you no longer need in your workbook. You should always check the worksheet's contents before deleting it to avoid removing any important data. As soon as you delete a worksheet, Excel permanently removes it from the workbook file.

Delete a Worksheet

1 Right-click the worksheet tab.

2 Click **Delete**.

Note: You can also click the **Delete** ▾ on the Home tab and then click **Delete**.

4	Office	Contact	January	February	March
5	New York Office	Velvet Jones	$26,500.00	$31,420.00	$36,340.00
6	London Office	Cinder Calhoun	$15,600.00	$19,505.00	$23,410.00
7	Paris Office	R.R. Dana	$29,750.00	$34,650.00	$22,760.00
8	Dallas Office	Francois Dubois	$31,420.00	$21,050.00	$26,500.00
9	Denver Office	Steve White	$29,750.00	$34,650.00	$30,989.00
10	Detroit Office	Gladys Plaisance	$19,505.00	$20,750.00	$15,600.00
11	Frankfurt Office	Kate Proctor	$32,976.00	$29,002.00	$20,868.00
12	Hong Kong Office	Francois Boisson	$34,650.00	$30,989.00	$29,750.00
13	Indianapolis Office	Diane Weitz	$34,650.00	$24,780.00	$29,750.00
14	Johannesburg Office	Heidi Plant	$30,989.00	$29,750.00	$34,650.00
15	Kiev Office		$19,505.00	$27,890.00	$15,600.00
16	L.A. Office		$26,500.00	$31,420.00	$33,086.00
17	London Office		$15,600.00	$19,505.00	$20,750.00
18	Mexico City Office		$15,600.00	$19,505.00	$27,890.00
19	Miami Office		$29,750.00	$34,650.00	$30,989.00
20	Milan Office		$15,600.00	$19,505.00	$27,890.00
21	Minneapolis Office		$29,002.00	$20,868.00	$32,976.00
22	Montreal Office		$33,086.00	$22,588.00	$29,389.00
23	Mumbai Office		$27,890.00	$15,600.00	$19,505.00
24	Phoenix Office		$32,976.00	$29,002.00	$20,868.00
25	Rio Office		$34,298.00	$20,868.00	$29,535.00
26	San Francisco Office		$18,939.00	$27,090.00	$22,751.00

Menu: Insert... / Delete / Rename / Move or Copy... / View Code / Protect Sheet... / Tab Color ▸ / Hide / Unhide... / Select All Sheets

Tabs: 2nd Quarter / 1st Quarter (2) / 3rd Quarter / 4th Quarter

Ready

If the worksheet is blank, Excel deletes it immediately.

If the worksheet contains any data, Excel prompts you to confirm the deletion.

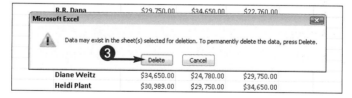

R.R. Dana $29,750.00 $34,650.00 $22,760.00

Microsoft Excel

⚠ Data may exist in the sheet(s) selected for deletion. To permanently delete the data, press Delete.

3 [Delete] [Cancel]

Diane Weitz $34,650.00 $24,780.00 $29,750.00
Heidi Plant $30,989.00 $29,750.00 $34,650.00

3 Click **Delete**.

Excel deletes the worksheet.

Find and Replace Data

You can use Excel's Find tool to search through your worksheet for a particular number, formula, word, or phrase. You can use the Replace tool to replace instances of text or numbers with other data. For example, you may need to sort through a long worksheet to replace a reference with another name.

Find and Replace Data

Find Data

1 Click the **Home** tab on the Ribbon.

2 Click the **Find & Select** button.

3 Click **Find**.

The Find and Replace dialog box appears, displaying the Find tab.

4 Type the data that you want to find.

5 Click **Find Next**.

● Excel searches the worksheet and finds the first occurrence of the data.

You can click **Find Next** again to search for the next occurrence.

6 When finished, click **Close** to close the dialog box.

Note: *Excel may display a prompt box when the last occurrence is found. Click OK.*

Replace Data

1 Click the **Home** tab on the Ribbon.

2 Click the **Find & Select** button.

3 Click **Replace**.

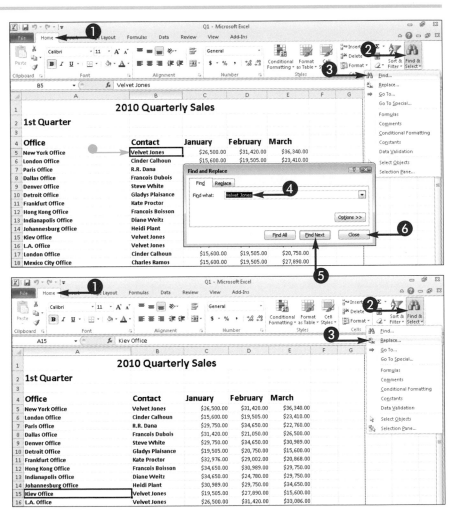

The Find and Replace dialog box appears, displaying the Replace tab.

④ Type the data that you want to find.

⑤ Type the replacement data.

⑥ Click **Find Next**.

● Excel locates the first occurrence of the data.

⑦ Click **Replace** to replace it.

● You can click **Replace All** to replace every occurrence in the worksheet.

● Excel replaces the data with the text you typed.

● Excel selects the next instance of the data.

⑧ When finished, click **Close**.

Note: *Excel may display a prompt box when the last occurrence is found. Click* **OK**.

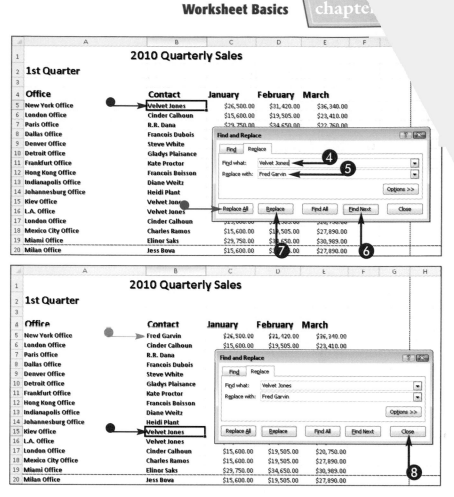

Where can I find detailed search options?

You can click the **Options** button in the Find and Replace dialog box to reveal additional search options. For example, you can search by rows or columns, matching data, and more. You can also search for specific formatting or special characters using Format options. To hide the additional search options, click the **Options** button again.

How can I search for and delete data?

You can search for a particular word, number, or phrase using the Find and Replace dialog box, and remove the data completely from the worksheet. Start by typing the text in the **Find what** field; then leave the **Replace with** field empty. When you activate the search, Excel looks for the data and deletes it without adding new data to the worksheet.

...xcel data to reorganize the
...is technique is particularly useful
...xcel to create database tables. For
..., you might want to sort a client table to
...e names alphabetically. Ascending sorts list
...cords from A to Z or from lowest number to
highest number; descending sorts list records from
Z to A or from highest number to lowest number.

Sort Data

Perform a Quick Sort

1 Click in the field name, or heading, that you want to sort.

2 Click the **Home** tab on the Ribbon.

3 Click the **Sort & Filter** button.

4 Click an ascending or descending sort command.

● Excel sorts the records.

Q1 - Microsoft Excel

	A	B	C	D	E
1		**2010 Quarterly Sales**			
2	**1st Quarter**				
3					
4	**Office**	Contact	**January**	**February**	**March**
5	New York Office	Fred Garvin	$26,500.00	$31,420.00	$36,340.00
6	London Office	Cinder Calhoun	$15,600.00	$19,505.00	$23,410.00
7	Paris Office	R.R. Dana	$29,750.00	$34,650.00	$22,760.00
8	Dallas Office	Francois Dubois	$31,420.00	$21,050.00	$26,500.00
9	Denver Office	Steve White	$29,750.00	$34,650.00	$30,989.00
10	Detroit Office	Gladys Plaisance	$19,505.00	$20,750.00	$15,600.00
11	Frankfurt Office	Kate Proctor	$32,976.00	$29,002.00	$20,868.00
12	Hong Kong Office	Francois Boisson	$34,650.00	$30,989.00	$29,750.00
13	Indianapolis Office	Diane Weitz	$34,650.00	$24,780.00	$29,750.00
14	Johannesburg Office	Heidi Plant	$30,989.00	$29,750.00	$34,650.00
15	Kiev Office	Fred Garvin	$19,505.00	$27,890.00	$15,600.00

Sort A to Z
Sort Z to A
Custom Sort...
Filter
Clear
Reapply

	A	B	C	D	E
1		**2010 Quarterly Sales**			
2	**1st Quarter**				
3					
4	**Office**	Contact	**January**	**February**	**March**
5	Dallas Office	Francois Dubois	$31,420.00	$21,050.00	$26,500.00
6	Denver Office	Steve White	$29,750.00	$34,650.00	$30,989.00
7	Detroit Office	Gladys Plaisance	$19,505.00	$20,750.00	$15,600.00
8	Frankfurt Office	Kate Proctor	$32,976.00	$29,002.00	$20,868.00
9	Hong Kong Office	Francois Boisson	$34,650.00	$30,989.00	$29,750.00
10	Indianapolis Office	Diane Weitz	$34,650.00	$24,780.00	$29,750.00
11	Johannesburg Office	Heidi Plant	$30,989.00	$29,750.00	$34,650.00
12	Kiev Office	Fred Garvin	$19,505.00	$27,890.00	$15,600.00
13	L.A. Office	Fred Garvin	$26,500.00	$31,420.00	$33,086.00
14	London Office	Cinder Calhoun	$15,600.00	$19,505.00	$23,410.00
15	London Office	Cinder Calhoun	$15,600.00	$19,505.00	$20,750.00
16	Mexico City Office	Charles Ramos	$15,600.00	$19,505.00	$27,890.00
17	Miami Office	Elinor Saks	$29,750.00	$34,650.00	$30,989.00
18	Milan Office	Jess Bova	$15,600.00	$19,505.00	$27,890.00
19	Minneapolis Office	James Stanton	$29,002.00	$20,868.00	$32,976.00
20	Montreal Office	Jacqueline Pfeiffer	$33,086.00	$22,588.00	$29,389.00

Perform a Custom Sort

1 Click in the worksheet you want to sort.

2 Click the **Home** tab on the Ribbon.

3 Click the **Sort & Filter** button.

4 Click **Custom Sort**.

The Sort dialog box appears.

5 Click the first **Sort by** ▾ and select the primary field to sort by.

● By default, the Sort On field is set to Values. To sort on another setting, you can click the **Sort On** ▾ and choose a setting.

6 Click the **Order** ▾ to sort the field in ascending or descending order.

● To specify additional sort fields, click **Add Level** and repeat Steps **5** and **6**.

7 Click **OK**.

● Excel sorts the data.

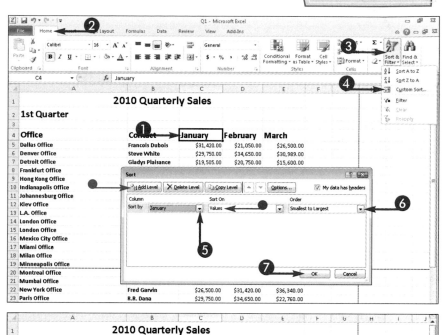

 TIPS

What are database tables?

A database is a list of related information; each entry in the list is called a *record*. You can create a variety of database lists in Excel to manage sales contacts, inventory, household valuables, and more. An entire list is called a *table*. Tables contain *fields* — typically columns — to break the list into manageable pieces. Rows contain each record in your list of data.

Can I sort data in rows?

Yes. If the data is across a row rather than down a column, you can activate the Sort left to right option. To do so, open the Sort dialog box as shown in this section, and click the **Options** button. In the Sort Options dialog box that appears, click **Sort left to right**.

Filter Data

When using Excel as a database, you can use an AutoFilter to view only portions of your data. Unlike a sort, which sorts the entire table, a filter selects certain records to display based on your criteria, while hiding records that do not match the criteria. (Refer to the previous section to learn how to sort data in Excel.)

Filter Data

① Select the field names for the data you want to filter.

② Click the **Home** tab on the Ribbon.

③ Click the **Sort & Filter** button.

④ Click **Filter**.

● Excel adds drop-down arrow buttons (▾) to your field names.

⑤ Click a field's ▾.

6 Click the data you want to use as a filter.

7 Click **OK**.

	A	B	C	D	E	F
1		**2010 Quarterly Sales**				
2	**1st Quarter**					
3						
4	**Office**	**Contact**	**January**	**February**	**March**	
5	London Office		$15,600.00	$19,505.00	$23,410.00	
6	London Office		$15,600.00	$19,505.00	$20,750.00	
7	Mexico City Office		$15,600.00	$19,505.00	$27,890.00	
8	Milan Office		$15,600.00	$19,505.00	$27,890.00	
9	San Francisco Offi		$18,939.00	$27,890.00	$32,751.00	
10	Detroit Office		$19,505.00	$20,750.00	$15,600.00	
11	Kiev Office		$19,505.00	$27,890.00	$15,600.00	
12	Singapore Office		$20,868.00	$32,976.00	$29,002.00	
13	Toronto Office		$20,868.00	$29,535.00	$34,298.00	
14	L.A. Office		$26,500.00	$31,420.00	$33,086.00	
15	New York Office		$26,500.00	$31,420.00	$36,340.00	
16	Tokyo Office		$26,500.00	$31,420.00	$33,086.00	
17	Mumbai Office		$27,890.00	$15,600.00	$19,505.00	
18	Vancouver Office		$27,890.00	$32,751.00	$18,939.00	
19	Minneapolis Offic		$29,002.00	$20,868.00	$32,976.00	
20	Tampa Office		$29,002.00	$30,089.00	$32,976.00	
21	Denver Office		$29,750.00	$34,650.00	$30,989.00	
22	Miami Office		$29,750.00	$34,650.00	$30,989.00	
23	Paris Office		$29,750.00	$34,650.00	$22,760.00	
24	Johannesburg Office	Heidi Plant	$30,989.00	$29,750.00	$34,650.00	

Filter dropdown: Sort A to Z, Sort Z to A, Sort by Color, Clear Filter From "Contact", Filter by Color, Text Filters, Search. Diane Weitz, Elinor Saks, Francois Boisson, Francois Dubois, ✓ Fred Garvin, Gemma Windsor, Gladys Plaisance, Heidi Plant, Jacqueline Pfeiffer, James Stanton. OK / Cancel.

● Excel filters the table.

To view all the records again, click the **Sort & Filter** button in the Home tab and choose **Clear**.

	A	B	C	D	E	F
1		**2010 Quarterly Sales**				
2	**1st Quarter**					
3						
4	**Office**	**Contact**	**January**	**February**	**March**	
11	Kiev Office	Fred Garvin	$19,505.00	$27,890.00	$15,600.00	
13	Toronto Office	Fred Garvin	$20,868.00	$29,535.00	$34,298.00	
14	L.A. Office	Fred Garvin	$26,500.00	$31,420.00	$33,086.00	
15	New York Office	Fred Garvin	$26,500.00	$31,420.00	$36,340.00	
28	Phoenix Office	Fred Garvin	$32,976.00	$29,002.00	$20,868.00	

TIP

Can I customize a filter?

Yes. In the Filter drop-down list, click **Text Filters** or **Number Filters**, and then click **Custom Filter** to open the Custom AutoFilter dialog box. Here, you can further customize the filter by selecting operators and values to apply on the filtered data. Here, a custom filter has been set to display all records whose Contact field contains the value Francois Boisson or Fred Garvin. To learn more about customizing AutoFilters, see Excel's help files.

Custom AutoFilter

Show rows where: Contact

equals — Francois Boisson

◯ And ◉ Or

equals — Fred Garvin

Use ? to represent any single character
Use * to represent any series of characters

OK / Cancel

Track and Review Worksheet Changes

If you share your Excel workbooks with others, you can use the program's Track Changes feature to help you keep track of what edits others have made, including formatting changes and data additions or deletions. The Track Changes feature uses different colors for each person's edits, making it easy to see who changed what in the workbook. When you review the workbook, you can choose to accept or reject the changes.

Turn On Tracking

1. Click the **Review** tab on the Ribbon.

2. Click the **Track Changes** 🔽.

3. Click **Highlight Changes**.

The Highlight Changes dialog box appears.

4. Select the **Track changes while editing** check box.

This option automatically creates a shared workbook file if you have not already activated the Share Workbook feature.

- You can select options to choose when, by whom, or where you track changes.

- You can leave this check box selected to view changes in the file.

5. Click **OK**.

Excel prompts you to save the workbook.

6 Click **OK**.

Excel activates the tracking feature.

7 Edit your worksheet.

● Excel highlights any cells that contain changes.

● To view details about a change, position the mouse pointer over the highlighted cell.

Microsoft Excel

⚠ This action will now save the workbook. Do you want to continue?

6 OK | Cancel

2010 Quarterly Sales

1st Quarter

	A	B	C	D	E
4	Office	Contact	January	February	March
5	London Office	Cinder Calhoun			$20,750.00
6	Mexico City Office	Murgatroyd Peterson			$27,890.00
7	Milan Office	Jess Bova			$27,890.00
8	San Francisco Office	Betsy Shoup			$32,751.00
9	Detroit Office	Gladys Plaisance			$15,600.00
10	Kiev Office	Fred Garvin	$19,505.00	$27,890.00	$15,600.00
11	Singapore Office	Lauren Esposito	$20,868.00	$32,976.00	$29,002.00
12	Toronto Office	Fred Garvin	$20,868.00	$29,535.00	$34,298.00
13	L.A. Office	Fred Garvin	$26,500.00	$31,420.00	$33,086.00
14	New York Office	Fred Garvin	$26,500.00	$31,420.00	$36,340.00
15	Tokyo Office	Aaron England	$26,500.00	$31,420.00	$33,086.00

, 12/20/2009 8:58 PM:
Changed cell B6 from 'Charles Ramos' to 'Murgatroyd Peterson'.

 TIP

What does the Share Workbook feature do?

The Share Workbook feature enables multiple users to work in a workbook at the same time. You use the Advanced tab of the Share Workbook dialog box to change various Share Workbook settings, such as when files are updated to reflect one user's changes and what should happen when changes made by two or more users conflict. You can also use this dialog box to remove a user from the shared workbook (click the **Editing** tab to access this option). To open this dialog box, click the **Share Workbook** button on the Ribbon.

Share Workbook

Editing | Advanced

Track changes
◉ Keep change history for: 30 days
○ Don't keep change history

Update changes
◉ When file is saved
○ Automatically every: 15 minutes
　◉ Save my changes and see others' changes
　○ Just see other users' changes

Conflicting changes between users
◉ Ask me which changes win
○ The changes being saved win

Include in personal view
☑ Print settings
☑ Filter settings

OK | Cancel

continued

When you activate the reviewing process, Excel goes through each change in the worksheet and allows you to accept or reject the edit. When the review is complete, you can turn the tracking feature off.

Review Changes

① Click the **Review** tab on the Ribbon.

② Click **Track Changes**.

③ Click **Accept/Reject Changes**.

	A	B	C	D	E	F	G	H
1		**2010 Quarterly Sales**						
2	**1st Quarter**							
3								
4	**Office**	**Contact**	**January**	**February**	**March**			
5	London Office	Cinder Calhoun	$15,600.00	$19,505.00	$20,750.00			
6	Mexico City Office	Murgatroyd Peterso	$15,600.00	$19,505.00	$27,890.00			
7	Milan Office	Jess Bova	$15,600.00	$19,505.00	$27,890.00			
8	San Francisco Office	Betsy Shoup	$18,939.00	$27,890.00	$32,751.00			
9	Detroit Office	Gladys Plaisance	$19,505.00	$20,750.00	$15,600.00			
10	Kiev Office	Fred Garvin	$19,505.00	$27,890.00	$15,600.00			
11	Singapore Office	Lauren Esposito	$20,868.00	$32,976.00	$29,002.00			
12	Toronto Office	Fred Garvin	$20,868.00	$29,535.00	$34,298.00			
13	L.A. Office	Fred Garvin	$26,500.00	$31,420.00	$33,086.00			
14	New York Office	Fred Garvin	$26,500.00	$31,420.00	$36,340.00			
15	Tokyo Office	Aaron England	$26,500.00	$31,420.00	$33,086.00			

Excel prompts you to save the file.

④ Click **OK**.

Microsoft Excel

This action will now save the workbook. Do you want to continue?

OK   Cancel

The Select Changes to Accept or Reject dialog box appears.

5 Click options for which changes you want to view.

6 Click **OK**.

Select Changes to Accept or Reject	? X
Which changes	
☑ When: Not yet reviewed ▼	
☑ Who: Everyone ▼	
☐ Where: 🔲	
OK Cancel	

The Accept or Reject Changes dialog box appears.

7 Specify an action for each edit.

● You can click **Accept** to add the change to the final worksheet.

● To reject the change, you can click **Reject**.

● You can click one of these options to accept or reject all of the changes at the same time.

Note: To turn off Track Changes, click the **Review** tab, click the **Track Changes** button, and choose **Highlight Changes**. In the Highlight Changes dialog box, deselect the **Track changes while editing** check box and click **OK**.

Contact	January	February	March
Cinder Calhoun	$15,600.00	$19,505.00	$20,750.00
Murgatroyd Peterso	$15,600.00	$19,505.00	$27,890.00
Jess Bova	$15,600.00	$19,505.00	$27,890.00
Betsy Shoup			
Gladys Plaisan			
Fred Garvin			
Lauren Esposit			
Fred Garvin			
Fred Garvin			
Fred Garvin			
Aaron England			
Katie Kitchel			
Lauren Esposit			
James Stanton	$29,002.00	$20,868.00	$32,976.00

Accept or Reject Changes ? X

Change 2 of 5 made to this document:

Katie, 12/20/2009 8:59 PM:

Changed cell B6 from 'Charles Ramos' to 'Murgatroyd Peterson'.

Accept   Reject   Accept All   Reject All   Close

TIP

Can I password-protect workbooks I share?

Yes. To do so, you must first disable sharing. Click the **Share Workbook** button in the Review tab to open the Share Workbook dialog box; then, in the Editing tab, deselect the **Allow Changes by More Than One User at the Same Time** check box and click **OK**. Excel prompts you to confirm that you no longer want to share the workbook; click **OK** again. Next, password-protect the workbook by clicking **Protect Workbook** in the Review tab; in the dialog box that appears, type a password (●), click **OK**, retype the password, and click **OK** again. Re-share the workbook by again clicking **Share Workbook** on the Ribbon, this time selecting the check box you deselected earlier before clicking **OK**. Finally, click **Protect Shared Workbook** in the Review tab. In the dialog box that appears, select the **Sharing with track changes** check box, type the password you set in the **Password** field, click **OK**, retype the password, and click **OK** again.

Protect Shared Workbook	? X
Protect workbook for	
☑ Sharing with track changes	
This shares your workbook and then prevents change tracking from being removed.	
If desired, a password must be chosen now, prior to sharing the workbook.	
Password (optional):	
●●●●●●	
OK Cancel	

Insert a Comment

You can add comments to your worksheets to make a note to yourself about a particular cell's contents or as a note for other users to see. For example, if you share your workbooks with other users, you can add comments to leave feedback about the data without typing directly in the worksheet. Excel displays comments in a balloon.

Insert a Comment

Add a Comment

① Click the cell to which you want to add a comment.

② Click the **Review** tab on the Ribbon.

③ Click the **New Comment** button.

You can also right-click the cell and choose **Insert Comment**.

A comment balloon appears.

④ Type your comment text.

⑤ Click anywhere outside the comment balloon to deselect the comment.

● Cells that contain comments
display a tiny red triangle in the
corner.

January	February	March
$15,600.00	$19,505.00	$20,750.00
$15,600.00	$19,505.00	$27,890.00
$15,600.00	$19,505.00	$27,890.00
$18,939.00	$27,890.00	$32,751.00
$19,505.00	$20,750.00	$15,600.00
$19,505.00	$27,890.00	$15,600.00
$20,868.00	$32,976.00	$29,002.00
$20,868.00	$29,535.00	$34,298.00
$26,500.00	$31,420.00	$33,086.00
$26,500.00	$31,420.00	$36,340.00
$26,500.00	$31,420.00	$33,086.00
$27,890.00	$15,600.00	$19,505.00
$27,890.00	$32,751.00	$18,939.00
$29,002.00	$20,868.00	$32,976.00

View a Comment

① Position the mouse pointer over
the cell.

● The comment balloon appears,
displaying the comment.

January	February	March
$15,600.00	$19,505.00	$20,750.00
$15,600.00	$19,505.00	$27,890.00
$15,600.00	$19,505.00	$27,890.00
$18,939.00	$27,890.00	$32,751.00
$19,505.00	$20,750.00	$15,600.00
$19,505.00	$27,890.00	$15,600.00
$20,868.00	$32,976.00	$29,002.00
$20,868.00	$29,535.00	$34,298.00
$26,500.00	$31,420.00	$33,086.00
$26,500.00	$31,420.00	$36,340.00
$26,500.00	$31,420.00	$33,086.00
$27,890.00	$15,600.00	$19,505.00
$27,890.00	$32,751.00	$18,939.00
$29,002.00	$20,868.00	$32,976.00

Katie:
Fred: I'm concerned
about the drop between
February and March.
Please explain.

TIPS

<table>
<tr><td>

How do I remove a comment?
If you no longer want a comment
to appear in a worksheet, you can
remove it. To remove a comment,
right-click the cell containing the
comment. A shortcut menu
appears; click **Delete Comment**.
Excel removes the comment from
the cell. Alternatively, click the comment to select it
and click the **Delete** button in the Review tab's
Comments area.

</td><td>

</td><td>

**How do I view all the
comments in a worksheet?**
If a worksheet contains several
comments, you can view them
one after another by clicking
the **Next** button in the Review
tab's Comments area. To view
a comment you have already seen, click the
Previous button. Alternatively, display all
comments at once by clicking the **Show All
Comments** button.

</td><td>

</td></tr>
</table>

Understanding Formulas

You can use formulas to perform all kinds of calculations on your Excel data. You can build formulas using mathematical operators, values, and cell references. For example, you can add the contents of a column of monthly sales totals to determine the cumulative sales total. If you are new to writing formulas, this section explains the basics of building your own formulas in Excel.

Formula Structure

Ordinarily, when you write a mathematical formula, you write the values and the operators, followed by an equal sign, such as 2+2=. In Excel, formula structure works a bit differently. All Excel formulas begin with an equal sign (=), such as =2+2. The equal sign tells Excel to recognize any subsequent data as a formula rather than as a regular cell entry.

Referencing Cells

Although you can enter specific values in your Excel formulas, you can also reference data in cells — for example, adding the contents of two cells together. Every cell in a worksheet has a unique address, called a *cell reference*, composed of the cell's column letter and row number. Cell D5, for example, identifies the fifth cell down in column D. To make your worksheets easier to use, you can also assign your own names to cells — for example, naming a cell that contains a figure totaling weekly sales "Sales."

Cell Ranges

A group of related cells in a worksheet is called a *range*. Excel identifies a range by the cells in the upper left and lower right corners of the range, separated by a colon. For example, range A1:B3 includes cells A1, A2, A3, B1, B2, and B3. You can also assign names to ranges to make it easier to identify their contents. Range names must start with a letter, underscore, or backslash, and can include uppercase and lowercase letters. Spaces are not allowed.

Mathematical Operators

You can use mathematical operators in Excel to build formulas. Basic operators include the following:

Operator	Operation
+	Addition
-	Subtraction
*	Multiplication
/	Division
%	Percentage
^	Exponentiation
=	Equal to
<	Less than
≤	Less than or equal to
>	Greater than
≥	Greater than or equal to
<>	Not equal to

Operator Precedence

Excel performs operations from left to right, but gives some operators precedence over others:

First	All operations enclosed in parentheses
Second	Exponential equations
Third	Multiplication and division
Fourth	Addition and subtraction

When you are creating equations, the order of operations determines the results. For example, suppose you want to determine the average of values in cells A2, B2, and C2. If you enter the equation =A2+B2+C2/3, Excel first divides the value in cell C2 by 3, and then adds that result to A2+B2 — yielding the wrong answer. The correct way to write the formula is =(A2+B2+C2)/3. By enclosing the values in parentheses, Excel performs the addition operations before dividing the sum by 3.

Reference Operators

You can use Excel's reference operators to control how a formula groups cells and ranges to perform calculations. For example, if your formula needs to include the cell range D2:D10 and cell E10, you can instruct Excel to evaluate all the data contained in these cells using a reference operator. Your formula might look like this: =SUM(D2:D10,E10).

Operator	Example	Operation
:	=SUM(D3:E12)	Range operator. Evaluates the reference as a single reference, including all of the cells in the range from both corners of the reference.
,	=SUM(D3:E12,F3)	Union operator. Evaluates the two references as a single reference.
[space]	=SUM(D3:D20 D10:E15)	Intersect operator. Evaluates the cells common to both references.
[space]	=SUM(Totals Sales)	Intersect operator. Evaluates the intersecting cell or cells of the column labeled Totals and the row labeled Sales.

Create a Formula

You can write a formula to perform a calculation on data in your worksheet. In Excel, all formulas begin with an equal sign (=) and contain the cell references of the cells that contain the relevant data. For example, the formula for adding the contents of cells C3 and C4 together is =C3+C4. You create formulas in the Formula bar; formula results appear in the cell to which you assign a formula.

Create a Formula

① Click in the cell to which you want to assign a formula.

② Type =.

● Excel displays the formula in the Formula bar and in the active cell.

③ Click the first cell that you want to reference in the formula.

● Excel inserts the cell reference into the formula.

④ Type an operator for the formula.

⑤ Click the next cell that you want to reference in the formula.

● Excel inserts the cell reference into the formula.

⑥ Repeat Steps **4** and **5** until all the necessary cells and operators have been added.

⑦ Press **Enter**.

● You can also click **Enter** (☑) on the Formula bar to accept the formula.

● You can click **Cancel** (☒) to cancel the formula.

● The formula results appear in the cell.

To view the formula in the Formula bar, you can simply click in the cell.

● The Formula bar displays any formula assigned to the active cell.

Note: If you change a value in a cell referenced in your formula, the formula results automatically update to reflect the change.

Q1 - Microsoft Excel

	January	February	March	Total
5	$15,600.00	$19,505.00	$20,750.00	=C5+D5+E5
6	$15,600.00	$19,505.00	$27,890.00	
7	$15,600.00	$19,505.00	$27,890.00	
8	$18,939.00	$27,890.00	$32,751.00	
9	$19,505.00	$20,750.00	$15,600.00	
10	$19,505.00	$27,890.00	$15,600.00	
11	$20,868.00	$32,976.00	$29,002.00	
12	$20,868.00	$29,535.00	$34,298.00	

F5 =SUM(C5:E5)

	January	February	March	Total
5	$15,600.00	$19,505.00	$20,750.00	$55,855.00
6	$15,600.00	$19,505.00	$27,890.00	
7	$15,600.00	$19,505.00	$27,890.00	
8	$18,939.00	$27,890.00	$32,751.00	
9	$19,505.00	$20,750.00	$15,600.00	
10	$19,505.00	$27,890.00	$15,600.00	
11	$20,868.00	$32,976.00	$29,002.00	
12	$20,868.00	$29,535.00	$34,298.00	

TIPS

How do I edit a formula?

To edit a formula, click in the cell containing the formula and make any corrections in the Formula bar. You can also double-click in the cell to make edits to the formula from within the cell itself. When finished, press **Enter** or click **Enter** (☑) on the Formula bar.

Can I reference cells in other worksheets?

Yes. To reference a cell in other worksheet, you specify the worksheet name followed by an exclamation mark and then the cell address (Sheet2!D12). If the worksheet has been renamed to, say, Sales, you must use the name along with an exclamation mark followed by the cell or range reference (Sales!D12). If the worksheet name includes spaces, enclose the sheet name in single quote marks, as in 'Sales Totals'!D12.

Apply Absolute and Relative Cell References

Excel treats the location of the cells that you include in formulas as relative rather than absolute. This is called *relative cell referencing*. For example, when you copy a formula to a new location, the formula automatically adjusts using relative cell addresses. If you want to include a particular cell location no matter where the formula appears, you can assign an *absolute cell reference*. Absolute references are preceded with dollar signs, as in =$D$2+E2.

Apply Absolute and Relative Cell References

Assign Absolute References

1 Click in the cell containing the formula that you want to change.

2 Select the cell reference in the Formula bar.

3 Press **F4**.

Note: *You can also type dollar signs in the Formula bar to make a reference absolute.*

● Excel enters dollar signs ($) before each part of the cell reference, making the cell reference absolute.

Note: *You can continue pressing* **F4** *to cycle through mixed, relative, and absolute references.*

4 Press **Enter** or click **Enter** (☑).

Excel assigns the changes to the formula.

Assign Relative References

1 Click in the cell containing the formula that you want to change.

2 Select the cell reference.

3 Press F4 as many times as needed to cycle to relative addressing (that is, remove the dollar signs).

Note: *You can press F4 multiple times to cycle through mixed, relative, and absolute references.*

Note: *You can also delete the dollar sign characters in the Formula bar to make a reference relative.*

4 Press Enter or click **Enter** (☑).

● Excel assigns the changes to the formula.

	C	D	E	F
4	**January**	**February**	**March**	**Total**
5	$15,600.00	$19,505.00	$20,750.00	=$C$5+$D$5+$E$5
6	$15,600.00	$19,505.00	$27,890.00	
7	$15,600.00	$19,505.00	$27,890.00	
8	$18,939.00	$27,890.00	$32,751.00	
9	$19,505.00	$20,750.00	$15,600.00	
10	$19,505.00	$27,890.00	$15,600.00	
11	$20,868.00	$32,976.00	$29,002.00	
12	$20,868.00	$29,535.00	$34,298.00	

	C	D	E	F
4	**January**	**February**	**March**	**Total**
5	$15,600.00	$19,505.00	$20,750.00	=C5+D5+E5
6	$15,600.00	$19,505.00	$27,890.00	
7	$15,600.00	$19,505.00	$27,890.00	
8	$18,939.00	$27,890.00	$32,751.00	
9	$19,505.00	$20,750.00	$15,600.00	
10	$19,505.00	$27,890.00	$15,600.00	
11	$20,868.00	$32,976.00	$29,002.00	
12	$20,868.00	$29,535.00	$34,298.00	

TIPS

When would I use absolute cell references?

You use absolute referencing to always refer to the same cell in a worksheet. For example, suppose your worksheet contains columns of pricing information that refer to a discount rate disclosed in cell G10. When you create a formula that involves the discount rate, that formula must always reference cell G10, even if the formula is moved or copied to another cell. In this case, you would make cell G10 absolute.

When would I use mixed cell references?

You use mixed referencing to reference the same row or column, but different relative cells within. For example, referencing $C6 keeps the column absolute while the row remains relative. If the mixed reference is C$6, the column is relative but the row is absolute. You can press F4 while writing a formula to cycle through absolute, mixed, and relative cell referencing, or you can type the dollar signs ($) as needed.

Understanding Functions

If you are looking for a speedier way to enter formulas, you can use any one of a wide variety of functions. *Functions* are ready-made formulas that perform a series of operations on a specified range of values. Excel offers more than 300 functions that you can use to perform mathematical calculations on your worksheet data.

Function Elements

All functions must start with an equal sign (=). Functions are distinct in that each one has a name. For example, the function that sums data is called SUM, and the function for averaging values is called AVERAGE. You can create functions by typing them directly into your worksheet cells or Formula bar; alternatively, you can use the Insert Function dialog box to select and apply functions to your data.

Constructing Arguments

Functions use arguments to indicate which cells contain the values you want to calculate. Arguments are enclosed in parentheses. When applying a function to individual cells in a worksheet, you can use a comma to separate the cell addresses, as in =SUM(A5,B5,C5). When applying a function to a range of cells, you can use a colon to designate the first and last cells in the range, as in =SUM(B5:E12). If your range has a name, you can insert the name, as in =SUM(Sales).

Types of Functions

Excel groups functions into 12 categories, each of which includes a variety of functions:

Category	Description
Financial	Includes functions for calculating loans, principal, interest, yield, and depreciation.
Date & Time	Includes functions for calculating dates, times, and minutes.
Math & Trig	Includes a wide variety of functions for calculations of all types.
Statistical	Includes functions for calculating averages, probabilities, rankings, trends, and more.
Lookup & Reference	Includes functions that enable you to locate references or specific values in your worksheets.
Database	Includes functions for counting, adding, and filtering database items.
Text	Includes text-based functions to search and replace data and other text tasks.
Logical	Includes functions for logical conjectures, such as if-then statements.
Information	Includes functions for testing your data.
Engineering	Offers many kinds of functions for engineering calculations.
Cube	Enables Excel to fetch data from SQL Server Analysis Services, such as members, sets, aggregated values, properties, and KPIs.
Compatibility	Use these functions to keep your workbook compatible with earlier versions of Excel.

Common Functions

The following table lists some of the more popular Excel functions that you might use with your own spreadsheet work.

Function	Category	Description	Syntax
SUM	Math & Trig	Adds values	=SUM(number1,number2,...)
INT	Math & Trig	Rounds down to the nearest integer	=INT(number)
ROUND	Math & Trig	Rounds a number specified to a specified number of digits	=ROUND(number,number_digits)
ROUNDDOWN	Math & Trig	Rounds a number down	=ROUNDDOWN(number,number_digits)
COUNT	Statistical	Counts the number of cells in a range that contain data	=COUNT(value1,value2,...)
AVERAGE	Statistical	Averages a series of arguments	=AVERAGE(number1,number2,...)
MIN	Statistical	Returns the smallest value in a series	=MIN(number1,number2,...)
MAX	Statistical	Returns the largest value in a series	=MAX(number1,number2,...)
MEDIAN	Statistical	Returns the middle value in a series	=MEDIAN(number1,number2,...)
PMT	Financial	Finds the periodic payment for a fixed loan	=PMT(interest_rate,number_of_periods,present_value,future_value,type)
RATE	Financial	Returns an interest rate	=RATE(number_of_periods,payment,present_value,future_value,type,guess)
TODAY	Date & Time	Returns the current date	=TODAY()
IF	Logical	Returns one of two results that you specify based on whether the value is true or false	=IF(logical_text,value_if_true,value_if_false)
AND	Logical	Returns true if all of the arguments are true, false if any is false	=AND(logical1,logical2,...)
OR	Logical	Returns true if any argument is true, false if all arguments are false	=OR(logical1,logical2,...)

Apply a Function

You can use functions to speed up your Excel calculations. You use the Insert Function dialog box to look for a particular function from among Excel's 12 function categories. After you have selected your function, you build the formula using the Function Arguments dialog box.

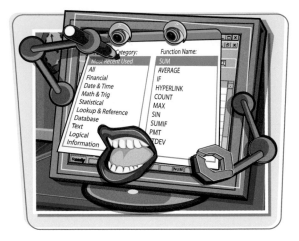

① Click in the cell to which you want to assign a function.

② Click the **Formulas** tab on the Ribbon.

③ Click the **Insert Function** button.

● Excel inserts an equal sign to denote a formula.

Excel launches the Insert Function dialog box.

④ Click the **Or select a category** ▾ and choose a function category.

● A list of functions in the selected category appears.

⑤ Click the function that you want to apply.

● A description of the selected function appears here.

⑥ Click **OK**.

The Function Arguments dialog box appears.

⑦ Select the cells for each argument required by the function.

If you select a cell or range of cells directly in the worksheet, Excel automatically adds the references to the argument.

You can also type a range or cell address (or range or cell name) into the various text boxes.

● The dialog box displays additional information about the function here.

⑧ When you finish constructing the arguments, click **OK**.

● Excel displays the function results in the cell.

● The function appears in the Formula bar.

Function Arguments

SUM

Number1 C5:C33 = {15600;15600;15600;18939;19505;...
Number2 = number

= 758139

Adds all the numbers in a range of cells.

Number1: number1,number2,... are 1 to 255 numbers to sum. Logical values and text are ignored in cells, included if typed as arguments.

Formula result = 758139

Help on this function   OK   Cancel

Q1 - Microsoft Excel

File Home Insert Page Layout Formulas Data Review View Add-Ins

C34   fx =SUM(C5:C33)

	C	D	E
17	$27,890.00	$32,751.00	$18,939.00
18	$29,002.00	$20,868.00	$32,976.00
19	$29,002.00	$30,089.00	$32,976.00
20	$29,750.00	$34,650.00	$30,989.00
21	$29,750.00	$34,650.00	$30,989.00
22	$29,750.00	$34,650.00	$22,760.00
23	$30,989.00	$29,750.00	$34,650.00
24	$30,989.00	$33,412.00	$27,890.00
25	$31,420.00	$21,050.00	$26,500.00
26	$32,976.00	$29,002.00	$20,868.00
27	$32,976.00	$29,002.00	$20,868.00
28	$33,086.00	$22,588.00	$29,389.00
29	$33,086.00	$26,500.00	$31,420.00
30	$34,298.00	$20,868.00	$29,535.00
31	$34,650.00	$30,989.00	$29,750.00
32	$34,650.00	$24,780.00	$29,750.00
33			
34	$758,139.00		
35			

TIPS

Can I edit a function?
Yes. To edit a function, click the cell containing the function that you want to edit; then click the **Insert Function** button in the Formulas tab. Excel displays the function's Function Arguments dialog box, where you can make changes to the cell references or values as needed.

=SUM(C5:C10)

How can I find help with a particular function?
Click the **Help on this function** link in either the Insert Function or Function Arguments dialog box to access Excel's help files to find out more about the function. The function help includes an example of the function being used and tips about how to use the function.

Total Cells with AutoSum

One of the most popular Excel functions is the AutoSum function. AutoSum automatically totals the contents of cells. For example, you can quickly total a column of sales figures. AutoSum works by guessing which surrounding cells you want to total, although you can also specify exactly which cells to sum.

Use AutoSum to Total Cells

1 Click in the cell where you want to insert a sum total.

2 Click the **Formulas** tab on the Ribbon.

3 Click the **AutoSum** button.

● If you click the **AutoSum** ▾, you can select another common function, such as Average.

You can also click the **AutoSum** button (Σ) on the Home tab.

● AutoSum generates a formula to total the adjacent cells.

4 Press **Enter** or click **Enter** (✓).

● Excel displays the AutoSum result in the cell.

	C	D	E	F	G	H	I
17	$27,890.00	$32,751.00	$18,939.00				
18	$29,002.00	$20,868.00	$32,976.00				
19	$29,002.00	$30,089.00	$32,976.00				
20	$29,750.00	$34,650.00	$30,989.00				
21	$29,750.00	$34,650.00	$30,989.00				
22	$29,750.00	$34,650.00	$22,760.00				
23	$30,989.00	$29,750.00	$34,650.00				
24	$30,989.00	$33,412.00	$27,890.00				
25	$31,420.00	$21,050.00	$26,500.00				
26	$32,976.00	$29,002.00	$20,868.00				
27	$32,976.00	$29,002.00	$20,868.00				
28	$33,086.00	$22,588.00	$29,389.00				
29	$33,086.00	$26,500.00	$31,420.00				
30	$34,298.00	$20,868.00	$29,535.00				
31	$34,650.00	$30,989.00	$29,750.00				
32	$34,650.00	$24,780.00	$29,750.00				
33		$763,015.00					
34	$758,139.00						
35							

Total Cells without Applying a Function

1 Click a group of cells whose values you want to total.

Note: To sum noncontiguous cells, press and hold Ctrl while clicking the cells.

● Excel adds the contents of the cells, displaying the sum in the status bar along the bottom of the program window.

● Excel also counts the number of cells you have selected.

● Excel also displays an average of the values in the selected cells.

Contact	January	February	March	Total
Cinder Calhoun	$15,600.00	$19,505.00	$20,750.00	
Murgatroyd Petersa	$15,600.00	$19,505.00	$27,890.00	
Jess Bova	$15,600.00	$19,505.00	$27,890.00	
Betsy Shoup	$18,939.00	$27,090.00	$32,751.00	
Gladys Plaisance	$19,505.00	$20,750.00	$15,600.00	
Fred Garvin	$19,505.00	$27,890.00	$15,600.00	
Lauren Esposito	$20,868.00	$32,976.00	$29,002.00	
Fred Garvin	$20,868.00	$29,535.00	$34,298.00	
Fred Garvin	$26,500.00	$31,420.00	$33,086.00	
Fred Garvin	$26,500.00	$31,420.00	$36,340.00	
Aaron England	$26,500.00	$31,420.00	$33,086.00	
Katie Kitchel	$27,890.00	$15,600.00	$19,505.00	
Lauren Esposito	$27,890.00	$32,751.00	$18,939.00	
James Stanton	$29,002.00	$20,868.00	$32,976.00	
Gemma Windsor	$29,002.00	$30,089.00	$32,976.00	
Steve White	$29,750.00	$34,650.00	$30,989.00	
Elinor Saks	$29,750.00	$34,650.00	$30,989.00	
R.R. Dana	$29,750.00	$34,650.00	$22,760.00	
Gemma Windsor	$30,989.00	$29,750.00	$34,650.00	
Francois Dubois	$30,989.00	$33,412.00	$27,890.00	
Francois Dubois	$31,420.00	$21,050.00	$26,500.00	
Kate Proctor	$32,976.00	$29,002.00	$20,868.00	

3rd Quarter 4th Quarter

Average: $26,785.71   Count: 7   Sum: $187,500.00

TIPS

Can I select a different range of cells to sum?

AutoSum takes its best guess when determining which cells to total. If it guesses wrong, simply click the cells you want to add together before pressing Enter or clicking **Enter** (✓).

Can I apply AutoSum to both rows and columns at the same time?

Yes. Simply select both the row and column of data that you want to sum, along with a blank row and column to hold the results. When you apply the AutoSum function, Excel sums the row and column and displays the results in the blank row and column.

Audit a Worksheet for Errors

If you see an error message, such as #DIV/0!, you should double-check your formula references to ensure that you referenced the correct cells. Locating the source of an error is difficult, however, in larger worksheets. If an error occurs, you can use Excel's Formula Auditing tools — namely, Error Checking and Trace Error — to examine and correct formula errors.

Apply Error Checking

1 Click the **Formulas** tab on the Ribbon.

2 Click the **Error Checking** button.

● Excel displays the Error Checking dialog box and highlights the first cell containing an error.

3 To fix the error, click **Edit in Formula Bar**.

● To find help with an error, you can click here to open the help files.

● To ignore the error, you can click **Ignore Error**.

● You can click **Previous** and **Next** to scroll through all of the errors on the worksheet.

4 Make edits to the cell references in the Formula bar.

5 Click **Resume**.

When the error check is complete, a prompt box appears.

6 Click **OK**.

Trace Errors

1. Click in the cell containing the error that you want to trace.

2. Click the **Formulas** tab on the Ribbon.

3. Click the **Error Checking** ⏷.

4. Click **Trace Error**.

● Excel displays trace lines from the current cell to any cells referenced in the formula.

You can make changes to the cell contents or changes to the formula to correct the error.

Note: Click the **Remove Arrows** button to turn off the trace lines.

TIP

What kinds of error messages does Excel display for formula errors?
Different types of error values appear in cells when an error occurs:

Error	Problem	Solution
######	The cell is not wide enough to contain the value	Increase the column width
#DIV/0!	Dividing by zero	Edit the cell reference or value of the denominator
#N/A	Value is not available	Ensure that the formula references the correct value
#NAME?	Does not recognize text in a formula	Ensure that the name referenced is correct
#NULL!	Specifies two areas that do not intersect	Check for an incorrect range operator or correct the intersection problem
#NUM!	Invalid numeric value	Check the function for an unacceptable argument
#REF!	Invalid cell reference	Correct cell references
#VALUE!	Wrong type of argument or operand	Double-check arguments and operands

Add a Watch Window

Suppose you want to view a cell containing a formula at the top of your worksheet while making changes to data referenced in the formula at the bottom of the worksheet. To do so, you can create a watch window. This displays the cell containing the formula, no matter where you scroll. You can also use a watch window to view cells in other worksheets or in a linked workbook.

Add a Watch Window

1 Click the **Formulas** tab on the Ribbon.

2 Click the **Watch Window** button.

The Watch Window opens.

3 Click **Add Watch**.

The Add Watch dialog box appears.

4 Select the cell or range that you want to watch.

● You can also type the cell reference.

5 Click **Add**.

Note: You can add multiple cells to the watch window.

● Excel adds the cells to the watch window, including any values or formulas within the cells.

If you scroll away from the original cells, the watch window continues to display the cell contents.

To return to the original cell, you can double-click the cell name.

6 Click the **Close** button (⊠) to close the watch window.

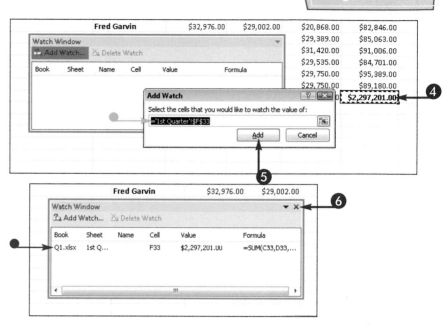

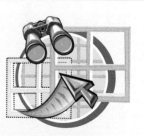

How do I remove and add cells in the watch window?

To remove a cell from the watch window, click the cell name, and then click the **Delete Watch** button in the watch window. Excel removes the cell from the window. You can add more cells by clicking the **Add Watch** button and selecting the cell that you want to add to the window.

How can I move and resize the watch window?

To move the watch window, simply click and drag the window's title bar. You can reposition the window anywhere on-screen. You can also dock the window to appear with the toolbars at the top of the Excel program window. To resize the columns within the watch window, position the mouse pointer over a column in the watch window, and drag to resize the column.

Create a Chart

You can quickly convert your spreadsheet data into easy-to-read charts, choosing from a wide variety of chart types to suit your needs. Excel makes it easy to determine exactly what type of chart works best for your data. After you create a chart, you can use the Chart Tools on the Ribbon to fine-tune the chart to best display and explain the data.

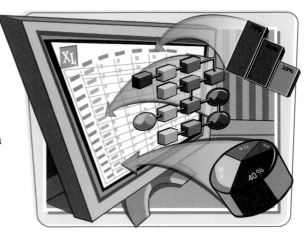

1 Select the range of data that you want to chart.

You can include any headings and labels, but do not include subtotals or totals.

2 Click the **Insert** tab on the Ribbon.

3 Click a chart type from the Charts group.

4 Click a chart style.

● Excel creates a chart and places it in the worksheet.

● You can click the **Design** tab to find tools for controlling design elements in the chart, such as the chart layout, style, and type.

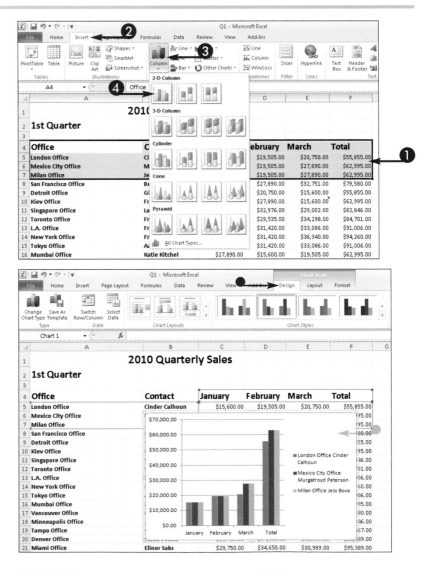

- You can click the **Layout** tab to find tools for controlling how the chart elements are positioned on the chart.

- You can click the **Format** tab to find tools for formatting various chart elements, including chart text and shapes.

TIPS

Can I select noncontiguous data to include in a chart?

Yes. The cells that you select for a chart do not have to be adjacent to each other. To select noncontiguous cells and ranges, select the first range and then press and hold Ctrl while selecting additional ranges that you want to include.

How do I create an organizational chart in Excel?

You can add an organizational chart to track the hierarchy of an organization or method. When you insert an organizational chart, Excel creates four shapes to which you can add your own text. You can add additional shapes and branches to the chart as needed. To create an organizational chart, click the **Insert** tab on the Ribbon, and then click the **SmartArt** button.

Move and Resize Charts

You can move and resize an embedded chart on your worksheet. For example, you may want to reposition the chart at the bottom of the worksheet or resize it to make the chart easier to read.

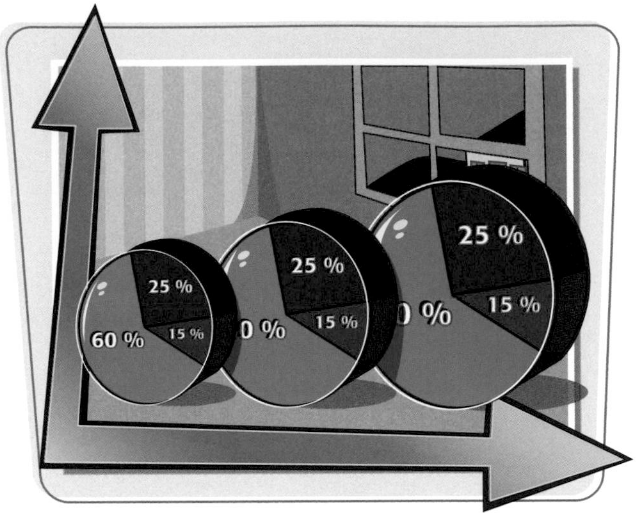

Move and Resize Charts

Resize a Chart

1. Click an empty area of the chart.
   - Excel selects the chart and surrounds it with handles.
2. Position the mouse pointer over a handle.

   The ⇖ changes to ⤢.

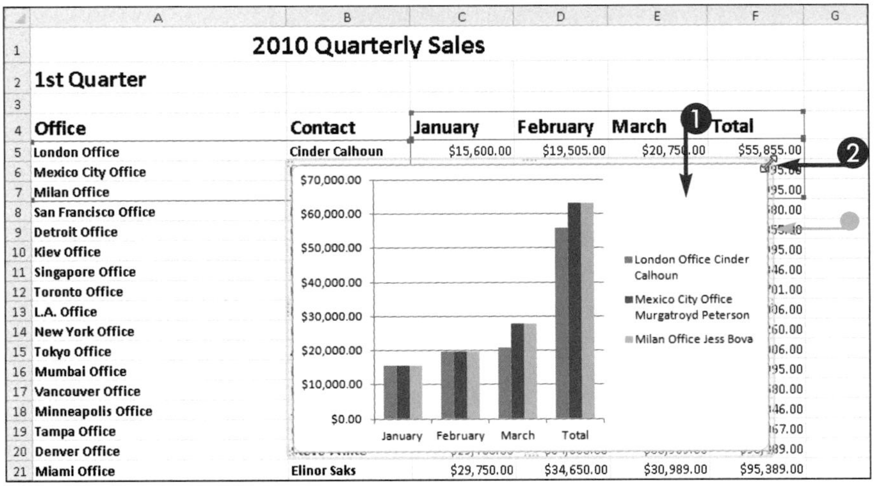

3. Click and drag a handle to resize the chart.
   - A frame appears, representing the chart as you resize it on the worksheet.
4. Release the mouse button.

   Excel resizes the chart.

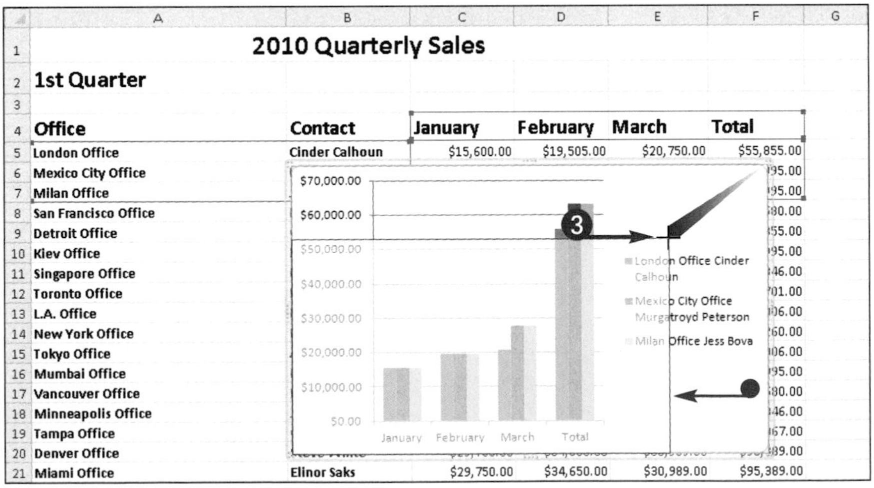

Move a Chart

① Click an empty area of the chart.

● Excel selects the chart and surrounds it with handles.

② Position the mouse pointer over an empty area of the chart.

The ↖ changes to ↖.

2010 Quarterly Sales

Contact	January	February	March	Total
Cinder Calhoun	$15,600.00	$19,505.00	$20,750.00	$55,855.00
Murgatroyd Peterso	$15,600.00	$19,505.00	$27,890.00	$62,995.00
Jess Bova	$15,600.00	$19,505.00	$27,890.00	$62,995.00
Betsy Shoup	$18,939.00	$27,890.00	$32,751.00	$79,580.00
Gladys Plaisance	$19,505.00	$20,750.00	$15,600.00	$55,855.00

③ Click and drag the chart to a new location on the worksheet.

● A frame appears, representing the chart as you move it on the worksheet.

④ Release the mouse button.

Excel moves the chart.

Can I move a chart to its own worksheet?

Yes. Select the chart, click the **Design** tab on the Ribbon, and click the **Move Chart** button. This opens the Move Chart dialog box. Click the **New Sheet** option and click **OK**. Excel adds a new worksheet to the workbook and places the chart on the worksheet.

How do I delete a chart that I no longer want?

To remove an embedded chart, simply select the chart and press Delete. Excel removes the chart from the worksheet. If your chart appears on its own worksheet, you can delete the worksheet — and the chart along with it — by right-clicking the worksheet's tab in the bottom left corner of the screen and clicking **Delete**. When Excel asks you to confirm the deletion, click **Delete**.

Change the Chart Type

You can change the chart type at any time to present your data in a different way. For example, you might want to change a bar chart to a line chart.

① Click an empty area of the chart to select the chart.

② Click the **Design** tab on the Ribbon.

③ Click the **Change Chart Type** button.

The Change Chart Type dialog box appears.

④ Click a new chart type.

⑤ Click a chart style.

⑥ Click **OK**.

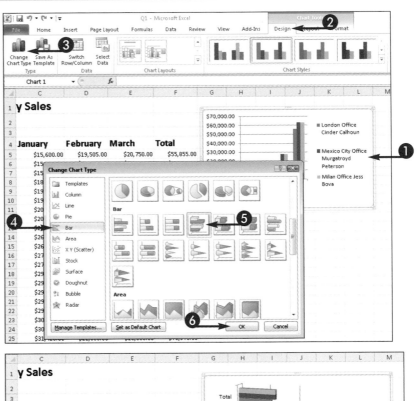

● Excel changes the chart to the chart type that you selected.

Change the Chart Style

You can change the chart style to change the appearance of a chart. For example, you might prefer a brighter color scheme for the chart. You can choose from a wide variety of styles to find just the look you want.

Change the Chart Style

① Click an empty area of the chart to select the chart.

② Click the **Design** tab on the Ribbon.

③ Click a new chart style from the Chart Styles group.

● Click the **More** button (⬇) to view the full palette of styles.

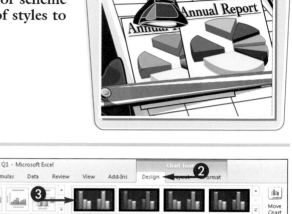

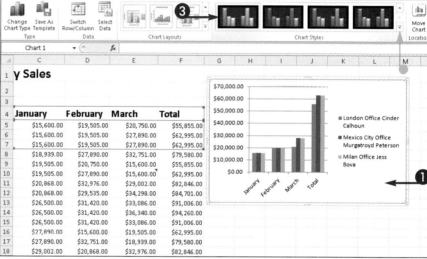

● Excel applies the new style to the existing chart.

Change the Chart Layout

You can change the chart layout to change how chart elements are positioned. For example, you may prefer to show a legend on the top of the chart rather than on the side. You can use Excel's layout options to further customize your chart's appearance.

Change the Chart Layout

1. Click an empty area of the chart to select the chart.

2. Click the **Design** tab on the Ribbon.

3. Click a new layout from the Chart Layouts group.

- You can click the **More** button (⊡) to view the full palette of layouts.

- Excel applies the new layout to the existing chart.

Add Axis Titles

Axes are used to show the scale of all of the values in a chart. The x-axis is the horizontal value display in a chart, and the y-axis is the vertical value display. You can add titles to the axes on your chart to identify your chart data, positioning them as desired. If your chart already has axis titles, you can change them.

Add Axis Titles

① Click an empty area of the chart to select the chart.

② Click the **Layout** tab on the Ribbon.

③ Click the **Axis Titles** button.

④ Click the **Primary Horizontal Axis Title** or **Primary Vertical Axis Title**.

⑤ Click an axis option.

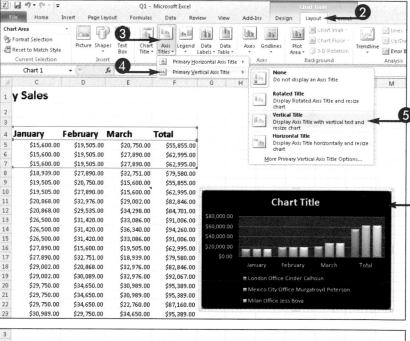

● Excel adds the axis title to the chart.

⑥ Select the placeholder text and type over it with your own title text.

⑦ Click anywhere outside the axis title to deselect it.

Format Chart Objects

You can change the formatting of any element, or *object*, in a chart, such as the background pattern for the plot area or the color of a data series. To do so, you use the Format dialog box. The settings in this dialog box change depending on what object you select. This section covers changing the data series and data labels; you can apply these same techniques to format other chart objects.

Format Chart Objects

Format Data Series Objects

1 Click the data series object that you want to edit.

● Excel automatically selects all corresponding objects in the series.

2 Click the **Format** tab on the Ribbon.

3 Click the **Format Selection** button.

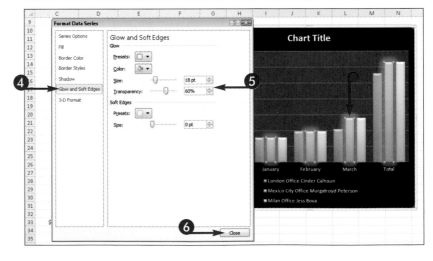

The Format Data Series dialog box appears.

4 Click the type of formatting that you want to change.

5 Change the desired settings.

6 Click **Close** to apply the changes.

● Excel applies your changes.

Format Data Labels

1 Click the data label that you want to format.

2 Click the **Format** tab on the Ribbon.

3 Click the **Format Selection** button.

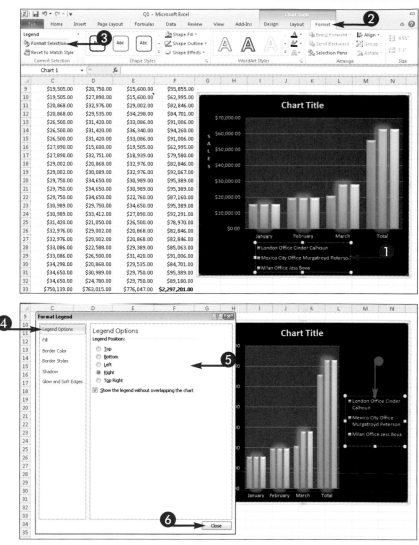

The Format Legend dialog box appears.

4 Click the type of formatting that you want to change.

5 Change the desired settings.

6 Click **Close** to apply the changes.

● Excel applies your changes.

How do I change the font for my chart text?

The quickest way to change the font is to select the chart element that contains text and then right-click the element to display the mini toolbar. From there, you can change the font, font size, font color, and font alignment, as well as apply bold and italics formatting.

How do I print my chart?

To print only the chart — not any worksheet data around it — click the chart to select it, click the **File** tab, and then click **Print**. The Print dialog box appears; ensure that the **Selected Chart** option is selected, and then click **Print**.

Add Gridlines

As long as your chart is not a pie chart, you can add gridlines to it to make it easier to read. You do so via the Layout tab. This tab includes chart objects that you can turn on or off in your chart; although this section shows how to add gridlines, you can use this same technique to add other objects.

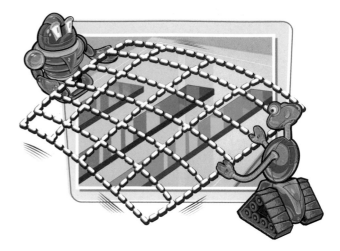

Add Gridlines

1 Click an empty area in the chart that you want to edit.

2 Click the **Layout** tab on the Ribbon.

3 Click the **Gridlines** button.

4 Click the type of gridlines that you want to add.

Select **Primary Horizontal Gridlines** to add horizontal gridlines.

Select **Primary Vertical Gridlines** to add vertical gridlines.

5 Click a gridline option.

Excel adds the gridlines to the chart.

● This example adds horizontal gridlines.

Change the Chart Data

Whenever you change data referenced in your chart, Excel automatically updates the chart data. If you are dealing with a large spreadsheet, however, locating the data you need to change can be difficult. Fortunately, Excel includes a special tool to help you do just that.

Change the Chart Data

1 Select the chart that you want to edit.

2 Click the **Design** tab on the Ribbon.

3 Click the **Select Data** button.

● Excel highlights the source data in the worksheet with a dashed border and displays the Select Data Source dialog box.

4 Edit the data range here, or click and drag the corner handle of the source range to add or subtract cells.

● You can edit the series or axis labels using these options.

5 Click **OK**.

Excel updates the chart.

Use Sparklines to View Data Trends

New in Excel 2010 are sparklines. Simple cell-sized graphics, *sparklines* show data trends, helping to bring meaning and context to the data they describe. There are three types of sparklines: Line sparklines, which display a simple line chart within a single cell; Column sparklines, which display a simple column chart within a single cell; and Win/Loss sparklines, which display a win/loss chart in a single cell.

Use Sparklines to View Data Trends

① Select the data for which you want to create a sparkline.

② Click the **Insert** tab on the Ribbon.

③ In the Sparklines group, choose the type of sparkline you want to create.

In this example, **Column** is chosen.

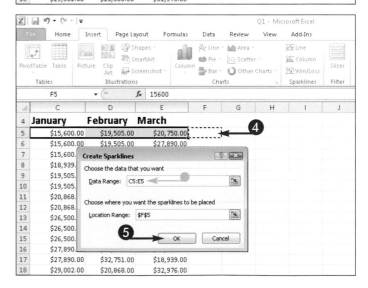

The Create Sparklines dialog box opens.

● The Data Range field already includes the data you selected in Step **1**.

④ Click the cell in your spreadsheet where you want to insert the sparkline.

A dotted line appears around the selected cell.

⑤ Click **OK**.

- Excel inserts the sparkline.

- Excel displays the Sparkline Tools tab. Here, you can choose a different type of sparkline, change the sparkline style and color, and more.

6 To change the style of the sparkline, click a style in the Style group.

- To view more styles, click the **More** button (▾).

- Excel changes the sparkline style.

Can I edit my sparkline data?

Yes. To edit your sparkline data, simply edit the value in any cell to which your sparkline data refers. Excel updates the sparkline to reflect your changes. Alternatively, click the cell containing the sparkline. Excel displays the Design tab; click the **Edit Data** button to display the Edit Sparklines dialog box. Here, you can change the data range or the cell in which the sparkline graphic appears. When you finish, click **OK**.

PART

IV

PowerPoint

PowerPoint is a presentation program you can use to convey all kinds of messages to an audience. You can use PowerPoint to create slide shows to present ideas to clients, explain a concept or procedure to employees, or teach a class. In this part, you learn how to create slide shows, add text and artwork, and package your show on a CD-ROM. You also learn how to add special effects to make your slide show lively and engaging to watch.

Create a Photo Album Presentation

You can quickly turn any collection of digital photos on your computer into a slide show in PowerPoint. You can then share the presentation with others or e-mail the file to family and friends.

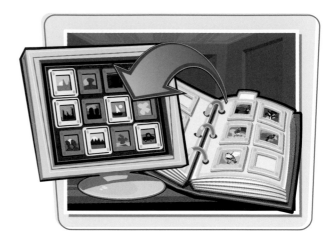

1 Click the **Insert** tab on the Ribbon.

2 Click **Photo Album**.

3 Click **New Photo Album**.

The Photo Album dialog box appears.

4 Click the **File/Disk** button.

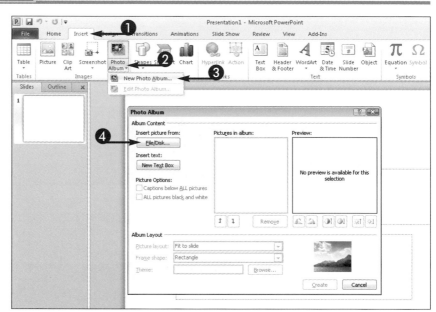

The Insert New Pictures dialog box appears.

5 Navigate to the folder or drive containing the digital pictures that you want to use.

6 Click the pictures that you want to use.

To use multiple pictures, you can press and hold Ctrl while clicking the pictures that you want to use.

7 Click **Insert**.

220

- You can change the picture order using these buttons.

- To remove a picture, you can click it in the Pictures in Album list and then click **Remove**.

- You can use the tool buttons to change the picture orientation, contrast, and brightness levels.

8 Click **Create**.

- PowerPoint creates the slide show as a new presentation file.

Note: The first slide in the show is a title slide, containing the title "Photo Album" and your user name.

Can I fit multiple pictures onto a single slide?

Yes. By default, PowerPoint displays one picture per slide, but you can use the Picture Layout setting in the Photo Album dialog box to display as many as four, with or without title text. You can also control the shape of the image (via the Frame Shape drop-down list) and add a background theme to the slide (click the **Browse** button next to the Theme field).

Can I add captions to my photos?

Yes. To add captions below images, click to select the **Captions Below All Pictures** check box in the Photo Album dialog box. (If this option is grayed out, choose a different layout option from the Picture Layout drop-down list.) Alternatively, add a text slide after each photo slide by clicking the **New Text Box** button. Type your text after closing the Photo Album dialog box.

Create a Presentation with a Template

PowerPoint installs with a wide variety of templates featuring various types of designs and color schemes. In addition, you can download PowerPoint templates from Office.com. You can use PowerPoint's templates to help you create a new presentation, regardless of its subject matter.

1 Click the **File** tab.

2 Click **New**.

3 Click **Sample templates**.

● You can click **New from existing** to create a new presentation based on the template of an existing one.

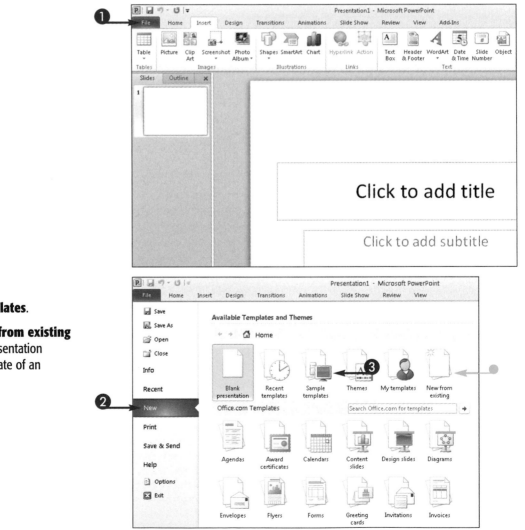

④ Click a template.

● PowerPoint displays a preview of the template design.

⑤ Click **Create**.

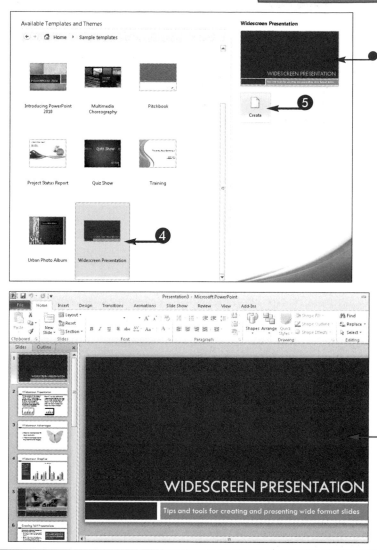

● PowerPoint creates the presentation using the template you chose and displays it in Normal view.

You can add your own text to each slide.

 TIPS

Where can I find more presentation templates?
You can download additional presentation templates from Office.com. To view available templates, click the **File** tab, click **New**, and click the Office.com template category that you want to view, such as **Design Slides**. Click the template that you want, and then click the **Download** button to start downloading the file.

How do I navigate between slides in a new presentation?
Click the **Outline** tab to view the new presentation in outline form. This allows you to build the slide show by typing text into the Outline pane. You can also type text directly onto a slide. Click the **Slides** tab to view individual slides in the presentation. You can click a slide to view the larger slide in the work area and add your own presentation content.

Build a Blank Presentation

Whenever you start PowerPoint, it displays a blank slide. You can use this blank slide as the first slide in your presentation, adding more slides and formatting them as needed. Alternatively, if you are already working on a presentation, you can create a new blank one using the File menu. This approach allows you the freedom to create your own color schemes and design touches.

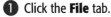

1 Click the **File** tab.

2 Click **New**.

❸ Click **Blank presentation**.

❹ Click **Create**.

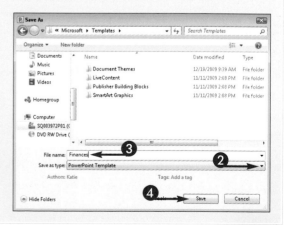

● PowerPoint creates a new presentation with one blank slide.

TIP

Can I save a presentation I create as a template?
Yes. To turn a presentation you create into a template file that you can reuse to make new presentations, follow these steps:

❶ Click the **File** tab and then click **Save As**.

❷ In the Save As dialog box, click the **Save as type** ▾ and choose **PowerPoint Template**.

❸ Type a name for the template in the **File name** field.

❹ Click **Save**.

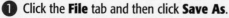

Change PowerPoint Views

You can use PowerPoint's views to change how your presentation appears on-screen. By default, PowerPoint displays your presentation in Normal view, with the Slides tab showing the order of slides in your presentation. You can view the Outline tab to see your presentation in an outline format, or switch to Slide Sorter view to see all the slides at the same time.

Use Outline View

1 While in Normal view, click the **Outline** tab.

PowerPoint displays the presentation in an outline format.

● You can click the outline text to edit it.

● You can click a slide icon to view the slide.

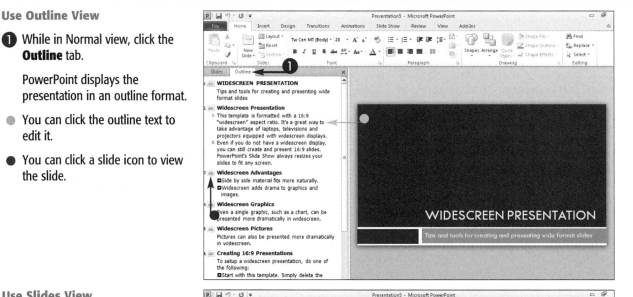

Use Slides View

1 Click the **Slides** tab.

● PowerPoint displays the current slide in the presentation.

● To view a particular slide, you can click the slide in the Slides tab.

● To close the tabs pane entirely and free up on-screen workspace, you can click the ⊠.

Note: To redisplay the tabs pane, you can click the **View** tab on the Ribbon, and then click the **Normal** button.

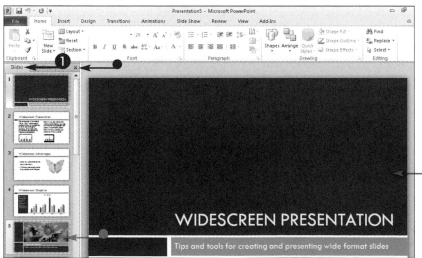

Use Slide Sorter View

1 Click the **View** tab.

2 Click the **Slide Sorter** button.

● PowerPoint displays all of the slides in the presentation.

Use Normal View

1 Click the **View** tab.

2 Click the **Normal** button.

● PowerPoint returns to the default view, displaying the current slide in the presentation.

How do I zoom my view of a slide?

To zoom your magnification of a slide, you can drag the **Zoom** bar on the Status bar at the bottom of the PowerPoint window. You can also click the **View** tab on the Ribbon, click the **Zoom** button, and choose the desired magnification in the Zoom dialog box that opens. Click the **Fit to Window** button on the Ribbon to return to the default view.

Can I resize the PowerPoint panes?

Yes. You can resize any of the panes shown in the PowerPoint window, including the tabs pane. Simply position the mouse pointer over the pane's border. When the ⌖ changes to ◄╫►, click and drag inward or outward to resize the pane.

227

PowerPoint makes it easy to add more slides to a presentation using buttons on the Ribbon's Home tab. You can add and remove slides on the Slides tab in Normal view, or you can switch to Slide Sorter view and manage your presentation's slides.

Insert Slides

1 In the Slides pane, click the slide after which you want to insert a new slide.

2 Click the **Home** tab.

3 Click the bottom half of the **New Slide** button.

Note: Clicking the top half of the New Slide button adds a slide with the same layout as the one you selected in the Slides pane.

4 Click a slide design.

● PowerPoint adds a new slide.

PowerPoint includes several predesigned slide layouts that you can apply to your slide. For example, you might apply a layout that includes a title with two content sections or a picture with a caption. For best results, you should assign a new layout before adding content to your slides; otherwise, you may need to make a few adjustments to the content's position and size to fit the new layout.

Change the Slide Layout

① Click the slide whose layout you want to change in the Slides tab.

② Click the **Home** tab on the Ribbon.

③ Click the **Layout** button.

④ Click a layout.

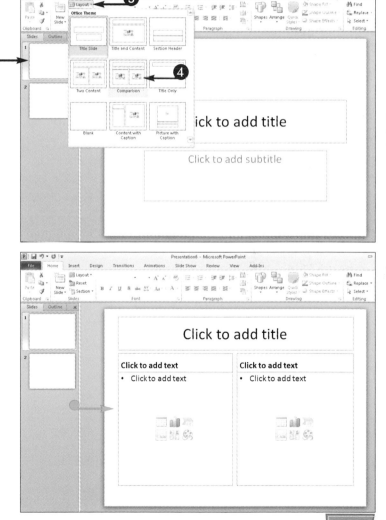

● PowerPoint assigns the layout to the slide.

Create a Custom Layout

In addition to choosing from a variety of preset layouts, you can create your own custom layouts, which you can reuse as needed by selecting them from the Layout button. When you create a custom layout, you control how many slide elements, also called objects, appear on the slide. These include text boxes, pictures, tables, charts, and more.

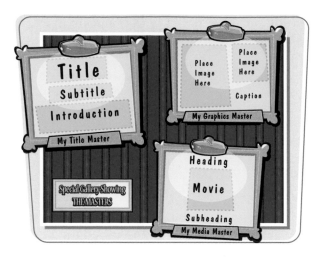

Create a Custom Layout

① Click the **View** tab on the Ribbon.

② Click the **Slide Master** button.

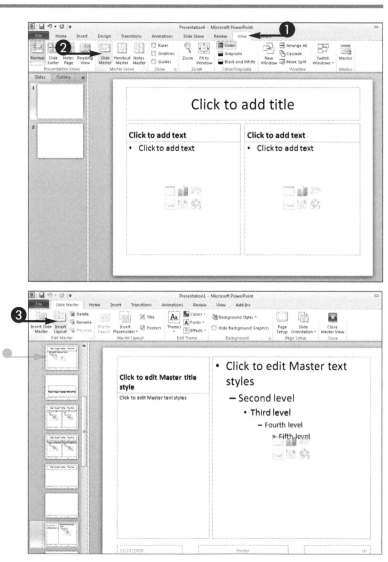

● PowerPoint displays the Slide Master view and opens the Slide Master pane.

③ Click the **Insert Layout** button on the Slide Master tab.

PowerPoint inserts a new layout that you can customize to suit your needs.

④ Click the bottom half of the **Insert Placeholder** button.

⑤ Click a slide object type.

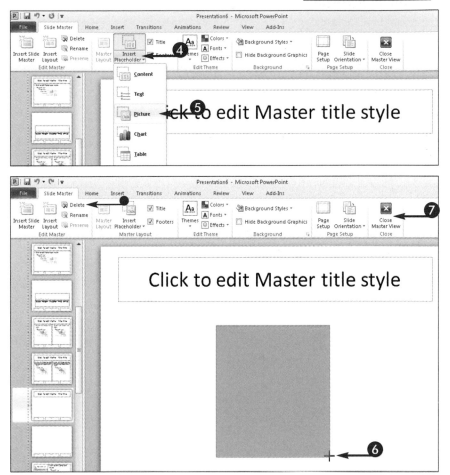

⑥ Click and drag to set the object's size and placement.

You can add more elements.

● You can delete an object on the slide by selecting it and clicking the **Delete** button or pressing **Delete**.

Note: *A quick way to delete the title and footer placeholders that appear in each new layout by default is to deselect the Title and Footers check boxes in the Slide Master tab's Master Layout group.*

⑦ Click the **Close Master View** button to close Slide Master view.

How do I apply my custom layout?

When you create a custom layout, you apply it to a slide the same way you do any predefined PowerPoint layout: by clicking the **Home** tab, clicking the **Layout** button, and choosing the layout from the list that appears (●), as outlined in the preceding section.

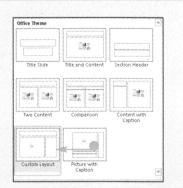

Add and Edit Slide Text

When you apply one of PowerPoint's text layouts to a slide, the text box appears with placeholder text. You can replace the placeholder text with your own text. After you add your text, you can change its font, size, color, and more, as you learn in the next section.

Add and Edit Slide Text

Add Slide Text

1 Click the text box to which you want to add text.

PowerPoint hides the placeholder text and displays a cursor.

2 Type the text that you want to add.

232

Edit Slide Text

❶ Click in the text box where you want to edit.

PowerPoint selects the text box and adds a cursor to the text box.

Off-Season Objectives

- Sign second driver
- Hire crew for second car
- Find at least three more sponsers ❶

- Click to add text

❷ Make any changes that you want to the slide text.

You can use the keyboard arrow keys to move the cursor in the text, or you can click where you want to make a change.

Off-Season Objectives

- Sign second driver
- Hire crew for second car
- Find at least three more sponsors ❷

- Click to add text

TIP

Is there another way to add text to a slide?
Yes. Notice that when you view a slide, you see a pane on the left side of the screen that contains a Slides tab and an Outline tab. The Outline tab enables you to view your entire presentation in outline format. You can also add text to slides in Outline view. To do so, follow these steps:

❶ Click the **Outline** tab.

❷ Click the slide that you want to edit.

❸ Type the text that you want to add or change.

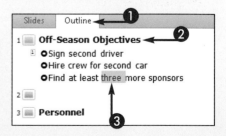

Slides Outline ◀ ❶

1 ▢ **Off-Season Objectives** ◀ ❷
  ▢ ●Sign second driver
     ●Hire crew for second car
     ●Find at least three more sponsors
2 ▢
3 ▢ **Personnel**
     ❸

Change the Font, Size, and Color

After you add text to a slide, you can change its font, size, color, and style to change its appearance. For example, you might want to increase the size of a slide's title text, or change the font of the body text to match the font used in your company logo. Alternatively, you might change the text's color to make it stand out against the background color.

Change the Font

1. Select the text that you want to edit.

2. Click the **Home** tab on the Ribbon.

3. Click the **Font** [ ].

4. Click a font.

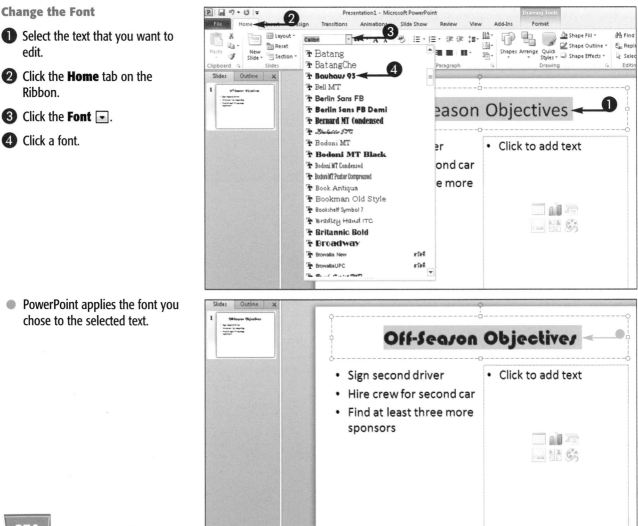

● PowerPoint applies the font you chose to the selected text.

Change the Size

1. Select the text that you want to edit.

2. Click the **Home** tab on the Ribbon.

3. Click the **Font Size** ▼.

4. Click a size.

● PowerPoint applies the font size you chose to the selected text.

TIPS

Is there a quicker way to change the text size?

Yes. To quickly increase or decrease the font size, you can select the text you want to change and then click the **Increase Font Size** (A̅) or **Decrease Font Size** (A̱) button in the Home tab's Font group as many times as needed until the text is the desired size.

Can I change the font style?

Yes. Simply select the text whose style you want to change, and then click the **Bold** button (B) to make the text bold, the **Italic** button (I) to italicize the text, the **Underline** button (U) to underline the text, the **Shadow** button (S) to add a shadow effect, or the **Strikethrough** button (abc) to draw a line through the text.

continued

Change the Font, Size, and Color *(continued)*

As mentioned, in addition to changing the text's font and size, you can change its color. You might do so to make the text better stand out against the background. In addition to choosing from among several more commonly used colors, you can apply your own custom color to text.

Choose a Coordinating Color

① Select the text that you want to edit.

② Click the **Home** tab on the Ribbon.

③ Click the ▼ next to the **Font Color** button (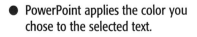).

● PowerPoint displays coordinating theme colors designed to go with the current slide design.

④ Click a color.

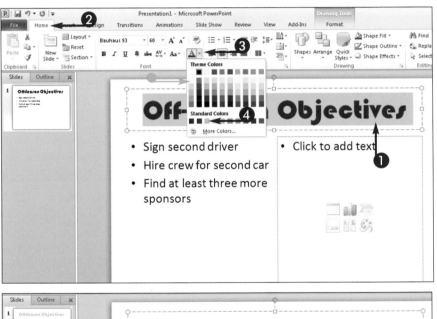

● PowerPoint applies the color you chose to the selected text.

Open the Colors Dialog Box

1 Select the text that you want to edit.

2 Click the **Home** tab on the Ribbon.

3 Click the ▼ next to the **Font Color** button (🅰).

4 Click **More Colors**.

The Colors dialog box appears.

5 Click the **Standard** tab.

6 Click a color.

7 Click **OK**.

● PowerPoint applies the color you chose to the selected text.

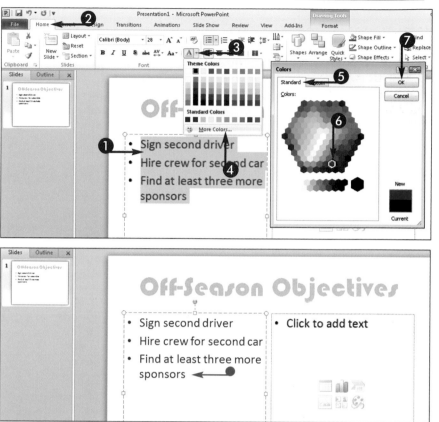

TIP

How do I set a custom color?

You can use the Colors dialog box to set your own custom color for use with the slide text or other slide elements. To set a custom color, follow these steps:

1 Open the Colors dialog box, as shown in this section, and click the **Custom** tab.

2 Click the color that you want to customize.

3 Drag the intensity arrow to adjust the color intensity.

● You can also adjust the color channel settings.

4 Click **OK**.

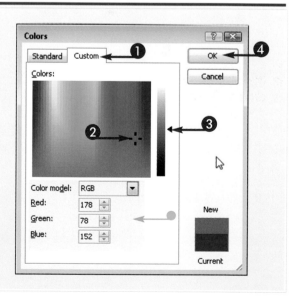

Apply a Theme

PowerPoint includes a variety of designs, called *themes*, which enable you to give every slide in your presentation the same look and feel. Alternatively, you can apply a theme to selected slides in your presentation. Themes include preset fonts, colors, and backgrounds.

Apply a Theme

1 Click the **Design** tab on the Ribbon.

● You can scroll through the available themes and click the **More** button (⬚) to view the full palette of themes.

2 Right-click a theme from the Themes group.

3 Choose **Apply to All Slides** to apply the theme to the entire presentation.

Note: *To apply the theme to selected slides, you must first select the slides to which you want to apply the theme in the Slides pane and then choose* **Apply to Selected Slides** *in Step 3. You will learn more about the Slides pane in the next chapter.*

● PowerPoint applies the theme. Any slides you add will use the same theme.

● You can use these controls to customize various aspects of the theme, such as color and font.

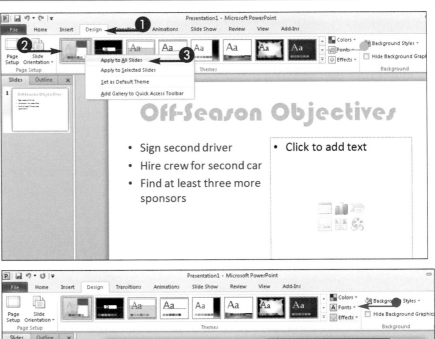

You can change the line spacing to create more or less space between lines of text. For example, you might want to increase line spacing so the text fills up more space in the text box, or to make the text easier to read. Alternatively, if you find that your text does not quite fit in its text box, you could reduce the line spacing to make room.

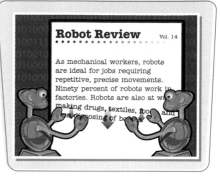

Robot Review Vol. 14

As mechanical workers, robots are ideal for jobs requiring repetitive, precise movements. Ninety percent of robots work in factories. Robots are also at work making drugs, textiles, food, and disposing of ...

Set Line Spacing

① Select the text that you want to edit.

② Click the **Home** tab on the Ribbon.

③ Click the ☐ next to the **Line Spacing** button (☰).

④ Click a line spacing amount.

PowerPoint applies the line spacing.

● This example applies 2.0 spacing.

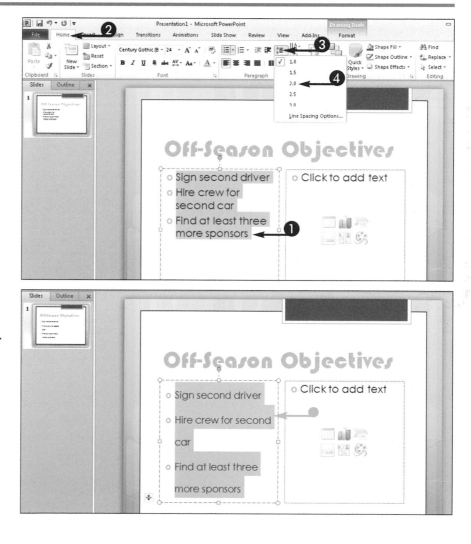

Align Text

By default, PowerPoint centers most text in text boxes (bulleted lists are left-aligned). You can change the horizontal alignment of text in a text box; however, left-aligning it or right-aligning it as desired. You can also justify text.

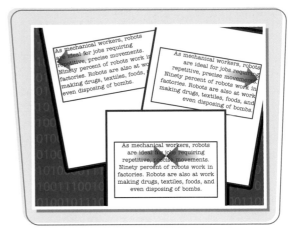

Align Text

1. Select the text that you want to edit.

2. Click the **Home** tab on the Ribbon.

3. Click an alignment button.

Click the **Align Left** button (▤) to align the text to the left side of the text box.

Click the **Center** button (▤) to align the text in the center of the text box.

Click the **Align Right** button (▤) to align the text to the right side of the text box.

Click the **Justify** button (▤) to justify text between the left and right margins.

PowerPoint assigns the formatting.

● In this example, the text is right-aligned.

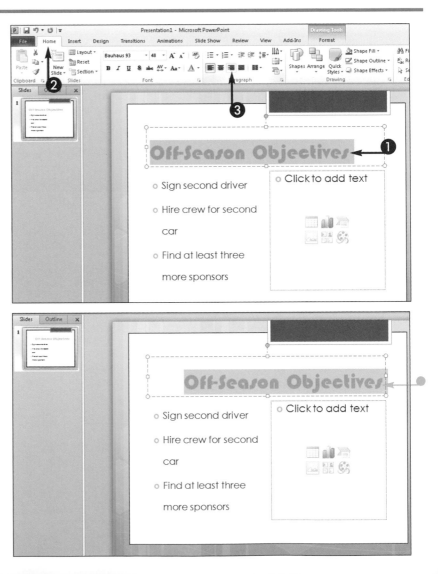

Add a Text Box to a Slide

You can add new text boxes to a slide when you need to customize a layout. Text boxes are simply receptacles for text in a slide. When you add a new text box, you can control the placement and size of the box.

Add a Text Box to a Slide

1 Click the **Insert** tab on the Ribbon.

2 Click the **Text Box** button.

3 Click and drag in the slide where you want to place a text box.

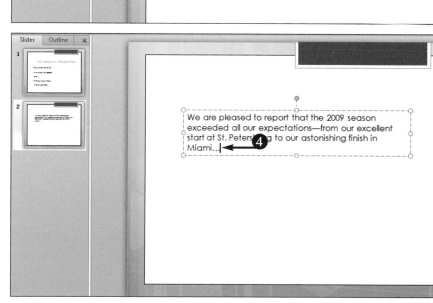

4 Click in the new text box and type your text.

You can click anywhere outside the text box to deselect it.

We are pleased to report that the 2009 season exceeded all our expectations—from our excellent start at St. Petersburg to our astonishing finish in Miami...

Add a Table to a Slide

You can add tables to your slides to organize data in an orderly fashion. Tables use a column-and-row format to present information. For example, you might use a table to display a list of products or classes.

Add a Table to a Slide

1. If an **Insert Table** icon (⊞) appears in your slide, click it.

● If no Insert Table icon appears in your slide, click the **Table** button on the Insert tab and choose **Insert Table**.

The Insert Table dialog box appears.

2. Type the number of columns that you want to appear in the table.

3. Type the number of rows that you want to appear in the table.

4. Click **OK**.

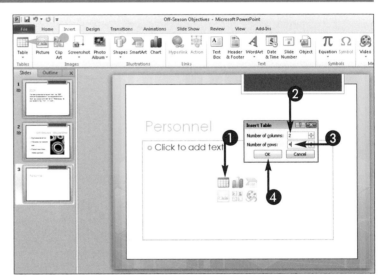

● PowerPoint inserts the table into the slide.

● PowerPoint displays the Table Tools tabs on the Ribbon.

● You can click an option in the Table Styles group to change the table style.

5. Click inside the first table cell and type your data.

You can press Tab to move from one table cell to the next.

6. Continue typing table cell data to fill the table.

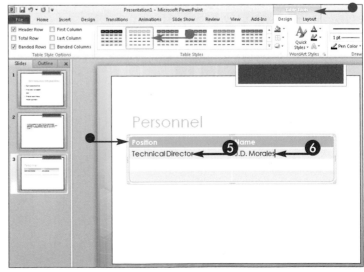

● You can use the tools in the Layout tab to merge table cells, split table cells, change alignment, add borders, and more.

● You can resize columns or rows by clicking and dragging the borders.

⑦ When you finish typing table data, click anywhere outside of the table area to deselect the table.

TIP

How do I add a column or a row to my table?

To add a column or a row to a table, follow these steps:

① Select a row or column adjacent to where you want to insert a new row or column. You can also click in a cell next to where you want to insert a new column or row.

② Click the **Layout** tab on the Ribbon.

③ Click an **Insert** button, such as **Insert Above** or **Insert Right**.

● PowerPoint inserts a new row or column.

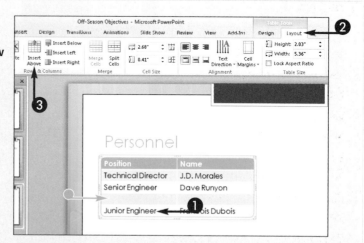

Add a Chart to a Slide

You can add a chart to a PowerPoint slide to turn numeric data into a visual element that your audience can quickly interpret and understand. When you add a chart, PowerPoint launches an Excel window, which you use to enter the chart data.

Add a Chart to a Slide

1 If an **Insert Chart** icon (▦) appears in your slide, click it.

● If no Insert Chart icon appears in your slide, click the **Chart** button on the Insert tab.

The Insert Chart dialog box appears.

2 Click a chart category.

3 Click a chart type.

4 Click **OK**.

- PowerPoint displays a sample of the chart type on the slide.

- The Excel program window opens.

5 Replace the placeholder data with the chart data that you want to illustrate.

You can press Tab to move from cell to cell.

- The chart is updated to reflect the data you enter.

6 Click the **Close** button ( ) to close the Excel window.

7 Click in the chart.

- PowerPoint displays the Chart Tools tabs on the Ribbon.

8 Click the **Design** tab.

- To edit the chart data, click the **Edit Data** button.

- Click a Chart Styles button to change the chart style.

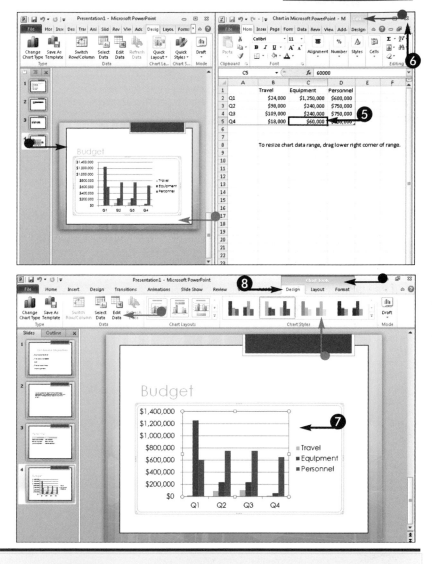

TIPS

Can I insert an existing Excel chart into my PowerPoint slide?

Yes. You can use the Copy and Paste commands to copy an Excel chart and insert it into a PowerPoint slide. You can also link and embed an Excel chart. To learn more about copying and pasting data between Office programs, see Chapter 2.

How do I make changes to my chart formatting?

As mentioned, when you click a chart in a PowerPoint slide, the Ribbon displays a collection of Chart Tools tabs. The **Design** tab contains options for changing the chart layout and style. The **Layout** tab offers tools for changing individual elements on the chart, such as the axis or legend. The **Format** tab includes tools for changing fill colors and shape styles.

Add a Picture to a Slide

One way to make your slides more visually appealing is to insert photographs or other pictures. After you insert a picture, you can resize and reposition it, as well as perform other types of edits on the image. In addition to inserting your own picture files into your PowerPoint slides, you can insert clip art, which is premade artwork supplied by Microsoft.

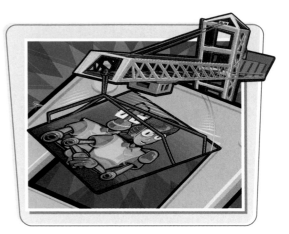

Add a Picture to a Slide

1 If an **Insert Picture** icon () appears in your slide, click it.

● If no Insert Picture icon appears in your slide, click the **Picture** button on the Insert tab.

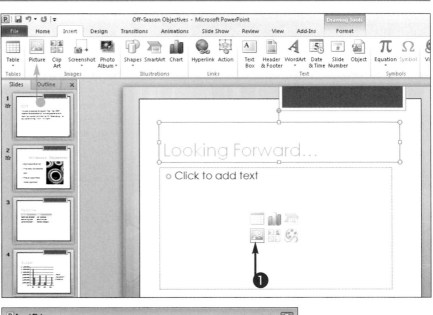

The Insert Picture dialog box opens.

2 Locate and select the picture you want to insert.

3 Click **Insert**.

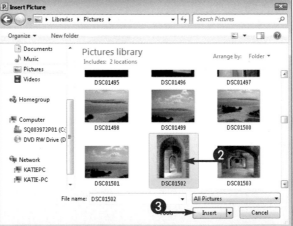

- PowerPoint inserts the picture into the slide.

- PowerPoint displays the Picture Tools Format tab on the Ribbon.

4 To edit the picture (in this example, to change its color), click the **Format** tab.

5 Click the **Color** button.

6 Choose a color option.

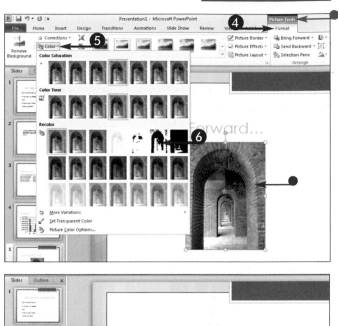

- PowerPoint updates the image to reflect your edits.

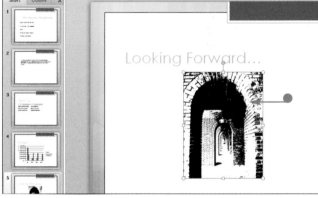

 TIP

How do I add clip art to a slide?
To add clip art to a slide, follow these steps:

1 Click the **Clip Art** icon (🖼) in your slide or click the **Clip Art Pane** button on the Insert tab.

2 In the Clip Art task pane, type a keyword or phrase for the type of clip art that you want to insert.

3 Click **Go**.

- The Clip Art task pane displays any matches for the keyword or phrase that you typed. To add a clip art image to your slide, click the image.

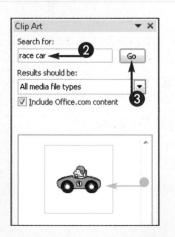

Add a Video Clip to a Slide

You can add video clips to your PowerPoint slides to play during a slide show presentation. For example, when creating a presentation showcasing the latest company product, you might place a video clip of the department head discussing the new item.

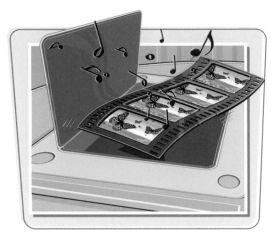

① If an **Insert Media Clip** icon (🎬) appears in your slide, click it.

● If no Insert Media Clip icon appears in your slide, click the **Video** button on the Insert tab.

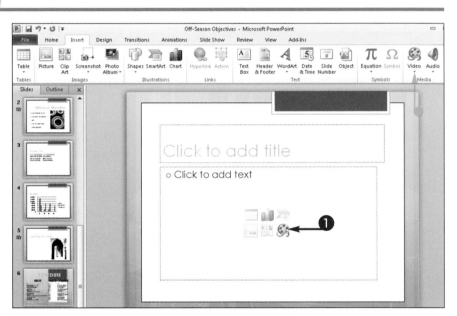

The Insert Video dialog box appears.

② Locate and select the video you want to insert.

③ Click **Insert**.

● PowerPoint inserts the clip into the slide.

● PowerPoint displays the Video Tools tabs on the Ribbon.

4 Click the **Format** tab.

● You can click an option in the Video Styles group to change the appearance of the video.

● You can use the options in the Size group to adjust the size of the clip on the slide.

● Click the **Play** button ( ) to play back the clip.

Note: You can click the Playback tab and use the settings in the Video Options group to specify when the clip should start playing, whether it should be looped, how loudly it should play, and so on.

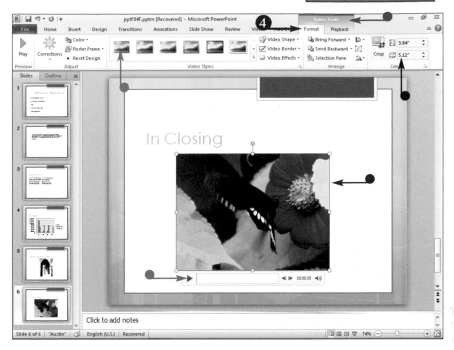

Can I edit my video clip in PowerPoint?

Yes. You can edit your video using the tools in the Playback tab's Editing group. Specifically, you can set up the clip to fade in and fade out using the **Fade In** and **Fade Out** fields. You can also click the **Trim Video** button to open the Trim Video dialog box, where you can change the duration of the video by trimming frames from the beginning or end of the clip.

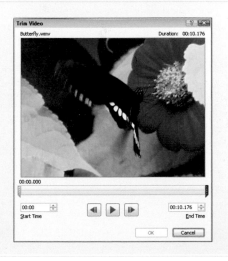

Move a Slide Object

You can move any slide element, often referred to as an object, to reposition it in the slide. For example, you can move a text box to make room for a clip-art object, or move a title to make the text fit better on a slide.

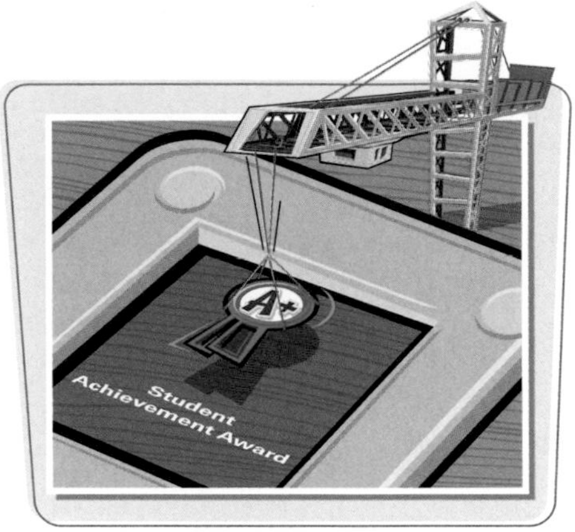

Move a Slide Object

1. Click the slide object that you want to move to select it.

   The ↖ changes to ✥.

2. Drag the object to a new location on the slide.

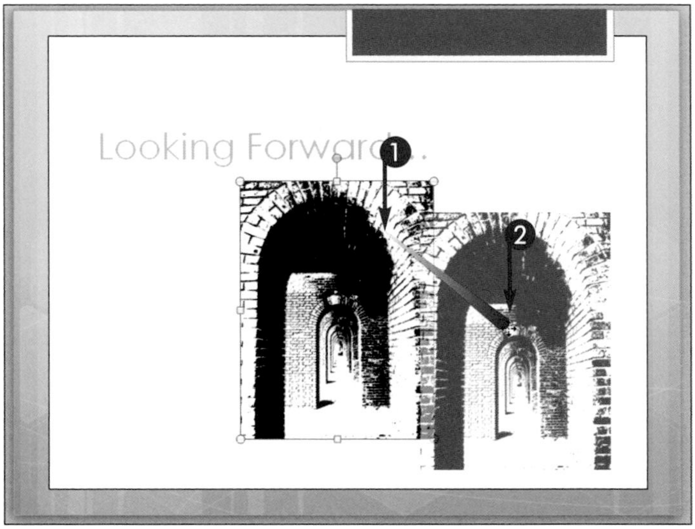

3. Release the mouse button.

- PowerPoint repositions the object.

4. Click outside the slide object to deselect it.

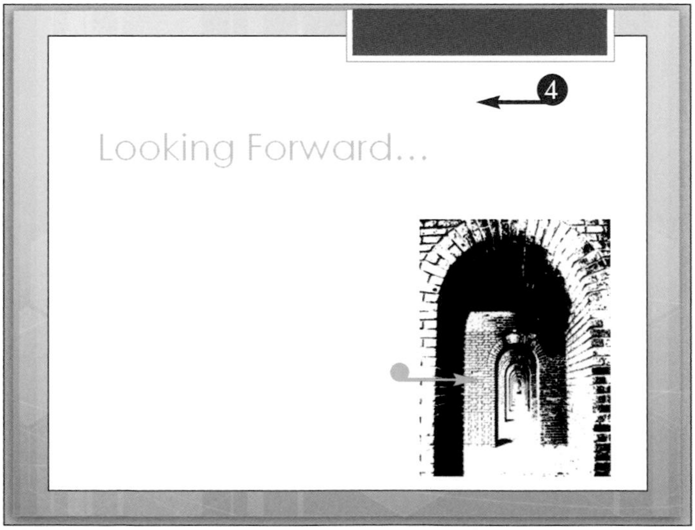

Resize a Slide Object

You can resize any slide element, or *object*, to make it larger or smaller on the slide. For example, you can resize a text box to make room for more text, or resize a picture object to enlarge the artwork.

Resize a Slide Object

① Click the slide object that you want to resize to select it.

● PowerPoint surrounds the object box with handles.

② Position your mouse pointer over a handle.

The ⤢ changes to ⤢.

③ Click and drag the handle inward or outward to resize the slide object.

Drag a corner handle to resize the object's height and width at the same time.

Drag a side handle to resize the object only along the one side.

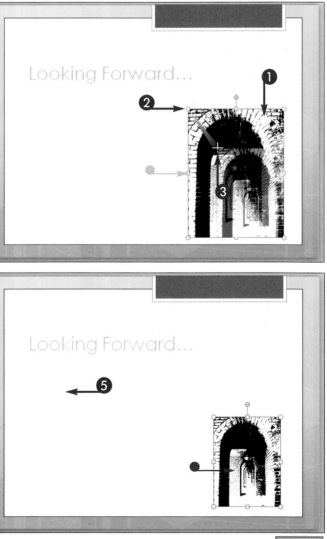

④ Release the mouse button.

● PowerPoint resizes the object.

⑤ Click outside the slide object to deselect it.

Note: *To delete a slide object that you no longer need, select the object and press* **Delete**.

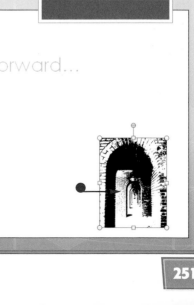

Reorganize Slides

You can change the order of your slides. For example, you may want to move a slide to appear later in the presentation, or swap the order of two side-by-side slides. PowerPoint makes it easy to change the slide order in Slide Sorter view or by using the Slides tab in Normal view.

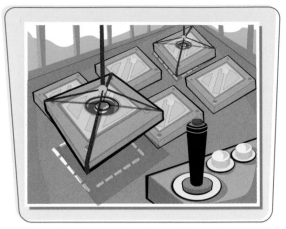

Reorganize Slides

Move Slides in Normal View

① In Normal view, click the slide that you want to move on the Slides tab.

Note: To switch to Normal view, click the **Normal** button in the View tab.

Note: You can move multiple slides at once. To do so, press and hold Ctrl as you click each slide, and then drag the slides to a new location.

② Drag the slide to a new location on the tab.

③ Release the mouse button.

● PowerPoint moves the slide.

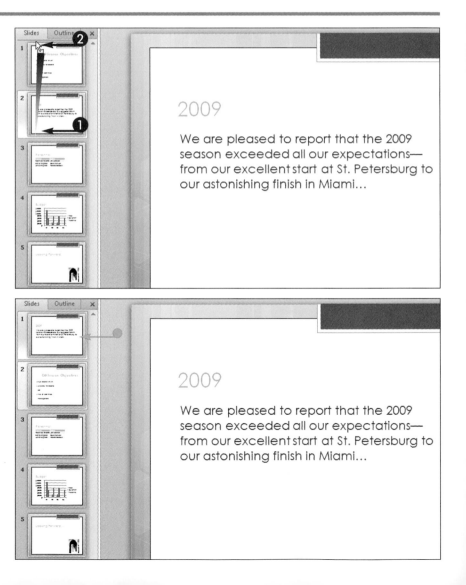

2009

We are pleased to report that the 2009 season exceeded all our expectations—from our excellent start at St. Petersburg to our astonishing finish in Miami...

Move Slides in Slide Sorter View

① In Slide Sorter view, click the slide that you want to move.

*Note: To switch to Slide Sorter view, click the **Slide Sorter** button in the View tab.*

Note: You can move multiple slides at once. To do so, press and hold Ctrl *as you click each slide, and then drag the slides to a new location.*

② Drag the slide to a new location in the presentation.

③ Release the mouse button.

● PowerPoint moves the slide.

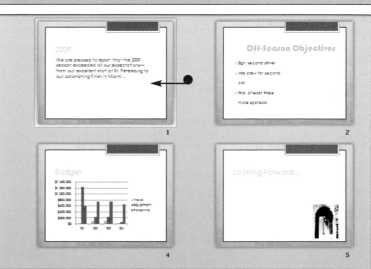

TIPS

How do I hide a slide in my presentation?

Suppose you frequently give the same presentation, but your next audience does not require the information in one of the presentation slides. In that case, you can hide the slide. To do so, switch to Slide Sorter view, click the **Slide Show** tab, and then click the **Hide Slide** button. The Hide Slide icon (🖾) appears next to the slide in Slide Sorter view. To unhide the slide, repeat these steps.

How do I delete slides?

To delete a slide, right-click it in Slide Sorter view or in the Slides tab and choose **Delete Slide** from the menu that appears. PowerPoint deletes the slide. If you realize you have deleted a slide in error, click the **Undo** button (🔄) in the Quick Access toolbar to undo the mistake.

Reuse a Slide

Suppose you are creating a new PowerPoint presentation, but you want to reuse a slide from an old one. Assuming the presentation containing the slide you want to reuse has been saved on your hard drive or is accessible to you via a network connection, you can easily do so.

Reuse a Slide

① In Slide Sorter view, click where you want the new slide to appear.

② Click the **Home** tab.

③ Click the bottom half of the **New Slide** button.

④ Click **Reuse Slides**.

The Reuse Slides pane opens.

⑤ Click the **Browse** button.

⑥ Click **Browse File**.

The Browse dialog box opens.

7 Locate and select the presentation containing the slide you want to reuse.

8 Click **Open**.

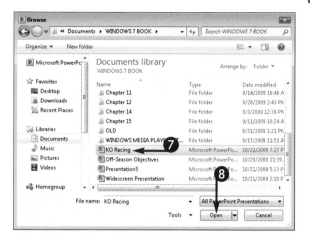

PowerPoint populates the Reuse Slides pane with slides in the presentation you selected.

9 Click the slide you want to reuse.

● PowerPoint adds the slide to your presentation.

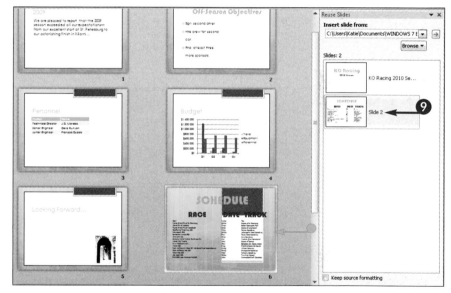

TIPS

Can I retain the reused slide's original formatting?

Yes. When you reuse a slide, PowerPoint updates the slide to match the formatting used in the new presentation. If you want the reused slide to retain its original formatting, select the **Keep Source Formatting** check box in the Reuse Slides pane. You can also change all the slides in the presentation to match the reused slide by right-clicking the slide in the Reuse Slides pane and choosing **Apply Theme to All Slides**.

How do I reuse all the slides in a presentation?

To reuse all the slides in a presentation, right-click any one slide in the Reuse Slides pane and choose **Insert All Slides** from the menu that appears. PowerPoint inserts all the slides from the existing presentation into the new presentation.

Organize Slides into Sections

If your presentation has a large number of slides, keeping it organized can be difficult. To make it easier to manage your slides, you can organize them into sections. For example, you might group all the slides that will be displayed during your introductory speech into a section called "Introduction," place the slides that pertain to your first topic of discussion into a section called "Topic 1," and so on.

Organize Slides into Sections

1 Click the slide that marks the beginning of the section you want to create.

2 Click the **Home** tab.

3 Click the **Section** button.

4 Choose **Add Section**.

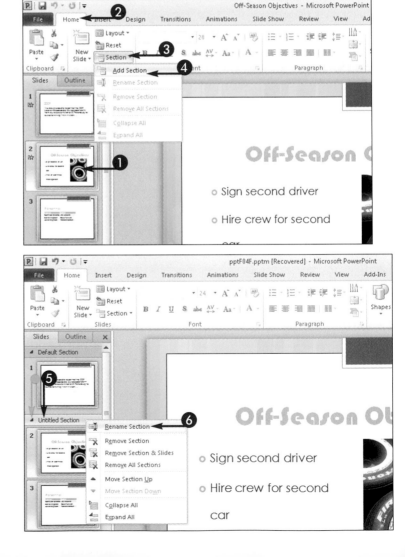

● PowerPoint adds a section marker before the slide you selected, adding all slides below the marker to the section.

5 Right-click the section marker.

6 Choose **Rename Section**.

The Rename Section dialog box appears.

⑦ Type a name for the new section.

⑧ Click the **Rename** button.

● PowerPoint applies the name to the section.

⑨ To collapse the section, hiding the slides it contains, click the section marker's ▲.

● PowerPoint collapses the section.

TIPS

How do I remove a section marker?

If you decide you no longer want to group a set of slides in a section, you can remove the section marker. To do so, right-click the section marker and choose **Remove Section** from the menu that appears. PowerPoint removes the marker.

Can I reorganize the sections in my presentation?

Yes. Instead of moving slides one by one to reorganize your presentation, you can reorganize it by moving sections. To do so, right-click a section's marker and choose **Move Section Up** or **Move Section Down** as many times as needed. PowerPoint moves the slides in the section accordingly.

Define Slide Transitions

You can add transition effects, such as fades, dissolves, and wipes, to your slides to control how one slide segues to the next. You control the speed of the transition to appear fast or slow. You can also specify how PowerPoint advances the slides, either manually or automatically. Take note: You must use good judgment when assigning transitions. Using too many different types of transitions may detract from your presentation.

① In Slide Sorter view, click the slide to which you want to apply a transition.

② Click the **Transitions** tab on the Ribbon.

● You can scroll through the available transition effects and click the **More** button (▾) to view all of the transition effects.

③ Click a transition.

● PowerPoint displays a preview of the transition effect.

● PowerPoint adds an animation icon (▭) below the slide.

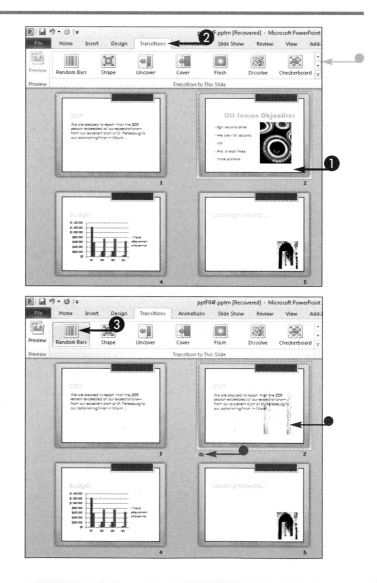

258

④ Click the **Duration** ⬦ to specify a speed setting for the transition.

● You can click **Apply To All** to apply the same transition to the entire slide show.

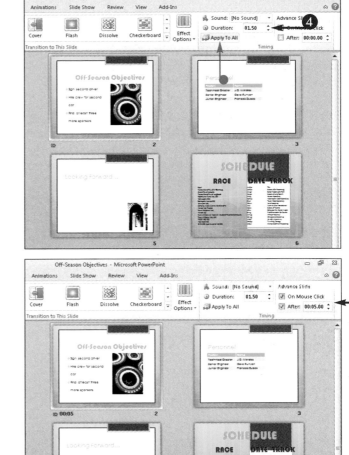

⑤ Under Advance Slide, click an advance option.

To use a mouse click to move to the next slide, select the **On Mouse Click** check box.

To move to the next slide automatically, select the **After** check box and use the ⬦ to specify a duration.

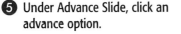

 TIPS

How do I remove a transition effect?

To remove a transition effect, first select the slide containing the transition that you want to remove in Slide Sorter view. Then click the **Transitions** tab and click the **None** option in the Transition to This Slide group. PowerPoint removes the transition that you assigned, returning the slide to the default state.

What does the sound option do?

You can assign sounds as transition effects with your slides. For example, you might assign the Applause sound effect for the first or last slide in a presentation. To assign a sound transition, click the **Sound** ⬦ in the Transitions tab's Timing group and select a sound. PowerPoint previews the sound with the slide transition.

Add Animation Effects

You can use PowerPoint's animation effects to add even more visual interest to your presentation. There are four types of animation effects: entrance effects, emphasis effects, exit effects, and motion paths. You can add any of these effects to any slide element, such as a text box or a picture. You can also edit your animations. To avoid overwhelming your audience, limit effects to slides in which they will make the most impact.

Add Animation Effects

Add a Simple Animation Effect

1 In Normal view, click the slide element to which you want to apply an animation.

You can assign an animation to any object on a slide, including text boxes, shapes, and pictures.

2 Click the **Animations** tab.

● You can scroll through the available animation effects and click the **More** button (⊟) to view all of the animation effects.

● You can also click the **Add Animation** button to view available animation effects.

3 Click an animation effect.

● PowerPoint applies the effect and previews the effect on the slide.

● You can click the **Preview** button to preview the effect again.

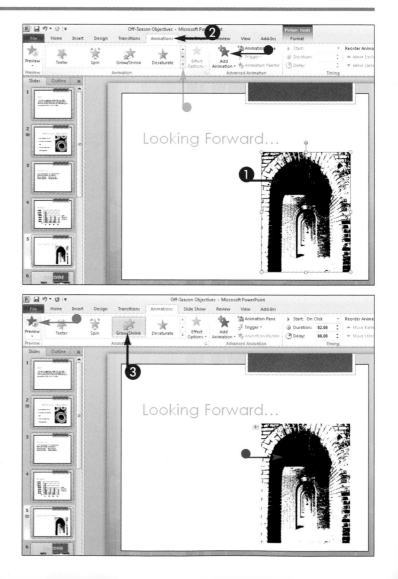

Edit an Animation

1 In Normal view, click the slide element containing the animation you want to edit.

2 Click the **Animations** tab on the Ribbon.

3 Click the **Effect Options** button.

A list of editing options for the animation appears.

4 Select an option from the list.

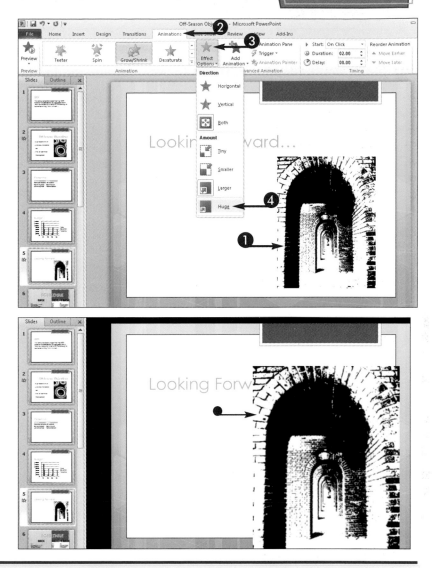

● PowerPoint applies the change and previews the effect on the slide.

TIPS

How do I access additional animations?

To access even more animations, click the **Add Animation** button in the Custom Animation group or the **More** button (⬇) in the Animation group and choose **More Entrance Effects**, **More Emphasis Effects**, **More Exit Effects**, or **More Motion Paths** from the menu that appears. A dialog box opens, displaying additional animation options; select the desired option, and then click **OK**.

Can I copy an effect to another slide object?

Yes. PowerPoint's Animation Painter feature enables you to copy an effect applied to one slide object to another slide object. To do so, select the slide object whose effect you want to copy; then, in the Animations tab's Advanced Animation group, click the **Animation Painter** button. Next, in the Slides tab, click the slide containing the object to which you want to apply the effect to display it; then click the object. PowerPoint copies the effect to the slide object.

Create a Custom Animation

In addition to applying one of PowerPoint's predesigned animation effects to a slide object, such as a text box or a picture, you can use these effects as building blocks to create your own custom effects. You create custom effects using PowerPoint's Animation pane.

Create a Custom Animation

① In Normal view, click the slide element to which you want to apply an animation.

② Click the **Animations** tab.

③ Apply an animation effect.

Note: *This effect is the first "building block" of your custom animation.*

PowerPoint applies the animation effect.

④ Click the **Animation Pane** button in the Advanced Animation group.

PowerPoint displays the Animation pane.

● The animation you applied appears in the pane.

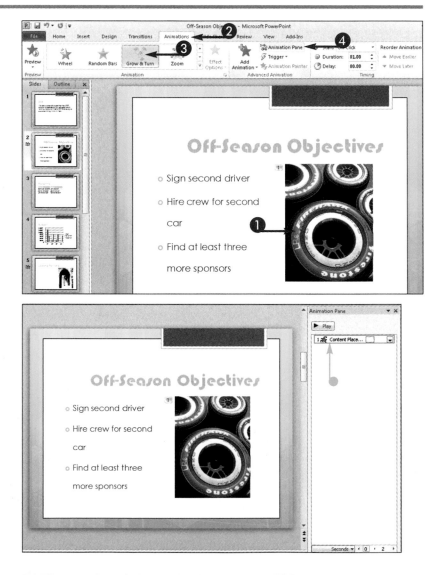

5 To add your next building block, click the **Add Animation** button in the Advanced Animation group.

Note: When applying multiple animation effects to a slide object, you must use the Add Animation button instead of choosing an effect from the Animation group. Otherwise, the new effect will overwrite the existing one.

6 Click an effect.

PowerPoint adds the effect to the Animation pane.

7 Repeat Steps **5** and **6** to add more building blocks.

● PowerPoint places each effect in the Animation pane, in the order you added them.

8 To preview your custom effect, click **Play**.

PowerPoint plays back your custom animation.

9 To change the order in which effects are played back, click an effect.

10 Click the **Re-Order** buttons (⬆ or ⬇) to move the selected effect up or down in the list.

TIPS

How do I remove an animation effect?

To remove an animation effect, first select the slide element containing the effect that you want to remove. Then click the **Animations** tab and, in the Animation group, click **No Animation**. PowerPoint removes the animation. If you assigned custom effects, click the **Animation Pane** button to display the Animation pane, click the effect that you want to remove, click the ▾ that appears, and click **Remove**.

Can I change the duration of an effect?

Yes. To change the duration of an effect, select the slide element containing the effect. Then, in the Animation pane, click the effect whose duration you want to change. Click the ▾ that appears and choose **Timing**; a dialog box opens, enabling you to set the duration of the effect, how many times it should repeat, whether there should be a delay before the effect launches, and more.

Record Narration

If your presentation needs narration, you can use PowerPoint's Record Narration feature to record a narration track to go a long with the show. If your computer has a microphone, you can record a narration for your presentation; PowerPoint saves it along with the presentation file. When you finish recording, an audio icon appears at the bottom of each slide to which you have assigned narration.

Record Narration

1. Click the **Slide Show** tab on the Ribbon.

2. Click **Record Slide Show**.

   The Record Slide Show dialog box appears.

   ● Make sure the **Narrations and laser pointer** check box is selected.

3. Click **Start Recording**.

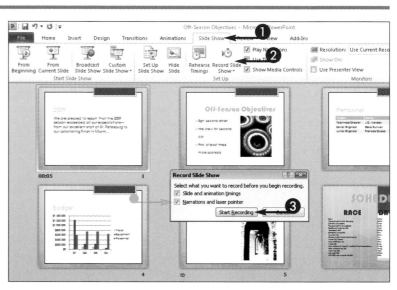

PowerPoint starts the show, and you can begin talking into the computer's microphone to record your narration.

● Click ➡ to move to the next slide in the show.

● Click ⏸ to pause the recording.

● Click ↻ to start over on the current slide.

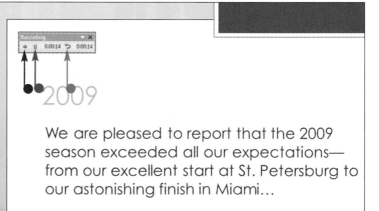

2009

We are pleased to report that the 2009 season exceeded all our expectations—from our excellent start at St. Petersburg to our astonishing finish in Miami...

You can set up how you want your presentation to run. For example, you can specify whether it should loop continuously, be played back in full, be shown without narration or animations, and more. If the presentation will be presented by a speaker (rather than, for example, run at a kiosk), you can choose a pen color and a laser pointer color; the speaker can then use his or her mouse pointer to draw on or point to slides.

Set Up a Slide Show

① Click the **Slide Show** tab on the Ribbon.

② Click **Set Up Slide Show**.

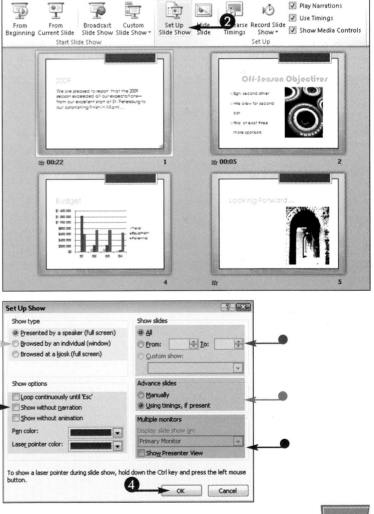

The Set Up Show dialog box appears.

③ Set any options that you want to assign to the show.

● The Show Type settings specify how the slide show is presented.

● The Show Options settings control looping, narration, and animation.

● The Show Slides settings specify which slides appear in the show.

● The Advance Slides settings specify how each slide advances.

● If your system has multiple monitors, you can use the Multiple Monitors settings to specify which monitor to use for your presentation.

④ Click **OK**.

PowerPoint assigns the new settings.

Create Speaker Notes

You can create speaker notes for your presentation. Speaker notes, also called notes pages, are notations that you add to a slide and that you can print out and use to help you give a presentation. You can also use speaker notes as handouts for your presentation. When creating notes pages, PowerPoint includes any note text that you add, as well as a small picture of the actual slide.

① In Normal view, click a slide in the Slides tab to which you want to add notes.

② Click in the Notes pane.

③ Type any notes about the current slide that you want to include.

You can repeat Steps **1** to **3** for other slides to which you want to add notes.

④ Click the **View** tab.

⑤ Click **Notes Page**.

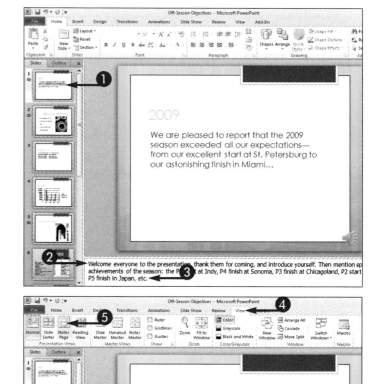

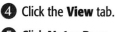

The Notes Page view opens and displays the first page in your slide show.

● You can use the scroll bars to scroll through the notes.

● You can drag the Zoom slider to magnify your view of the notes.

● You can edit and format your notes text.

Note: To return to Normal view, click the **View** tab and click the **Normal** button.

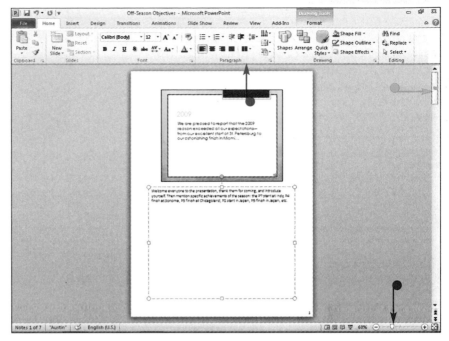

How do I print my notes?

Before you can print your notes, you must configure PowerPoint to do so. Follow these steps:

1 Click the **File** tab and then click **Options**.

The PowerPoint Options dialog box appears.

2 Click **Advanced**.

3 Under When Printing This Document, click the **Use the following print settings** radio button.

4 Click the **Print what** ⬇ and choose **Notes**.

5 Click **OK**.

6 Print your PowerPoint presentation as you would any other Office document: by clicking the **File** tab, choosing **Print**, and choosing the desired settings.

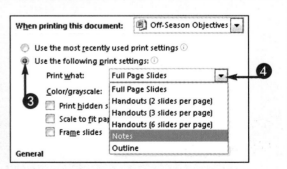

Rehearse a Slide Show

You can time exactly how long each slide displays during a presentation using PowerPoint's Rehearse Timings feature. When rehearsing a presentation, you should rehearse what you want to say during each slide, as well as allow the audience time to read the entire content of each slide. After you record the timings, PowerPoint saves them for use when you present the slide show to your audience.

Rehearse a Slide Show

① Click the **Slide Show** tab.

② Click the **Rehearse Timings** button.

● PowerPoint switches to Slide Show mode and displays the first slide.

● PowerPoint displays the Record Slide Show toolbar and starts a timer.

③ Rehearse what you want to say while the slide plays.

● Click the **Pause** button (⏸) to pause the timer. To restart the timer, you can click ⏸ again.

④ When you finish with the first slide, click the **Next** button (➡).

PowerPoint displays the next slide.

⑤ Repeat Steps **3** and **4** for each slide in your presentation.

When the slide show is complete, a dialog box appears, displaying the total time for the slide show.

⑥ Click **Yes**.

● PowerPoint saves the timings and displays them below each slide.

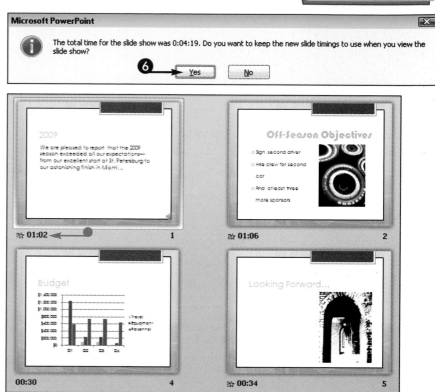

TIP

How do I create handouts for my audience?
One way to create handouts is to send your presentation to Microsoft Word. Follow these steps:

① Click the **File** tab and then click **Share**.

② Click **Create Handouts**.

③ Click **Create Handouts**.

The Send To Microsoft Word dialog box appears.

④ Choose a page layout.

⑤ Click **OK**.

Office launches Microsoft Word, with your presentation pasted in.

⑥ Print the handouts as you would any other Office document: by clicking the **File** tab, choosing **Print**, and choosing the desired settings.

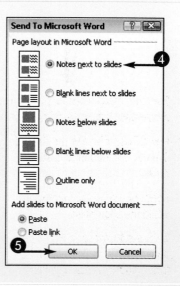

Run a Slide Show

You can view a presentation using PowerPoint's Slide Show view. Slide Show view displays full-screen images of your slides. You can advance each slide manually, or instruct PowerPoint to advance the slides for you.

① Click the **Slide Show** tab.

② Click the **From Beginning** button.

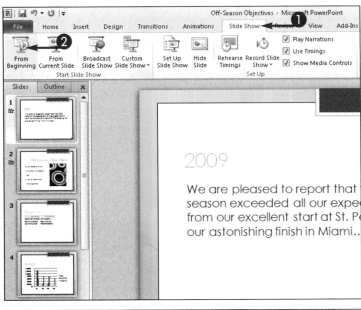

PowerPoint switches to Slide Show mode and displays the first slide.

● When you move the mouse pointer to the bottom left corner, faint slide show control buttons appear.

③ Click anywhere in the slide to advance to the next slide or click the **Next** button (▣).

● To return to a previous slide, you can click the **Previous** button (▣).

● To view a menu of slide show commands, click 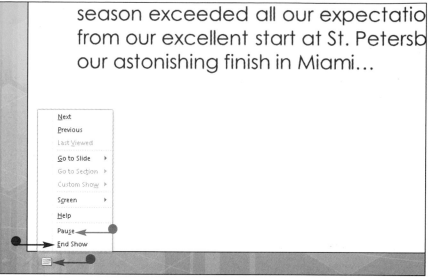.

● You can pause the show by clicking the **Pause** command.

● You can end the show early by clicking the **End Show** command.

Note: You can end a slide show at any time by pressing `Esc`.

④ When the slide show is complete, click anywhere on the screen.

PowerPoint closes the presentation.

TIP

Can I draw on my slides as I present the show?

Yes. You can use PowerPoint's pointer options to draw directly on the screen using the mouse pointer. You can choose from several pen tools and colors. Follow these steps:

① During the slide show, click the **Pen** button (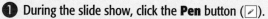).

② Click a pen style.

● You can click here to choose a pen color.

③ Click and drag to draw on the slide.

To erase your markings, press `E`.

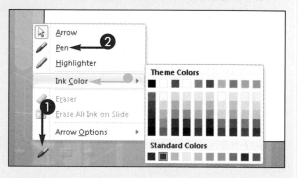

Package Your Presentation on a CD

You can save your PowerPoint presentation to a CD to enable you to share your presentation with others. With the Package for CD feature, PowerPoint bundles the presentation along with all of the necessary clip art, multimedia elements, and other items needed to run your show. The CD even includes a PowerPoint Viewer with the file in case the recipient does not have PowerPoint installed on his or her computer.

Package Your Presentation on a CD

1. Click the **File** tab.

2. Click **Save & Send**.

3. Click **Package Presentation for CD**.

4. Click **Package for CD**.

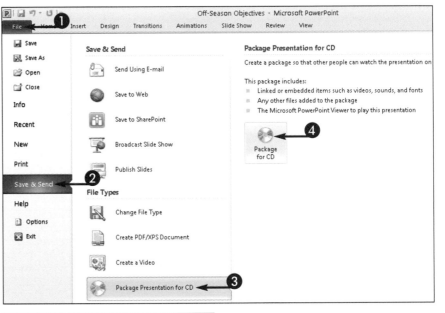

The Package for CD dialog box appears.

5. Type a name for the CD.

6. Click **Copy to CD**.

Note: *If your presentation contains linked files, PowerPoint asks you if you want to include those files on the CD. If you trust the source of each linked file, click Yes.*

● PowerPoint copies the presentation files.

Depending on the size of the presentation, the copying process can take a few minutes.

When the copying process is complete, a dialog box appears.

⑦ Click **No**.

If you want to continue packing additional copies of the presentation, you can click **Yes**.

⑧ Click **Close**.

The Package for CD dialog box closes.

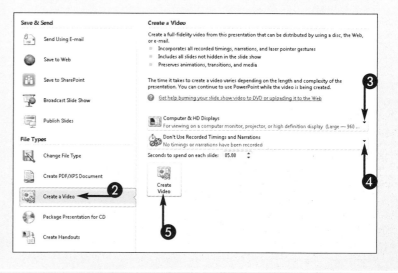

Copying Files to CD

Preparing to burn the CD...

Cancel

Microsoft PowerPoint

The files were successfully copied to the CD.
Do you want to copy the same files to another CD?

Yes   No   ⑦

Was this information helpful?

Can I save my presentation as a video?

Yes. You can save your presentation as a WMV movie file that includes any narration and timings you record. Follow these steps:

① Click the **File** tab and then click **Save & Send**.

② Click **Create a Video**.

③ Choose a quality level.

④ Specify whether recorded narration and timings should be used.

⑤ Click **Create Video**.

⑥ In the Save As dialog box, specify the folder in which the video should be saved.

⑦ Click the **Save** button.

PowerPoint saves the presentation as a movie file in the folder you specified.

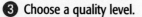

PART

V

Access

Access is a robust database program you can use to store and manage large quantities of data. You can use Access to manage anything from a home inventory to a giant warehouse of products. Access can help you organize your information into tables, speed up data entry with forms, and perform powerful analysis using filters and queries. In this part, you learn how to build and maintain a database file, add tables, create forms, and analyze your data using filters, sorting, and queries.

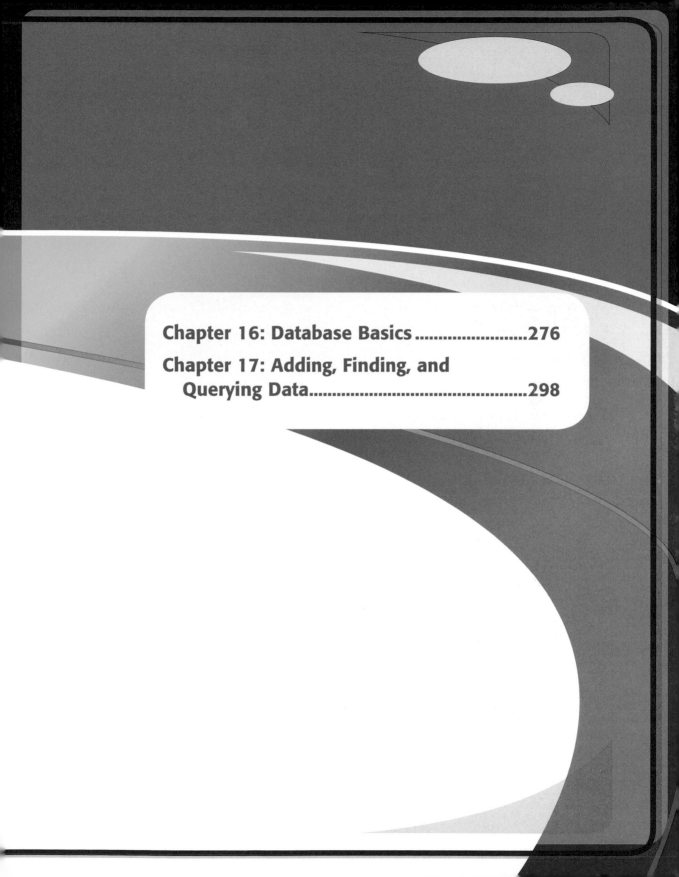

Understanding Database Basics

Access is a popular database program that you can use to catalog and manage large amounts of data. You can use Access to manage anything, from a simple table of data to large, multifaceted lists of information. If you are new to Access, you should take a moment and familiarize yourself with the basic terms associated with the program.

Defining Databases

Simply defined, a *database* is a collection of information. Whether you are aware of it or not, you use databases every day. Common databases include telephone directories or television program schedules. Your own database examples might include a list of contacts that contains addresses and phone numbers. Other examples of real-world databases include product inventories, client invoices, and employee payroll lists.

Tables

The heart of any Access database is a table. A table is a list of information organized into columns and rows. In the example of a client contact database, the table might list the names, addresses, phone numbers, company names, titles, and e-mail addresses of your clients. You can have numerous tables in your Access database. For example, you might have one table listing client information and another table listing your company's products.

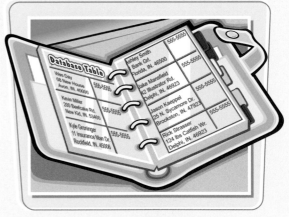

Records and Fields

Every entry that you make in an Access table is called a *record*. Records always appear as rows in a database table. You can organize the information for each record in a separate column, called a *field*. For example, in a client contact list, you might include fields for first name, last name, company name, title, address, city, ZIP code, phone number, and e-mail address. Field names appear at the top of the table.

Forms

You can enter your database records directly into an Access table or you can simplify the process by using a *form*. Access forms present your table fields in an easy-to-read, fill-in-the-blank format. Forms allow you to enter records one at a time. Forms are a great way to speed up data entry, particularly if other users are adding information to your database list.

Reports and Queries

You can use the report feature to summarize data in your tables and generate printouts of pertinent information, such as your top ten salespeople and your top selling products. You can use queries to sort and filter your data. For example, you can choose to view only a few of your table fields and filter them to match certain criteria.

Planning a Database

The first step to building an Access database is deciding what sort of data you want it to contain. What sorts of actions do you want to perform on your data? How do you want to organize it? How many tables of data do you need? What types of fields do you need for your records? What sort of reports and queries do you hope to create? Consider sketching out on paper how you want to group the information into tables and how the tables will relate to each other. Planning your database in advance can save you time when you build the database file.

Create a Database Based on a Template

You can build a new database based on any of the pre-defined Access templates. When you create a new database using a template, the database includes pre-built tables and forms, which you can populate with your own data. You control the structure of your database by determining which preset tables and fields are included in the file.

Create a Database Based on a Template

1 Click the **File** tab.

2 Click **New**.

3 Click **Sample templates**.

● You can also download templates from the Office Web site by clicking a template category under Office.com Templates.

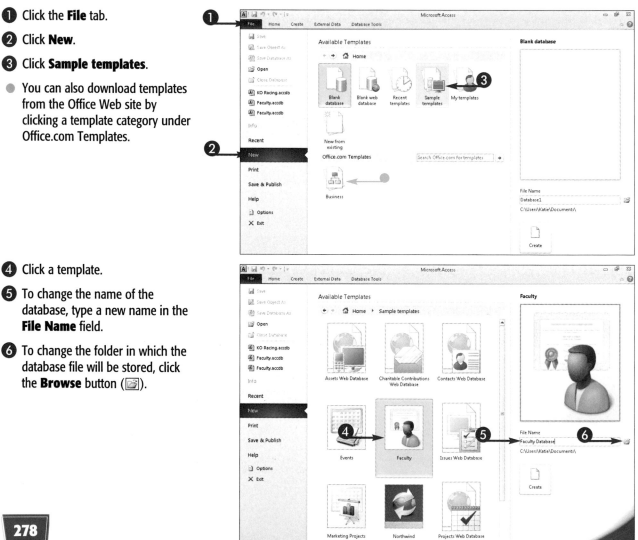

4 Click a template.

5 To change the name of the database, type a new name in the **File Name** field.

6 To change the folder in which the database file will be stored, click the **Browse** button ( ).

278

Access launches the File New Database dialog box.

⑦ Locate and select the folder in which you want to store the database file.

⑧ Click **OK**.

⑨ Click **Create**.

● Access creates a new, blank database based on the template you chose and opens a new table, ready for data.

TIPS

How do I know what fields to keep in or remove from my table?

To determine what fields you need in your database, do a little pre-planning. Decide what kinds of information you want to track in your database and what sorts of reports and queries you want to generate to view your data. For best results, use the suggested fields; you can always remove fields that you do not use at a later time.

What kinds of templates can I find to use for a database?

Microsoft offers all kinds of templates in a variety of categories. For example, the Business category includes templates for creating contact lists, assets, marketing projects, and events. The Education category includes templates for creating student and faculty database lists. You can also log onto the Office Web site to find new featured templates you can download.

Create a Blank Database

If none of the templates suits your purposes, you can create a new, blank database. You can then decide what tables and fields your database will include. When you create a new database file, Access prompts you to assign a name to the file. You also specify the folder and drive in which the database file will be stored.

Create a Blank Database

1. Click the **File** tab.

2. Click **New**.

3. Click **Blank database**.

4. Type a name for the database in the **File Name** field.

5. To change the folder in which the database file will be stored, click the **Browse** button ( ).

Access launches the File New Database dialog box.

6. Locate and select the folder in which you want to store the database file.

7. Click **OK**.

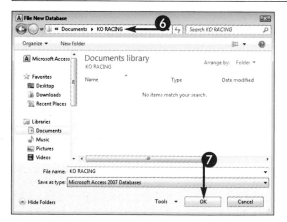

8 Click **Create**.

Available Templates

Home

Blank database   Blank web database   Recent templates   Sample templates   My templates

New from existing

Office.com Templates   Search Office.com for templates →

Business

Blank database

File Name
KO RACING.accdb
C:\Users\Katie\Documents\KO RACING\

Create **8**

● Access creates a new, blank database and opens a new table, ready for data.

Table Tools   KO RACING : Database (Access 2007) - Microsoft Access

File   Home   Create   External Data   Database Tools   Fields   Table

View   Text   Number   Currency   Date & Time   Yes/No   More Fields ▼   Delete   Name & Caption   Default Value   Field Size   Modify Lookups   Modify Expression   Memo Settings   Data Type: Format: Formatting $ %   ,   .00   .00

Views   Add & Delete   Properties   Formatting

All Access Objects   ⊽ «   Table1

Search...   ID   ▼   Click to Add   ▼

Tables   ⊼   *   (New)

Table1

TIPS

What is the pane on the left?

The pane on the left is the Navigation pane. You can use this pane to open various objects. You can collapse the pane to increase the on-screen workspace; simply click the **Shutter Bar Open/Close** button (⟪) in the top right corner of the pane. Click the button again to expand the pane.

How do I open an existing database?

If the database you want to open is one you have accessed recently, click the **File** tab and click **Recent**, and click the database in the Recent Databases list that appears. Otherwise, click the **File** tab and choose **Open** to launch an Open dialog box; then locate and select the database file and click **Open**.

Create a New Table

Access stores all data in tables. Tables consist of columns and rows that intersect to form *cells* for holding data. Each row is considered a *record*. You can use columns to hold *fields*, which are the individual units of information contained within a record. When creating a new table, you can give the table a unique name. All table objects that you create appear listed in the Navigation pane.

Create a New Table

① With your database open in Access, click the **Create** tab.

② Click the **Table** button.

● Access creates a new table and displays it in Datasheet view.

Note: See the upcoming "Change Table Views" section to learn more about Datasheet view.

③ To name a field, click the **Click to Add** link at the top of the field column.

④ Click the type of field you want to add (here, **Text**).

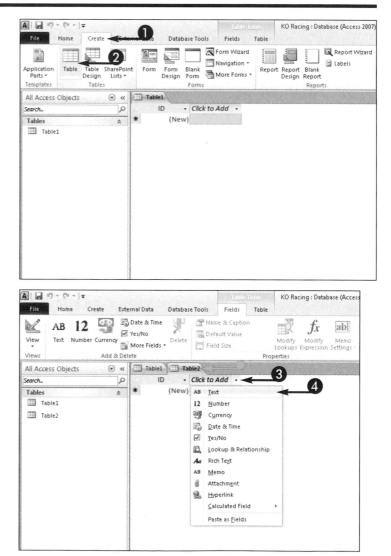

⑤ Type a name for the field and press **Enter**.

⑥ Repeat Steps **3** to **5** to create more fields for the table.

⑦ When you are finished adding fields, close the table by clicking the **Close** button (☒).

Access prompts you to save the table changes.

⑧ Click **Yes**.

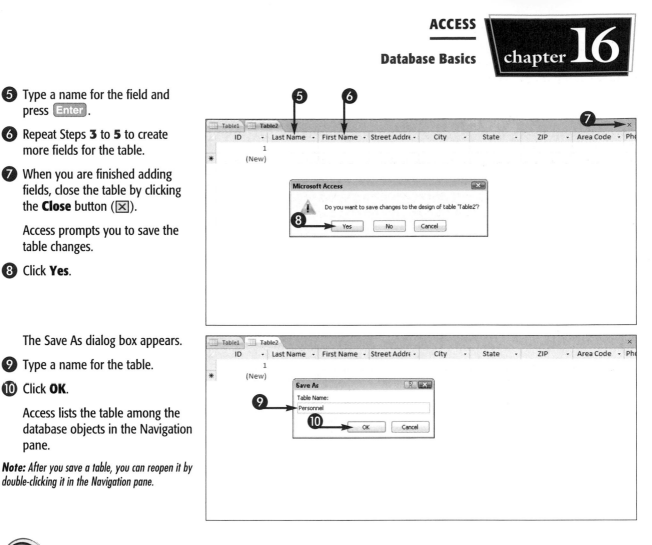

The Save As dialog box appears.

⑨ Type a name for the table.

⑩ Click **OK**.

Access lists the table among the database objects in the Navigation pane.

Note: After you save a table, you can reopen it by double-clicking it in the Navigation pane.

TIPS

Can I rename table fields?

Yes. You can rename fields in any table by double-clicking the field label and typing a new name. When you finish, press **Enter**. To add new fields, see the "Add a Field to a Table" section later in this chapter. To delete a field, see the "Delete a Field from a Table" section.

How do I remove a table that I no longer want?

Before attempting to remove a table, ensure that it does not contain any important data that you need. To delete the table, select it in the Navigation pane and press **Delete**. Access asks you to confirm the deletion before permanently removing the table, along with any data that it contains.

Change Table Views

You can view your table data using two different view modes: Datasheet view and Design view. In Datasheet view, the table appears as an ordinary grid of intersecting columns and rows where you can enter data. In Design view, you can view the skeletal structure of your fields and their properties. You can use Design view to modify the design of the table.

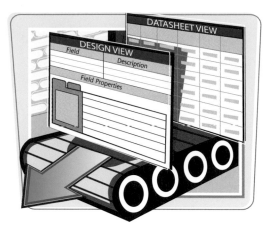

Switch to Design View

1 Click the **Home** tab on the Ribbon.

2 Click the bottom half of the **View** button.

3 Click **Design View**.

Note: An even quicker way to switch from Datasheet view to Design view is to click the top half of the **View** button.

● Access displays the table in Design view, showing the table's field properties.

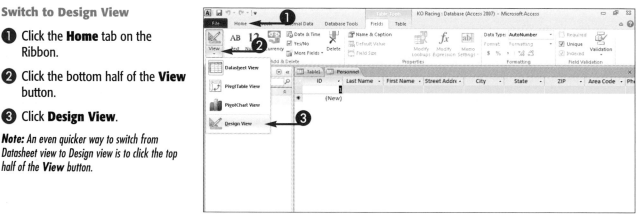

Switch to Datasheet View

1 Click the **Home** tab on the Ribbon.

2 Click the bottom half of the **View** button.

3 Click **Datasheet View**.

Note: *An even quicker way to switch from Design view to Datasheet view is to click the top half of the **View** button.*

● Access displays the default Datasheet view of the table.

TIPS

What sort of modifications can I make in Design view?

You can add fields by typing new field names in the **Field Name** column. You can also change the field names or change the type of data that is allowed within a field, such as text or number data. The Field Properties area enables you to change the design of the field itself, specifying how many characters the field can contain, whether fields can be left blank, and other properties.

What do the PivotTable and PivotChart views do?

If you create a PivotTable, you can use PivotTable view to summarize and analyze data by viewing different fields. You can use the PivotChart feature to create a graphical version of a PivotTable, and use the PivotChart view to see various graphical representations of the data. See the Access help files to learn more about the PivotTable and PivotChart features.

Add a Field to a Table

You can add fields to your table to include more information in your records. For example, you may need to add a separate field to a Contacts table for mobile phone numbers. After you add a field, you can name it whatever you want. To do so, double-click the field label, type a new name, and press Enter.

① Open the table to which you want to add a field in Datasheet view.

② Click the column header where you want to insert a new field. Access will add the new field to the right of the column you select.

③ Click the **Fields** tab.

④ In the Add & Delete group, click the button for the type of field you want to add (here, **Text**).

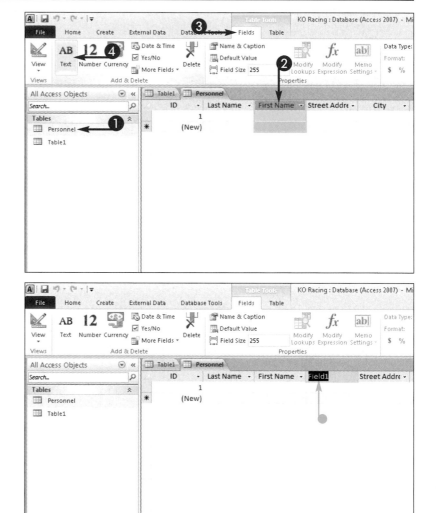

● Access adds the new field.

Note: As mentioned, you can rename the field by double-clicking the field label, typing a new name, and pressing Enter.

Delete a Field from a Table

You can delete a field that you no longer need in a table. When you remove a field, Access permanently removes any data contained within the field for every record in the table.

Delete a Field from a Table

① Open the table that you want to edit in Datasheet view.

② Click the **Fields** tab.

③ Click the column header for the field you want to remove.

④ Click the **Delete** button.

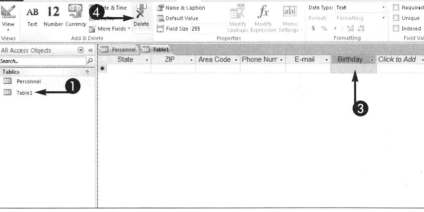

● Access removes the field and any record content for the field from the table.

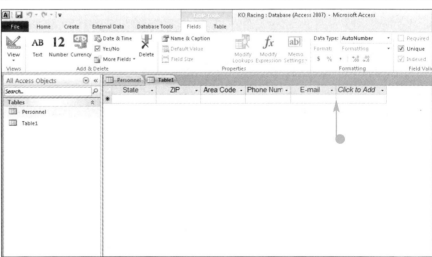

Hide a Field in a Table

You can hide a field in your table by hiding the entire column of data. You might hide a field to focus on other fields for a printout or to prevent another user on your computer from seeing the field.

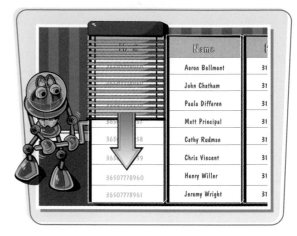

Hide a Field in a Table

① Click the column header for the field you want to hide.

② Right-click the selection.

③ Click **Hide Fields**.

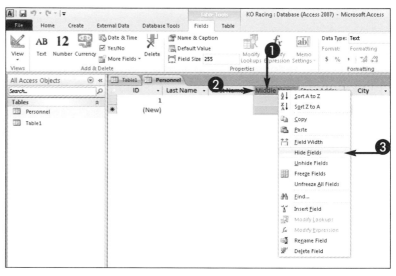

● Access hides the field.

Note: To view the field again, right-click the field next to the hidden field, click **Unhide Fields**, select the column that you want to display again, and click **OK**.

Move a Field in a Table

You can move a field in your table to rearrange how you view and enter record data. For example, you may want to move a field to appear before another field to suit the way you type your record data.

Move a Field in a Table

① Click the column header for the field you want to move.

② Drag the column to a new position in the table.

The 🖟 changes to 🖎.

● A bold vertical line marks the new location of the column as you drag.

③ Release the mouse button.

● Access moves the field to the new location.

One way to enter data into your database is to type it directly into an Access table. Alternatively, you can create a form based on your table to simplify data entry. Forms present your table fields in an easy-to-read, fill-in-the-blank format. When you create a form based on a table, Access inserts fields into the form for each field in the table.

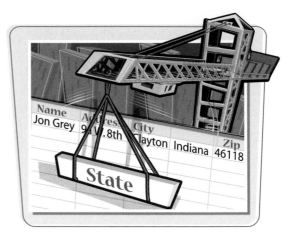

Create a Form

① With the table on which you want to base a form open in Access, click the **Create** tab.

② Click the **Form** button.

● Access creates the form.

③ Click the **Close** button (☒) to close the form.

Access prompts you to save your changes.

④ Click **Yes**.

Personnel

ID   1

Last Name

First Name

Street Ad

City

State

Microsoft Access

⚠ Do you want to save changes to the design of form 'Personnel'?

④ → Yes   No   Cancel

The Save As dialog box appears.

⑤ Type a name for the form.

⑥ Click **OK**.

Access lists the form among the database objects in the Navigation pane.

Note: After you save a form, you can reopen it by double-clicking it in the Navigation pane.

Personnel

ID   1

Last Na

First Name

Street Address

City

State

Save As

Form Name:

⑤ → Personnel

⑥ → OK   Cancel

TIPS

How do I delete a form that I no longer need?

To delete a form, click it in the Navigation pane. Then press Delete or click the **Delete** button on the Home tab. Access asks you to confirm the deletion; when you click **Yes**, Access permanently removes the form.

Can I create a blank form?

Yes. You can click the **Blank Form** button on the **Create** tab to open a blank form and a field list containing all the fields from all of the tables in the database. To add a field to the form, drag it from the list onto the form. You can populate the form with as many fields as you need.

Change Form Views

You can customize your form using Design view and Layout view. In Design view, each form object appears as a separate, editable element. For example, in this view, you can edit both the box that contains the data as well as the label that identifies the data. In Layout view, you can rearrange the form controls and adjust their sizes directly on the form.

Change Form Views

Switch to Design View

1 Click the **Home** tab on the Ribbon.

2 Click the bottom half of the **View** button.

3 Click **Design View**.

● Access displays the form in Design view.

Switch to Layout View

1 Click the **Home** tab on the Ribbon.

2 Click the bottom half of the **View** button.

3 Click **Layout View**.

● Access displays the form in Layout view.

To return to Form view, you can click the bottom half of the **View** button and then click **Form View**.

Move a Field in a Form

You can move a field to another location on your form. When you select a field for editing, the field label is also selected, making it easy to move both the field and the label at the same time. Although you can move a field in Design view or in Layout view, you might find it easier to make changes to your form in Layout view.

Move a Field in a Form

1 Open the form that you want to edit in Layout view.

2 Click the field that you want to move.

3 Click and drag the field to the new location on the form.

The ℞ changes to .

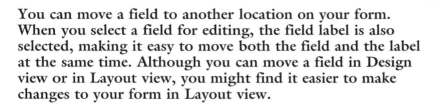

● Access repositions the field.

Delete a Field in a Form

You can delete a field that you no longer need in a form. When you remove a field, you need to remove both the data box and the field label. Removing a form field does not remove the field from the table upon which the form is originally based.

① Open the form that you want to edit in Layout view.

② Click the field that you want to delete.

③ Press Delete or click the **Delete** button on the Home tab.

● Access removes the field and label from the form.

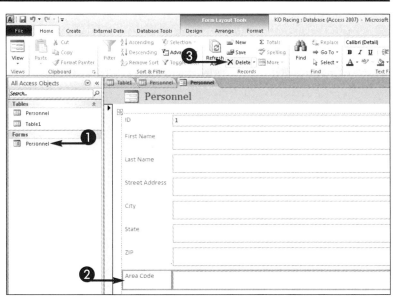

294

You can change the look of the forms and tables in your database by applying an Office theme. Each theme includes a variety of preset designs, fonts, and colors. When you apply a theme, that same theme is applied to all forms and tables in your database.

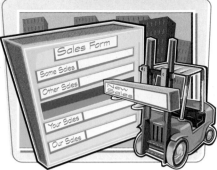

Apply a Database Theme

1. Open a database form in Layout view.

2. Click the **Design** tab on the Ribbon.

3. Click the **Themes** button.

4. Click the theme you want to apply.

● Access applies the theme to all forms in the database.

To change the look of a form, you can apply formatting to fields in the form. You might format a form field to draw attention to it in order to make it easier to locate that field for data-entry purposes.

① Open the form that you want to format in Layout view.

② Click to select the field whose text you want to format.

③ Click the **Format** tab.

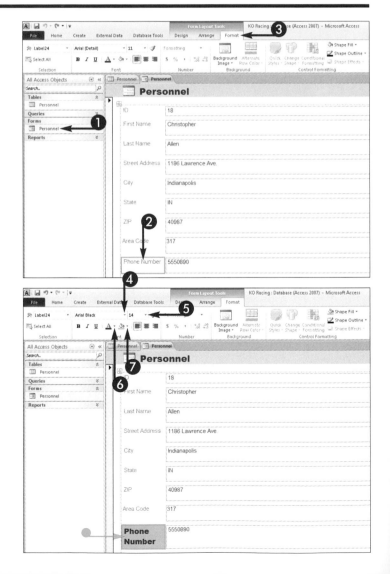

④ Click the **Font** 🔽 and choose a font.

⑤ Click the **Font Size** 🔽 and choose a font size.

⑥ Click the 🔽 to the right of the **Font Color** button (🅰) and choose a color from the palette that appears.

⑦ Click the 🔽 to the right of the **Background Color** button (🖊) and choose a color from the palette that appears.

● Access formats the text in the selected field according your selections.

Add a Background Image

You can add a background image to a form to make it more pleasant to look at. For example, you could add a company logo, or a photograph that appears in your company's marketing materials.

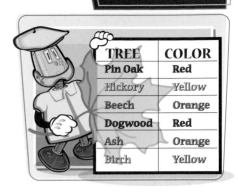

TREE	COLOR
Pin Oak	Red
Hickory	Yellow
Beech	Orange
Dogwood	Red
Ash	Orange
Birch	Yellow

Add a Background Image

1 Open the form to which you want to apply a background image in Layout view.

2 Click the **Format** tab.

3 Click the **Background Image** button.

4 Click **Browse**.

The Insert Picture dialog box opens.

5 Locate and select the image you want to use.

6 Click **OK**.

● Access applies the image to the form background.

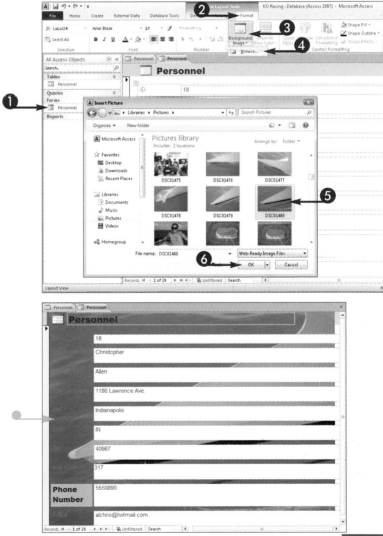

Add a Record to a Table

You can start building your database by adding records to a database table. Any new records that you add appear at the end of the table. As your table grows longer, you can use the navigation buttons on your keyboard to navigate it. You can press `Tab` to move from cell to cell or you can press the keyboard arrow keys. To move backward to a previous cell, press `Shift` + `Tab`.

Add a Record to a Table

1 In the Navigation pane, double-click the table to which you want to add a record.

● Access opens the table, placing the cursor in the first cell of the first blank row.

● By default, the first field in each table is an ID field, containing a unique ID number for the record. This value is set automatically.

2 Press `Tab`.

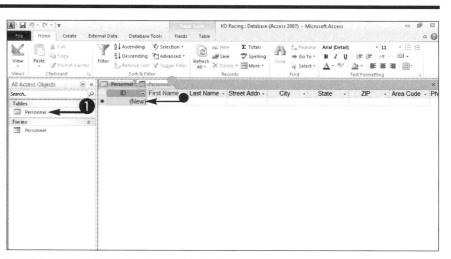

Access moves your cursor to the next cell in the row.

3 Type the desired data in the selected cell.

4 Press `Tab`.

5 Repeat Steps **3** and **4** until you have filled the entire row.

6 Press `Enter` or press `Tab` to move to the next row or record.

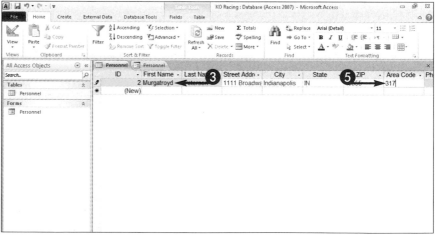

- Access adds the new record.

- Access moves your cursor to the first cell in the next row.

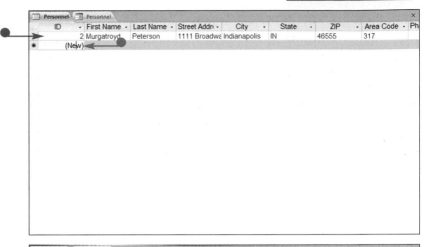

7 Repeat Steps **2** to **6** to add more records to the table.

Access adds your records.

- You can resize a column by dragging the column border left or right.

- You can use the scroll bars to view different portions of the table.

TIPS

How do I edit a record in a table?

To edit a record in a table, open the table in Datasheet view, click in the cell whose data you want to change, double-click the data to select it, and type over the data to replace it.

What is a primary key?

A *primary key* uniquely identifies each record in a table. For many tables, the primary key is the ID field, which stores a unique number for each record as it is entered into the database. You can also designate another field (or even multiple fields) as a primary key. To do so, switch the table to Design view, select the field that you want to set as the primary key, and click the **Primary key** button on the Design tab.

Add a Record to a Form

You can use forms to quickly add records to your Access databases. Forms present your record fields in an easy-to-read format. The form window presents each field in your table as a box that you can use to enter data.

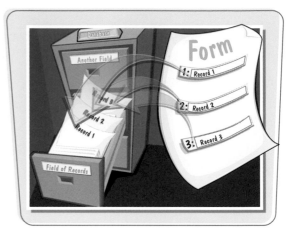

1 In the Navigation pane, double-click the form to which you want to add a record.

Note: *If the form is not visible in the Navigation pane, click the [⊙] along the top of the pane, choose* **Object Type***, and locate the desired form under the Forms heading.*

● Access opens the form.

2 Click the **Home** tab.

3 Click the **New** button in the Records group.

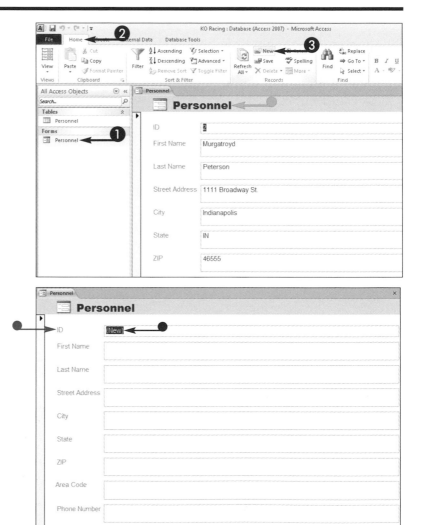

● Access opens a blank form, placing the cursor in the first cell of the first field.

● By default, the first field in the table associated with this form is an ID field, containing a unique ID number for the record. This value is set automatically.

4 Press Tab.

Access moves your cursor to the next field in the form.

5 Type the desired data in the selected field.

6 Press Tab.

Access moves to the next field in the form.

7 Repeat Steps **5** and **6** until you have filled the entire form.

8 Press Enter or Tab.

Access displays another blank record, ready for data.

● To close the form window, you can click the **Close** button (⊠).

 TIPS

Are there other ways to insert a new record?	

Yes. In addition to clicking the **New** button in the Home tab of the Ribbon to open a new, blank record in your form, you can click the **New (Blank) Record** button (▶) on the form window's navigation bar (located along the bottom of the form) to create a new, blank record.

How do I edit a record in a form?	

You can reopen the form, navigate to the record that you want to change, and make your edits directly to the form data. When you save your changes, Access automatically updates the data in your table. To learn how to display a particular record in a form, see the next section, "Navigate Records in a Form."

Navigate Records in a Form

You can navigate your table records using a form. The form window includes a navigation bar for viewing different records in your database. You may find it easier to read a record using a form rather than reading it from a large table containing other records.

Navigate Records in a Form

① In the Navigation pane, double-click the form whose records you want to navigate.

Note: If the form is not visible in the Navigation pane, click the ⊙ along the top of the pane, choose **Object Type**, and locate the desired form under the Forms heading.

● Access displays the form.

● The Current Record box indicates which record you are viewing.

② Click the **Previous Record** (◁) or **Next Record** (▷) buttons to move back or forward by one record.

● Access displays the previous or next record in the database.

● You can click the **First Record** (◁◁) or **Last Record** (▷▷) buttons to navigate to the first or last record in the table.

● You can click the **New (Blank) Record** button (▷✳) to start a new, blank record.

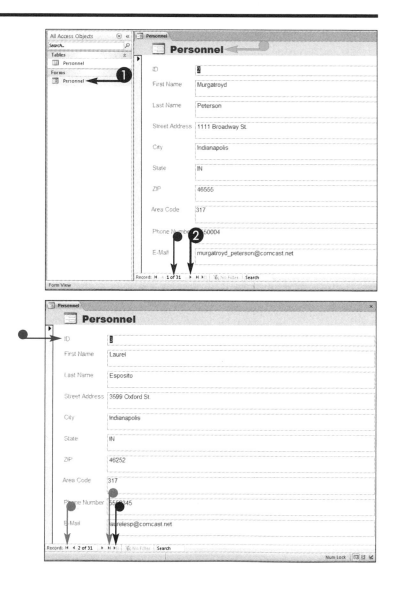

Although you can navigate the records in a form using the various buttons in the navigation bar, this method can become time-consuming if the form contains numerous records. An easier approach is to search for the record using Access's search functionality.

Search for a Record in a Form

1 In the Navigation pane, double-click the form containing the record you want to find.

Note: If the form is not visible in the Navigation pane, click the ⊙ along the top of the pane, choose **Object Type**, and locate the desired form under the Forms heading.

● Access displays the form.

2 Click in the **Search** field.

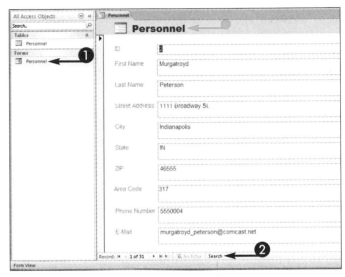

3 Type a keyword that relates to the record you want to find (here, a person's last name).

● As you type, Access displays matching records.

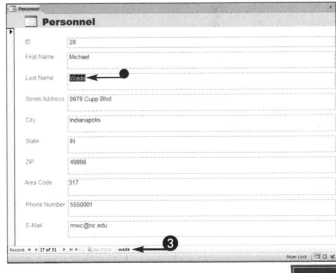

Delete a Record from a Table

You can remove a record from your database if it holds data that you no longer need. Removing old records can reduce the overall file size of your database and make it easier to manage. When you delete a record, all of the data within its fields is permanently removed.

Delete a Record from a Table

1 In the Navigation pane, double-click the table that contains the record you want to delete.

● Access opens the table.

2 Position your mouse pointer over the gray box to the left of the record that you want to delete (the mouse pointer changes to ➡) and click.

● The record is selected.

3 Click the **Home** tab.

4 Click the **Delete** button in the Records group.

*Note: You can also right-click the record, and then click **Delete Record**.*

Access displays a warning box about the deletion.

5 Click **Yes**.

● Access permanently removes the record from the table.

Delete a Record from a Form

In addition to removing records directly from a table, you can remove records that you no longer need by using a form. Removing old records can reduce the overall file size of your database and make it easier to manage. When you delete a record, whether from a table or a form, all the data within its fields is permanently removed.

Delete a Record from a Form

1 In the Navigation pane, double-click the form containing the record you want to delete.

*Note: If the form is not visible in the Navigation pane, click the ☑ along the top of the pane, choose **Object Type**, and locate the desired form under the Forms heading.*

● Access displays the form.

2 Navigate to the record you want to delete.

3 Click the **Home** tab on the Ribbon.

4 Click the **Delete** button's ☑.

5 Click **Delete Record**.

Access displays a warning box about the deletion.

6 Click **Yes**.

Access permanently removes the record.

Sort Records

Sorting enables you to arrange your database records in a logical order to match any criteria that you specify. For example, with a contacts database, you might sort the records alphabetically or based on the ZIP code. You can sort in ascending order or descending order. You can either sort records in a table, or you can use a form to sort records.

Sort Records

Sort a Table

1 Open the table you want to sort.

2 Position your mouse pointer over the column header for the field by which you want to sort (the mouse pointer changes to ↓) and click.

3 Click the **Home** tab on the Ribbon.

4 Click a sort button.

Click **Ascending** to sort the records in ascending order.

Click **Descending** to sort the records in descending order.

Access sorts the table records based on the field you choose.

● This example sorts the records alphabetically by last name in ascending order.

● In the prompt box that appears when you close the table, you can click **Yes** to make the sort permanent or **No** to leave the original order intact.

Sort Using a Form

1 Open the form you want to sort.

2 Click in the field by which you want to sort.

3 Click the **Home** tab on the Ribbon.

4 Click a sort button.

Click **Ascending** to sort the records in ascending order.

Click **Descending** to sort the records in descending order.

Access sorts the table records based on the field you choose.

● This example sorts the records alphabetically by last name in ascending order.

● You can use the navigation buttons to view the sorted records.

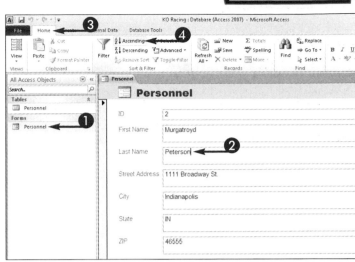

TIPS

What happens if I have empty records and perform a sort?

If you perform a sort on a field without any data for some of your records, those records are included in the sort. Records with empty fields are sorted first when you perform an ascending sort, or last with a descending sort.

How do I remove a sort order?

With the sorted table or form open, click the **Remove Sort** button in the Sort & Filter group on the Home tab. This returns the table to its original sort order. You can also use this technique to remove a sort from a query or report. (Queries and reports are covered later in this chapter.)

Filter Records

You can use an Access filter to view only specific records that meet criteria you set. For example, you may want to view all clients buying a particular product or anyone in a contacts database who has a birthday in June. You can apply a simple filter on one field in your database using the Selection tool, or you can filter several fields using the Filter by Form command.

Filter Records

Apply a Simple Filter

1 Open the form you want to filter.

2 Click in the field by which you want to filter.

3 Click the **Home** tab on the Ribbon.

4 Click the **Selection** button.

5 Click a criterion.

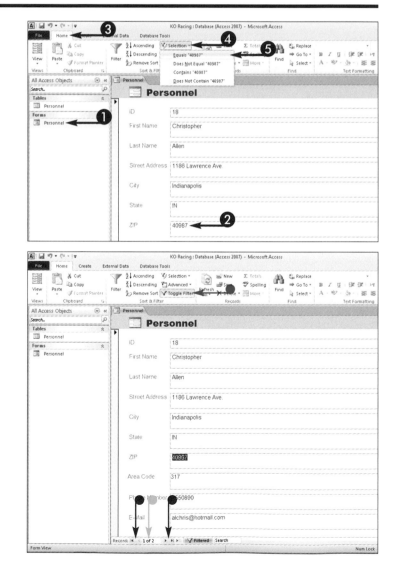

Access filters the records.

● In this example, Access finds two records matching the filter criterion.

● You can use the navigation buttons to view the filtered records.

● To undo a filter, click the **Toggle Filter** button.

Filter by Form

1 Open the form you want to filter.

2 Click the **Home** tab on the Ribbon.

3 Click the **Advanced** button.

4 Click **Filter By Form**.

● A blank form appears.

5 Click in the field by which you want to filter.

6 Click the ▾ that appears and choose a criterion.

7 Repeat Steps **5** and **6** to add more criteria to the filter.

● You can set OR criteria using the tabs at the bottom of the form.

8 Click the **Toggle Filter** button.

Access filters the records.

To remove the filter, you can click the **Toggle Filter** button again.

TIPS

Can I filter by exclusion?

Yes. You can filter out records that do not contain the search criteria that you specify. To do so, first click in the field that you want to filter in the form, click the **Selection** button on the Home tab, and then click an exclusion option. Access filters out any records that do not contain the data found in the field that you selected.

What are OR criteria?

Setting OR criteria enables you to display records that match one set of criteria or another. For example, you might set up your filter to display only those records with the value 46989 in the ZIP field OR the value 46555 in the ZIP field.

Apply Conditional Formatting

You can use conditional formatting to draw attention to certain data in your form. For example, you might apply a yellow highlight to any fields containing negative values in order to make them stand out. You apply conditional formatting by creating a rule, which specifies the criteria that the value in a field must meet. Values that meet the criteria are formatted using settings you specify.

Apply Conditional Formatting

1. Open the form to which you want to apply conditional formatting in Layout view.

2. Click the field to which you want to apply conditional formatting.

3. Click the **Format** tab.

4. Click the **Conditional Formatting** button.

The Conditional Formatting Rules Manager dialog box opens.

5. Click the **New Rule** button.

The New Formatting Rule dialog box opens.

6. Set the criteria you want to use to apply conditional formatting.

7. Specify how values that meet your criteria should be formatted.

8. Click **OK**.

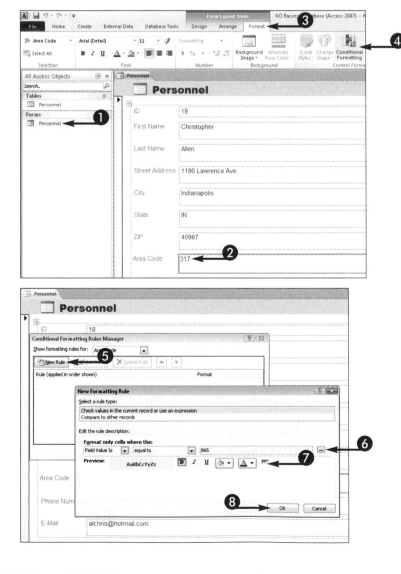

● Access creates a rule based on the criteria you set.

⑨ Click **OK**.

Conditional Formatting Rules Manager

Show formatting rules for: Area Code

🔳 New Rule   📝 Edit Rule   ✕ Delete Rule

Rule (applied in order shown)	Format
Value = 865	AaBbCcYyZz

OK   Cancel   Apply

● Access applies the conditional formatting.

Personnel

Personnel

ID	26
First Name	Becky
Last Name	Hyatt
Street Address	414 Montana Ave.
City	Indianapolis
State	IN
ZIP	40987
Area Code	**865**

TIP

How do I remove conditional formatting?

To remove conditional formatting, follow these steps:

① Open the Conditional Formatting Rules Manager dialog box. (To open this dialog box, follow Steps **1** to **4** in this section.)

② Click the conditional formatting rule you want to remove.

③ Click the **Delete Rule** button.

④ Click **OK**.

Access removes the conditional formatting.

Conditional Formatting Rules Manager

Show formatting rules for: Area Code

🔳 New Rule   📝 Edit Rule   ✕ Delete Rule

Rule (applied in order shown)	Format
Value = 865	AaBbCcYyZz

OK   Cancel   Apply

Perform a Simple Query

You can use a query to extract information that you want to view in a database. Queries are especially useful when you want to glean data from multiple tables. Queries are similar to filters, but offer you greater control when it comes to viewing records. You can use the Query Wizard to help you select what fields you want to include in the analysis.

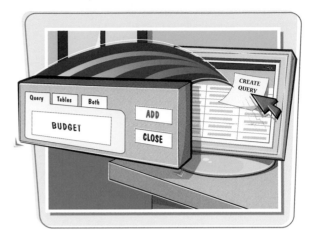

Perform a Simple Query

Create a Query

1. Open the table or form for which you want to perform a simple query.

2. Click the **Create** tab on the Ribbon.

3. Click the **Query Wizard** button.

The New Query dialog box appears.

4. Click **Simple Query Wizard**.

5. Click **OK**.

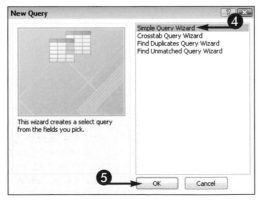

The Simple Query Wizard opens.

⑥ Click the **Tables/Queries** ▾ and choose the table containing the fields on which you want to base the query.

⑦ In the Available Fields list, click a field that you want to include in the query.

⑧ Click the **Add** button (>).

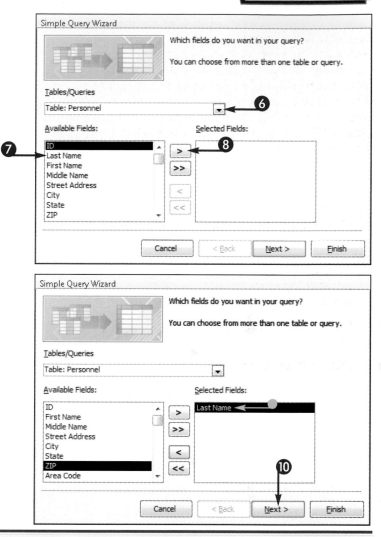

● The field is added to the Selected Fields list.

⑨ Repeat Steps **7** and **8** to add more fields to your query.

You can repeat Step **6** to choose another table from which to add fields.

Note: When using fields from two or more tables, the tables must have a prior relationship.

⑩ Click **Next**.

TIPS

What is a table relationship?

Table relationships enable you to combine related information for analysis. For example, you might define a relationship between one table containing customer contact information and another table containing customer orders; then, you could perform a query to locate all customers ordering the same product. To define table relationships, click **Database Tools** and then click **Relationships**. (If you created your database from a template, then certain table relationships are predefined.)

Are there other types of queries that I can create?

Yes. When you display the New Query dialog box, you can choose from several other query types to create a query. The Crosstab Query Wizard creates a query to display information in a spreadsheet-like format, the Find Duplicates Query Wizard creates a query that finds records with duplicate field values, and the Find Unmatched Query Wizard creates a query that finds records in one table with no related records in another table.

During the process of creating a new query, the wizard asks you to give the query a unique name. This is so that you can refer to the query later. All queries that you create are saved in the Navigation pane; you can open a query to perform it again, or open it in Design view to edit it.

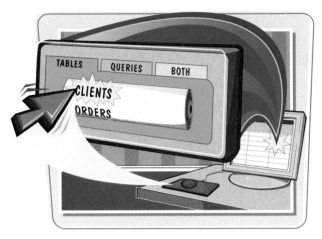

Perform a Simple Query (continued)

⑪ Type a name for the query.

⑫ Click the **Open the query to view information** radio button.

⑬ Click **Finish**.

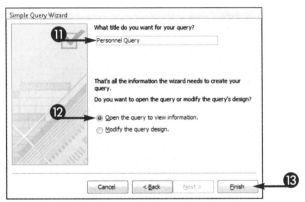

● A query datasheet appears, listing the fields.

Add Criteria to the Query

1 Double-click the query in the Navigation pane to open it.

Note: If the query is not visible in the Navigation pane, click the ⊙ along the top of the pane, choose Object Type, and locate the desired query under the Queries heading.

2 Click the **View** button to switch to Design view.

3 Click in the **Criteria** field and type the data that you want to view.

This example lists a ZIP code as the criterion.

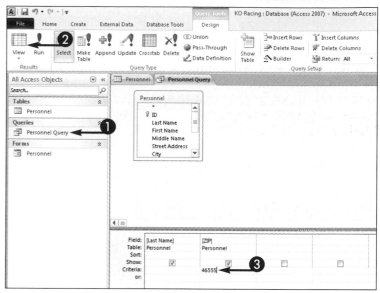

4 Click the **View** button again to switch back to Datasheet view to see the results.

● The table now shows only the records matching the criteria.

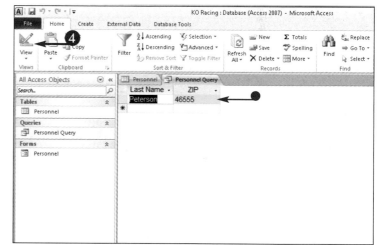

TIPS

How do I add another table to my query?

Switch to Design view, click the **Design** tab on the Ribbon, and then click the **Show Table** button. This opens the Show Table dialog box, where you can add another table to the query and choose from among the available fields to customize the query.

Can I sort or filter my query?

Yes. You can use the sorting and filtering features to further define your query results. To learn how to sort data, see the "Sort Records" section, earlier in this chapter. To learn how to apply a filter, see the "Filter Records" section, also earlier in this chapter.

Create a Report

You can use Access to create a report based on one or more database tables. This can be a simple report, which contains all the fields in a single table, or a custom report. To create a custom report, you can use the Report Wizard; it guides you through all the steps necessary to turn complex database data into an easy-to-read printout.

Create a Report

Create a Simple Report

1 Open the table for which you want to create a simple report.

2 Click the **Create** tab on the Ribbon.

3 Click the **Report** button.

● Access creates a simple report based on the table you selected.

Create a Custom Report

1. Open the table for which you want to create a custom report in Access.

2. Click the **Create** tab on the Ribbon.

3. Click the **Report Wizard** button.

   The Report Wizard opens.

4. Click the **Tables/Queries** ⏷ and choose the table containing the fields on which you want to base the report.

5. In the Available Fields list, click a field that you want to include in the report.

6. Click the **Add** button (>).

   ● The field is added to the Selected Fields list.

7. Repeat Steps **5** and **6** to add more fields to your report.

8. Click **Next**.

9. Optionally, click the field you want to use to group the data.

10. Click the **Add** button (>).

    ● A preview of the grouping appears here.

11. Click **Next**.

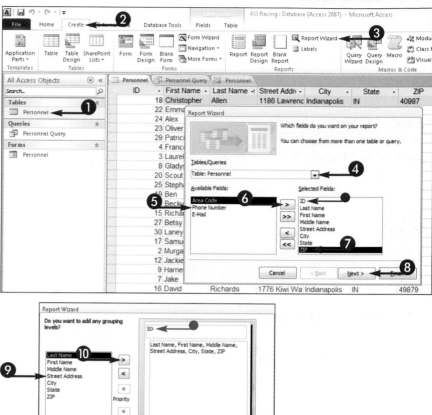

 TIPS

Can I choose different fields from different tables to create a custom report?

Yes. You can choose fields from multiple tables for your custom report. Simply repeat Step **3** under "Create a Custom Report" to select additional tables that contain the fields you want to include. Note that to use fields from two or more tables, the tables must have a prior relationship. (To learn more about table relationships, refer to the tip "What Is a table relationship?" in the preceding section.)

How do I remove a field from a custom report?

If you have not yet completed the wizard, you can remove a field from the report by clicking the **Back** button until you reach the wizard's first screen. Then click the field you want to remove in the **Selected Fields** list and click the **Remove** button (<) to remove the field. To remove all the fields, click the **Remove All** button (<<).

As the Report Wizard guides you through the steps for building a report, you are asked to decide upon a sort order and a layout for the report's appearance. After you create the report, you can print it.

Create a Report (continued)

12 To sort your data, click the first and click the field by which you want to sort.

You can add more sort fields as needed.

Note: Fields are sorted in ascending order by default. Click the **Ascending** button to toggle to descending order.

13 Click **Next**.

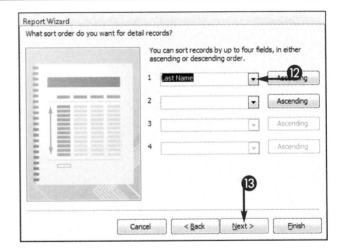

14 Click a layout option.

● You can set the page orientation for a report using these options.

15 Click **Next**.

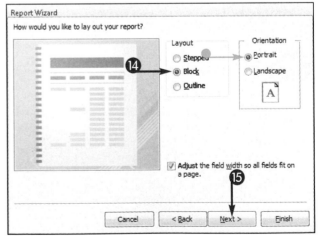

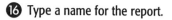
⑯ Type a name for the report.

⑰ Click the **Preview the report** radio button.

⑱ Click **Finish**.

Report Wizard

What title do you want for your report?

⑯ Personnel1

That's all the information the wizard needs to create your report.

Do you want to preview the report or modify the report's design?

⑰ ⦿ Preview the report.

○ Modify the report's design.

Cancel   < Back   Next >   Finish ⑱

● Access creates the report and displays the report in Print Preview mode.

Personnel | Personnel Query | Personnel | **Personnel1**

Personnel1

ID	Last Name	First Name	Mid
2	Peterson	Murgatroyd	
3	Esposito	Laurel	
4	Dubois	Francois	
5	Windsor	Gemma	
6	Welsh	Heidi	
7	Plant	Jake	
8	Farmer	Gladys	
9	Plaisance	Harriet	
10	White	Barbara	
11	Weitz	Diane	
12	Pfeiffer	Jackie	
13	Van Dyke	Steven	
14	Warren	Alfred	
15	James	Richard	
16	Richards	David	
17	Martin	Samuel	
18	Allen	Christopher	

Page: 1 ► ►I ► No Filter

TIPS

How do I print a report?

To print a report from Print Preview, click the **Print** button on the Print Preview tab on the Ribbon. You can also click the **File** button and then click **Print** to open the Print dialog box and assign any printing options before printing the report.

How can I customize a report in Access?

You can further customize a report using Design view. You can change the formatting of fields, move fields around, and more. You can even apply conditional formatting to the report by clicking the **Conditional Formatting** button in the Format tab. (For more about conditional formatting, refer to the section "Apply Conditional Formatting" earlier in this chapter.)

PART

VI

Outlook

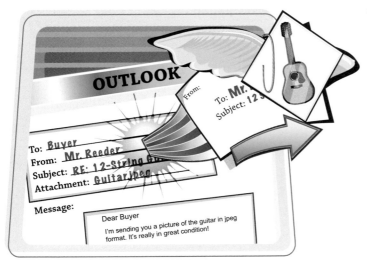

Outlook is a personal information manager for the computer desktop. You can use Outlook to manage your calendar, keep track of contacts, organize lists of things to do, and more. You can perform a wide variety of everyday tasks from the Outlook window, including sending and receiving e-mail messages, scheduling appointments, and organizing an address book of contacts. In this part, you learn how to put Outlook to work for you using each of the major components to manage everyday tasks.

View Outlook Components

You can use Outlook to manage everyday tasks and e-mail correspondence. Outlook works much like a personal organizer and contains components for certain tasks, such as a Mail component for sending and receiving e-mail messages and a Calendar component for scheduling appointments. In all, Outlook features four main components: Mail, Calendar, Contacts, and Tasks. You can switch between components, depending on the task that you want to perform.

View Outlook Components

① Click the **Calendar** button in the Navigation pane.

● You can use the To-Do Bar to see your daily items at a glance.

Outlook displays the Calendar component.

② Click the **Contacts** button in the Navigation pane.

Outlook displays the Contacts component.

③ Click the **Tasks** button in the Navigation pane.

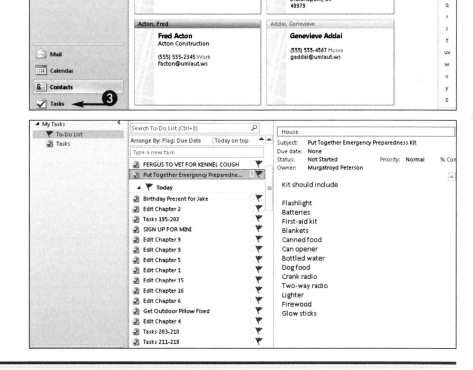

Outlook displays the Tasks component.

How I change what component opens by default when I start Outlook?

By default, Outlook opens the Mail component's Inbox folder when you start the program. To start with a different Mail folder or another component, such as Calendar, click the **File** tab, click **Options**, and click **Advanced** in the Outlook Options dialog box that opens. Under Outlook Start and Exit, click the **Browse** button. Then click the component or Mail folder that you want to set as the default component in the Select Folder dialog box, and click **OK** in both dialog boxes to close them.

Schedule an Appointment

You can use Outlook's Calendar component to keep track of your schedule. You can add notations on the calendar to remind you of appointments and other important events. When adding new appointments to the Calendar, you fill out appointment details, such as the name of the person with whom you are meeting, and the start and end times of the appointment.

Schedule an Appointment

❶ Click the **Calendar** button in the Navigation pane to open the Calendar component.

❷ Click the date for which you want to set an appointment.

● You can click the Date Navigator's arrow buttons to choose a different month.

❸ Double-click the time slot for the appointment that you want to set.

Outlook opens the Appointment window, displaying the Appointment tab.

❹ Type a name for the appointment.

● Outlook adds the name to the window's title.

❺ Type a location for the appointment.

❻ Click the **End time** ▼ and set an end time for the appointment.

● If you did not select the correct time slot in Step **3**, you can click the **Start time** ▼ and click a start time.

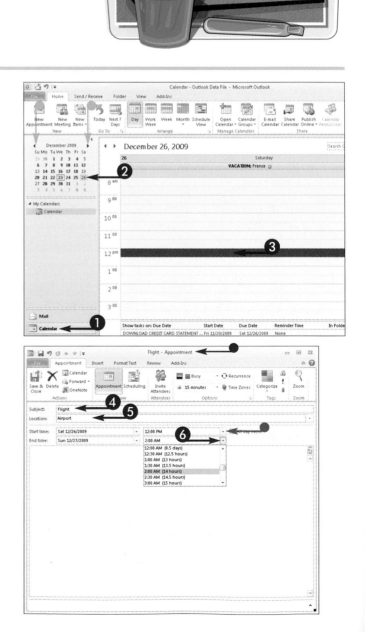

Outlook automatically sets a
reminder for the appointment.

● You can click the ⏷ to change
the reminder setting.

Note: *When a reminder is set, Outlook displays a
prompt box at the designated time to remind you
about the appointment (assuming, of course, that
Outlook is running).*

● You can type any notes about the
appointment here.

7 Click the **Save & Close** button.

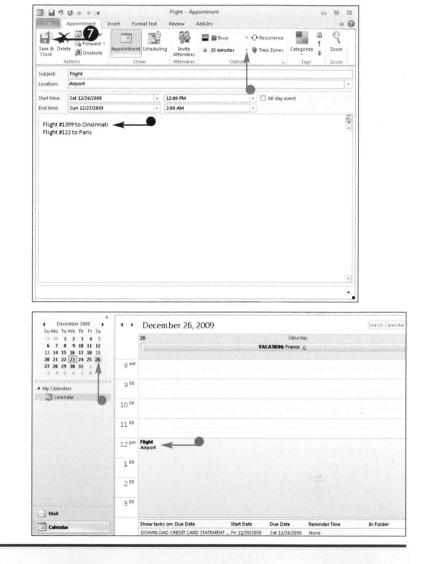

● Outlook displays the appointment
in the Calendar.

To view the appointment details
or make changes, you can double-
click the appointment to reopen
the Appointment window.

● The days on which you have any
appointments scheduled appear
bold in the Date Navigator.

How do I categorize an appointment?

You can click the **Categorize** button to
assign color categories to your
appointments to organize them in your
calendar. For example, you might
categorize all work appointments as blue and all non-
work appointments as red. You can also click **Tags** and
choose **High Importance** or **Low Importance** to
prioritize an appointment, or click **Private** to prevent
others from seeing the appointment in your calendar.

How do I delete an appointment from the Calendar?

To remove an appointment,
right-click the appointment in
the Calendar and click **Delete**.
You can also click the appointment to select it
and press Delete on your keyboard, or open
the appointment window and click the **Delete**
button. Outlook immediately deletes the
appointment from your schedule.

Schedule a Recurring Appointment

If your schedule includes a weekly department meeting or a lunch date with a friend on the second Friday of every month, you can set the appointment as a recurring appointment. Outlook adds the appointment to each week or month as you require. (Note that you can use this same technique to set recurring tasks in your Outlook Tasks.)

Tom Schroeder
9 am - Noon

① With the Appointment window for the recurring appointment open in Outlook, click the **Recurrence** button on the Appointment tab.

Note: For help creating an appointment, see the preceding section.

The Appointment Recurrence dialog box opens.

② Select the recurrence pattern.

● You can also set a range of the recurrence if the appointments will continue for only a set number of weeks or months.

③ Click **OK**.

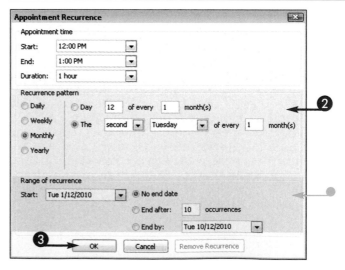

- Outlook marks the appointment as a recurring appointment.

4 Click the **Save & Close** button.

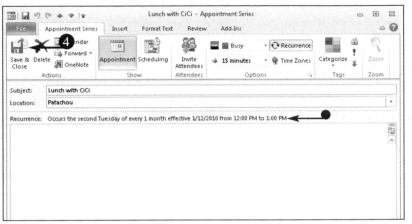

Outlook displays the appointment in the Calendar.

- Recurring appointments are indicated by a recurrence icon (🔁) in the lower right corner of the appointment on the Calendar.

TIPS

Is there an easy way to set an appointment with one of my contacts?

Yes. You can quickly create an appointment with anyone in your Contacts list. To do so, open the Contacts component and right-click the contact with whom you want to schedule an appointment. Next, click **Create**, and then click **Meeting**. This opens a Meeting window, where you can enter appointment details — such as the date and time — and e-mail a meeting request to the contact.

How do I add a holiday to my calendar?

By default, holidays do not appear in Outlook. To add a holiday, click the **File** tab, click **Options**, click **Calendar** in the Outlook Options dialog box, and click the **Add Holidays** button under Calendar Options. This opens the Add Holidays to Calendar dialog box; click the country or religion whose holidays you want to add to the calendar and click **OK**.

Schedule an Event

If you need to track an activity that lasts the entire day or spans several days, such as an anniversary or a conference, you can schedule the activity as an event. Events appear as banners at the top of the scheduled date.

Schedule an Event

1 Click the **Home** tab.

2 Click the **New Items** button.

3 Click **All Day Event**.

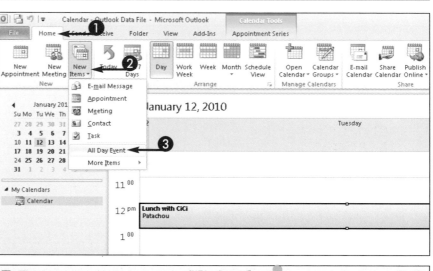

Outlook displays the Event window, which looks the same as the Appointment window.

4 Type a subject for the event.

● Outlook adds the subject to the window's title.

5 Type a location for the event, if applicable.

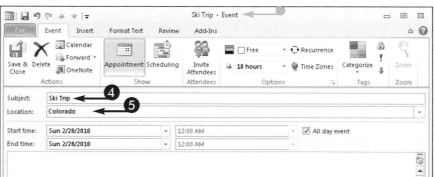

6 Enter the event's date in the **Start time** and **End time** fields.

● You can click each field's ⬇ to choose the date from a pop-up calendar.

7 Click the **Save & Close** button.

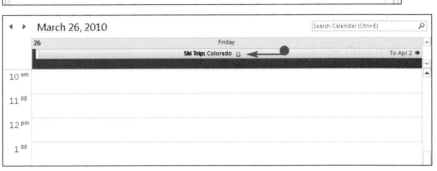

● Outlook displays the event as a banner in the Calendar for the date of the event.

To edit an event, you can double-click the event banner and make your changes in the appointment window that opens.

TIPS

How do I plan a meeting?
You can schedule meetings with other users, sending e-mail messages to invite attendees, tracking responses, and designating resources, such as conference rooms. To do so, click the **Home** tab and click the **New Meeting** button; a Meeting window opens, where you can enter the e-mail addresses of invitees, choose a meeting date and time, select a meeting room, and more.

Can I publish my calendar online so that others can see it?
Yes. To publish your calendar, click the **Home** tab, click **Publish Online**, and then click **Publish to Office.com**. Outlook prompts you to register with Office Online before launching a wizard to step you through the publication process. After your calendar is published, Outlook prompts you to invite others to view it; enter the e-mail addresses of people with whom you want to share your calendar and click **Send**.

Create a New Contact

You can use Outlook's Contacts component to keep a list of people that you contact most often, such as family members, co-workers, and clients. You can keep track of information such as addresses, e-mail addresses, phone numbers, and more.

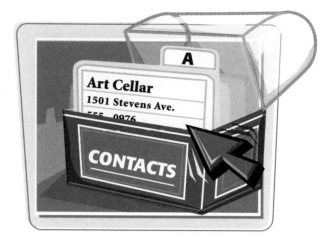

Create a New Contact

1 Click the **Contacts** button in the Navigation pane to open the Contacts component.

2 Click the **New Contact** button.

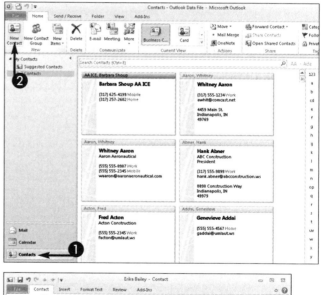

Outlook opens a Contact window.

3 Fill in the contact's information.

You can press Tab to move from field to field.

④ Click the **Show** button.

⑤ Click the **Details** button.

⑥ Fill in additional information about the contact, as needed.

⑦ Click the **Save & Close** button.

● Outlook saves the information and displays the contact in the Contacts list.

To edit contact details, you can double-click the contact to reopen the Contact window.

Can I import a list of contacts from another program?
Yes. Click the **File** tab, click **Open**, and then click **Import** to open the Import and Export Wizard. The wizard guides you through the steps for importing a list of contacts. (Note that to import contacts from another program, you must first export the contacts from that program to a special file. For details, see the program's help information.)

How do I send an e-mail to a contact?
You can right-click the contact name, click **Create**, and then click **E-mail**. Outlook opens a Message window with the contact's e-mail address in the To field; simply add a subject, type your message text, and click the **Send** button. To learn more about e-mailing with Outlook, see the next chapter.

You can use Outlook's Tasks component to keep track of things that you need to do, such as a daily list of activities or project steps that you need to complete. You can assign a due date to each task, as well as prioritize and categorize tasks.

Create a New Task

1 Click the **Tasks** button in the Navigation pane to open the Tasks component.

2 Click the **New Task** button.

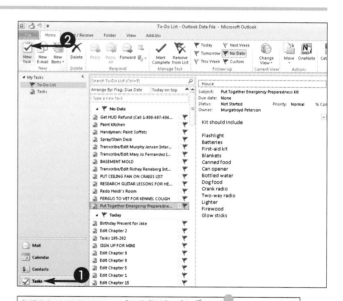

Outlook displays a Task window.

3 Type a subject for the task.

● Outlook adds the subject to the window's title.

4 Enter a due date for the task.

5 Click the **Status** 🔽 and click a progress option.

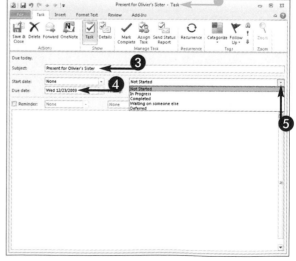

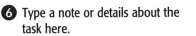

6 Type a note or details about the task here.

● You can set a priority level for the task using the **Priority** ▾.

● To set a completion amount, you can click the **% Complete** 🔾.

7 Click the **Save & Close** button.

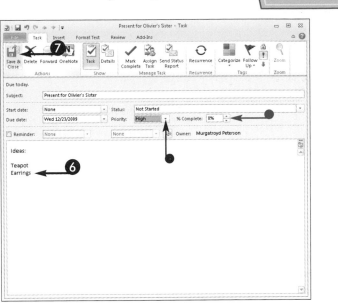

● Outlook displays the task in the Tasks list.

To view the task details again or make changes, you can double-click the task to reopen the Task window.

● To change your view of tasks in the Tasks list, you can click the **Change View** button and choose a view option from the menu that appears.

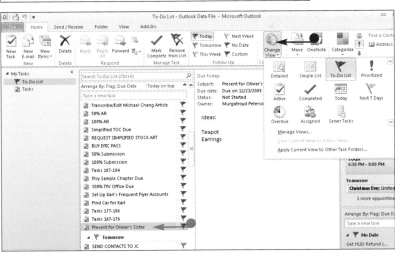

How do I mark a task as complete?

Click a task in the Tasks list and then click the **Mark Complete** button in the Home tab to mark the task as complete. Depending on the current view, completed tasks may appear with a strikethrough on the Tasks list or may be hidden. To remove a task from the list, click it to select it and then click the **Remove from List** button in the Home tab.

Can I turn a task into an e-mail?

Yes. You can assign a task to another user by turning the task into an e-mail message. Open the task and then click the **Assign Task** button in the Home tab to open the Task window. You can add an e-mail address and a message concerning the task, and then send the message. To learn more about e-mailing in Outlook, see the next chapter.

Add a Note

Outlook includes a Notes component, which you can use to create notes for yourself. Much like an electronic version of yellow sticky notes, Outlook's Notes enables you to quickly and easily jot down your ideas and thoughts. You can attach Outlook Notes to other items in Outlook as well as drag them from the Outlook window onto the Windows desktop for easy viewing.

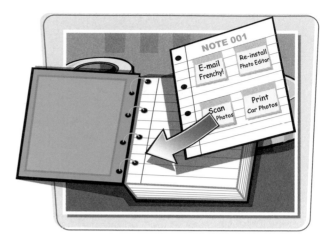

1 Click the **Notes** button (▣) in the Navigation pane to open the Notes component.

2 Click the **New Note** button.

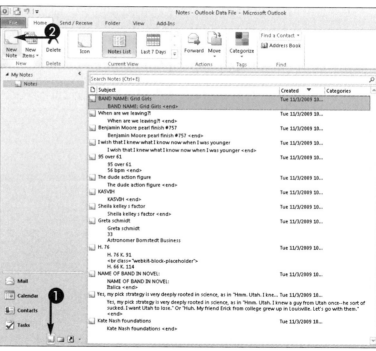

● Outlook displays a yellow note.

3 Type your note text.

4 When you finish, click the note's **Close** button (⊠).

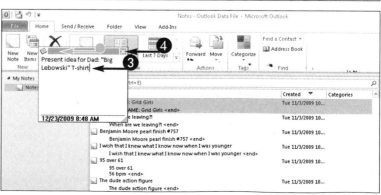

● Outlook adds the note to the Notes list.

To view the note again or to make changes, you can double-click the note to reopen it.

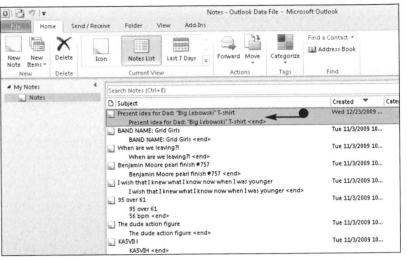

● To change your view of notes in the Notes list, you can click an option in the **Current View** group.

This example displays the Icon view.

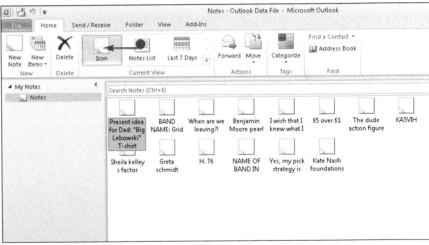

 TIPS

Can I forward the note to another user?

Yes. You can turn any note into an e-mail attachment. Simply right-click the note in the Notes list and click **Forward** to open an e-mail Message window with the note attached and the contents of the note in the Subject line. Enter the recipient's e-mail address and add any message text; then click the **Send** button. To learn more about e-mailing with Outlook, see the next chapter.

How do I delete a note that I no longer want?

Click the note in the Notes list and then click the **Delete** button in the Home tab or press `Delete`. Alternatively, right-click the note in the Notes list and click **Delete**. Outlook deletes the note. To delete multiple notes at the same time, press and hold `Ctrl` while clicking the notes and then press `Delete`.

Organize
Outlook Items

You can store your Outlook items, whether they are messages, tasks, or notes, in folders. By default, Outlook creates a set of folders for you to use when you install the program, including e-mail folders for managing incoming, outgoing, and deleted messages. You can use the Folders list to move items from one folder to another and create new folders in which to store Outlook items.

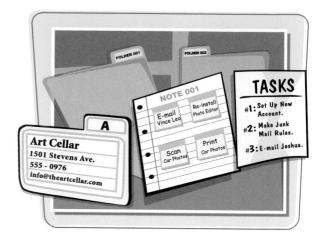

View the Folder List

① Click the **Folder List** button (▤) in the Navigation pane.

● Outlook displays the Folder List pane.

To move an item to another folder, you can click and drag the item and drop it on the folder's name.

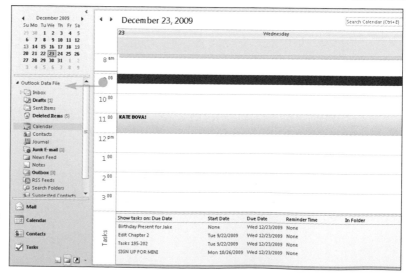

Create a New Folder

1 In the Folder list, right-click the folder in which you want to create a new folder.

2 Click **New Folder**.

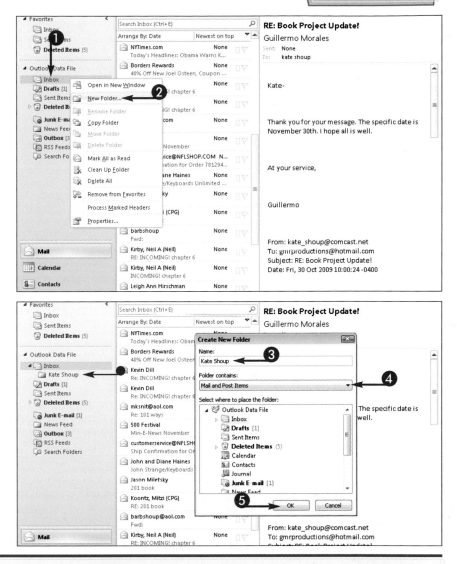

The Create New Folder dialog box appears.

3 Type a name for the new folder.

4 Click the **Folder contains** ▼ and choose an item type.

5 Click **OK**.

● Outlook creates the new folder.

TIPS

How do I delete an item from a folder?

Click the folder in the Folders list to display the items in that folder, select the item you want to delete, and click the **Delete** button in the Home tab. Outlook places deleted items in the Deleted Items folder; to empty the folder, right-click it and choose **Empty "Deleted Items" Folder**. To delete an entire folder and all of its items, click the folder in the Folders list and then press Delete.

Can I create subfolders for my work items and home items?

Yes. You can create as many folders as you need for each type of Outlook item or for a variety of items. For example, you might create a subfolder in your Inbox folder to place all the corporate correspondence that you send and receive, or create a folder in the Tasks folder for a special project.

Perform an Instant Search

You can use Outlook's search tool to quickly find an Outlook item such as an e-mail message, a calendar entry, a task, or a contact record. Each component includes an Instant Search box that you can use to quickly enter a keyword or phrase.

Perform an Instant Search

1 Click the Outlook component that you want to search.

2 Click in the **Search *Component*** box.

● Outlook displays a Search tab, with several search-specific tools.

3 Type your keyword or phrase.

● As you type, Outlook displays items that match your entry.

● Double-click an item to view it in its own window.

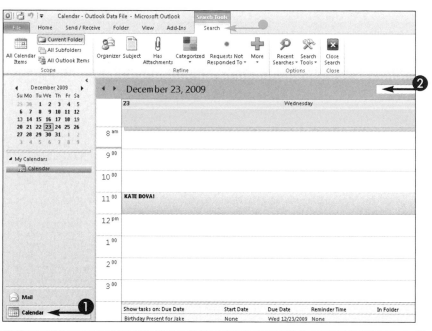

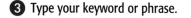

338

You can use Outlook's To-Do Bar to quickly view the Date Navigator and the current day's appointments and tasks, as well as to enter new tasks. You can customize the To-Do Bar to change what items appear in the list. If the To-Do Bar is not visible, click the Expand the To-Do Bar button (☐) on the right side of the Outlook screen.

Customize the To-Do Bar

1 Click the **View** tab.

2 Click **To-Do Bar**.

3 Click **Options**.

● You can click **Minimized** to minimize the bar.

The To-Do Bar Options dialog box appears.

4 Click a check box to deselect a feature on the To-Do Bar view.

● You can control the number of months or appointments that appear on the bar.

5 Click **OK**.

● Outlook applies the changes.

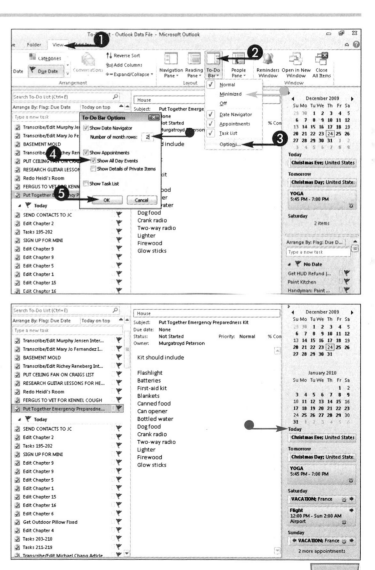

Compose and Send a Message

You can use Outlook to compose and send e-mail messages. When you compose a message, you designate the e-mail address of the message recipient (or recipients) and type your message text. You can also give the message a subject title to indicate to recipients what the message is about. Although you can compose a message offline, you must log on to your Internet connection to send a message.

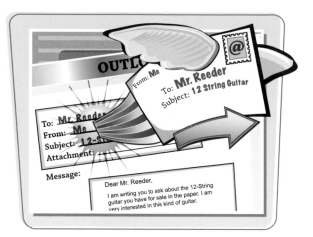

Compose and Send a Message

1 Click the **Mail** button in the Navigation pane to open the Mail component.

2 Click the **Home** tab.

3 Click the **New E-mail** button.

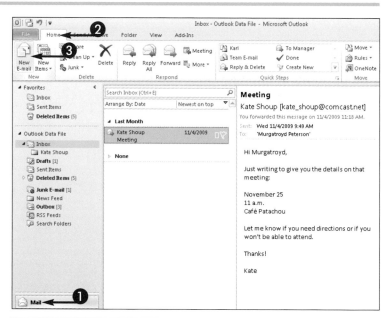

Outlook opens an untitled message window.

4 Type the recipient's e-mail address.

● If the e-mail address is already in your Address Book, you can click the **To** button and select the recipient's name.

If you enter more than one e-mail address, you must separate each address with a semicolon (;) and a space.

5 Type a subject title for the message.

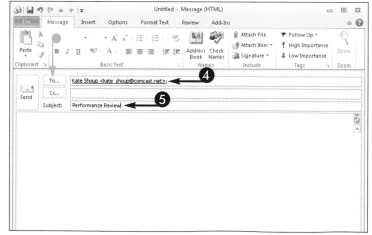

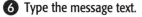

⑥ Type the message text.

● You can use Outlook's formatting buttons to change the appearance of your message text.

● To set a priority level for the message, you can click **High Importance** or **Low Importance**.

Note: By default, the message priority level is Normal.

⑦ Click **Send**.

Outlook sends the e-mail message.

Note: You must be connected to the Internet to send the message.

Messages you have sent are stored in the Sent Items folder.

⑧ Click the **Sent Items** folder in the Navigation pane.

● The message you sent appears in the Item list.

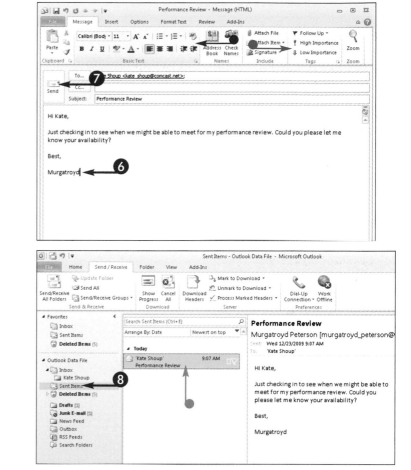

Can I save a message instead of sending it?

Yes. If, for example, you do not have time to finish composing your message, you can save it as a draft. To do so, click the message window's [x] button and click **Yes** when prompted to save the message. Outlook saves the message in the Drafts folder. When you are ready to recommence composing your message, click the **Drafts** folder in the Folders list and double-click the saved message to open it.

How do I carbon-copy my message to someone?

You can use the Cc field to copy the message to another recipient besides the main recipient. You can click **Cc** to open the Address Book and select the person's name. To send a copy of the message without revealing the Cc recipient's name, use the blind carbon copy, or Bcc, feature. Click **Cc**, click the person's name, and then click **Bcc**.

Send a File Attachment

You can send files stored on your computer to other e-mail recipients. For example, you might send an Excel file to a work colleague, or send a digital photo of your child's birthday to a relative. Note that some e-mail systems are not set up to handle large file attachments. If you are sending a large attachment, check with the recipient to see if his or her system can handle it.

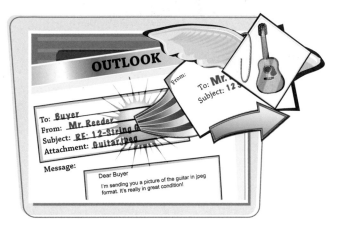

Send a File Attachment

① Create a new e-mail message, entering the recipient's e-mail address, a subject title, and the message text.

Note: *Refer to the preceding section for help creating a new e-mail message.*

② Click the **Message** tab.

③ Click the **Attach File** button.

The Insert File dialog box appears.

④ Locate and select the file you want to send.

⑤ Click **Insert**.

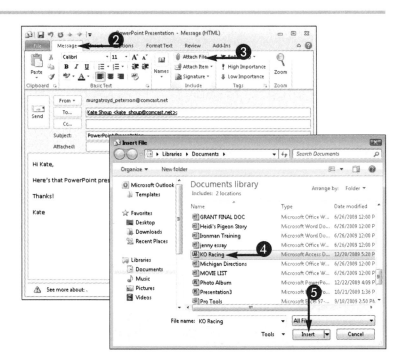

● Outlook adds the file attachment to the message and displays the filename and the file size.

⑥ Click **Send**.

Outlook sends the e-mail message and attachment.

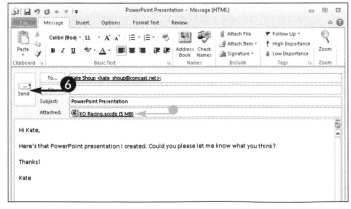

Read an Incoming Message

When you open Outlook's Mail feature, you can retrieve and view incoming e-mail messages. You can view a message in a separate message window or in the Reading pane. (Note that you need to log on to your Internet connection in order to receive e-mail messages.)

Read an Incoming Message

① Click the **Send/Receive** tab.

② Click **Send/Receive All Folders**.

Outlook accesses your e-mail account and downloads any new messages.

③ If the Inbox is not shown, you can click the **Inbox** folder.

④ Click a message in the Item list.

● The contents of the message are shown in the Reading pane.

Note: If the Reading pane is not visible, click the **View** tab, click **Reading Pane**, and choose a display option from the list that appears.

⑤ Double-click a message in the Item list.

● The message opens in a message window.

Note: If the message contains a file attachment, double-click it to open it. A warning dialog box appears; click **Open** to open and display the file in the appropriate program or click **Save** to save the attachment. Never open a file unless you trust the person who sent it.

Reply To or Forward a Message

You can reply to an e-mail message by sending a return message to the original sender. You can also forward the message to another recipient. Note that you must be connected to the Internet in order to send replies or forward e-mail messages.

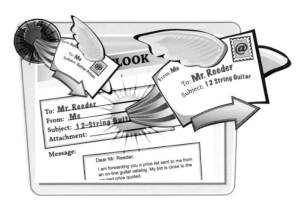

Reply To a Message

1 Open the message to which you want to reply.

Note: Refer to the preceding section to learn how to open an e-mail message.

2 Click the **Reply** button to reply to the original sender.

● To reply to the sender as well as to everyone else who received the original message, you can click the **Reply All** button.

● The original sender's address appears in the To field.

3 Type your reply.

4 Click **Send**.

Outlook sends the e-mail message.

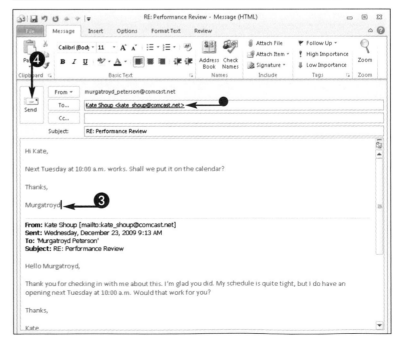

Forward a Message

1 Open the message that you want to forward.

Note: Refer to the preceding section to learn how to open an e-mail message.

2 Click the **Forward** button on the Message tab.

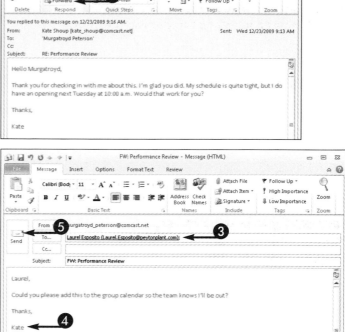

3 Enter the recipient's e-mail address in the **To** field.

4 Type any message that you want to add to the forwarded e-mail.

5 Click **Send**.

Outlook forwards the e-mail message.

TIP

How do I get rid of the original message in my reply?

By default, Outlook retains the original message when you click the **Reply** or **Reply All** button. To turn off this feature, click the **File** tab and then click **Options**. In the Outlook Options dialog box, click **Mail**. Under Replies and Forwards, click the **When replying to a message** ▾ and click **Do not include original message** (●). Click **OK**.

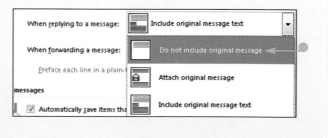

Add a Sender to Your Outlook Contacts

You can add the e-mail address of the sender of any message you receive to your Outlook Contacts. Then, if you want to send a new message to that person at a later time, you can click the To button in the message window and choose his or her name from the Select Names: Contacts dialog box that appears.

Add a Sender to Your Outlook Contacts

① Open the message whose sender you want to add to your Outlook Contacts.

Note: Refer to the section "Read an Incoming Message" earlier in this chapter to learn how to open an e-mail message.

② Right-click the sender's name.

③ Click **Add to Outlook Contacts**.

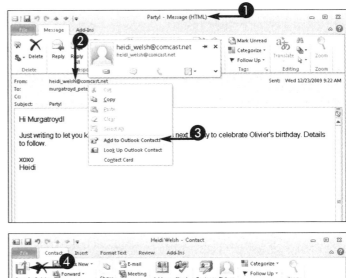

● The Contact window opens with the sender's name and e-mail address already filled in.

● You can add additional information as needed.

④ Click **Save & Close**.

Outlook saves the contact information.

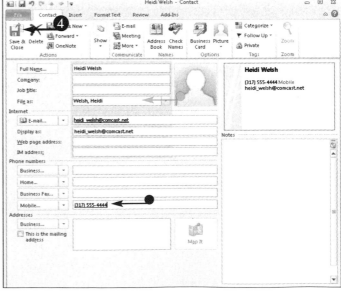

Delete a Message

You can remove messages from your Inbox to eliminate clutter and keep things manageable. When you delete a message, Outlook moves it to the Deleted Items folder. To maximize your computer's storage capacity, you should purge the Deleted Items folder on a regular basis.

Delete a Message

1 Locate and select the message that you want to delete.

2 Press Delete or click the **Delete** button on the Home tab.

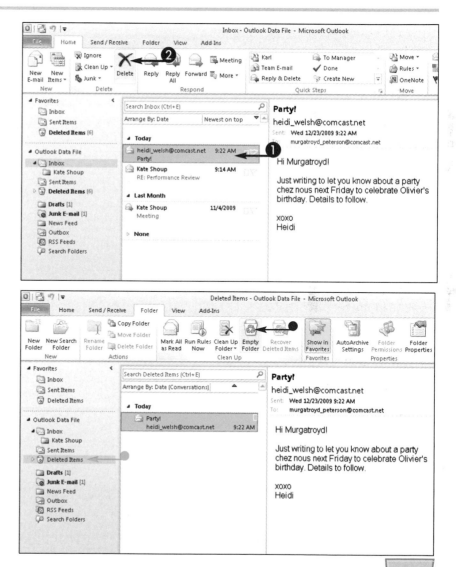

Outlook deletes the message from the Inbox and adds it to the Deleted Items folder.

● You can click the **Deleted Items** folder to view the message that you deleted.

● To empty the Deleted Items folder, click the **Deleted Items** folder, click the **Folder** tab, and click **Empty Folder**.

View Conversations

Outlook 2010 can group messages that are within the same thread, or conversation, in the Item list. This makes your Item list easier to navigate by compressing all related messages, including messages that you have sent as replies or forwarded to others, under a single heading. You can expand this heading to view these related messages.

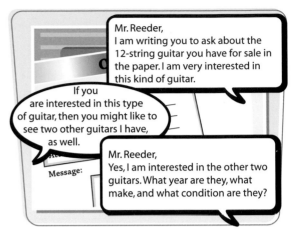

Mr. Reeder,
I am writing you to ask about the 12-string guitar you have for sale in the paper. I am very interested in this kind of guitar.

If you are interested in this type of guitar, then you might like to see two other guitars I have, as well.

Mr. Reeder,
Yes, I am interested in the other two guitars. What year are they, what make, and what condition are they?

View Conversations

① Click the **View** tab.

② Click the **Conversations** button in the Arrangement group.

③ Click **Show Messages in Conversations**.

● Outlook organizes your message by conversation.

④ Click the conversation heading.

⑤ Click the ▷ to expand the conversation.

● Outlook expands the conversation, displaying all the related messages.

⑥ Click the ◢ to compress the conversation.

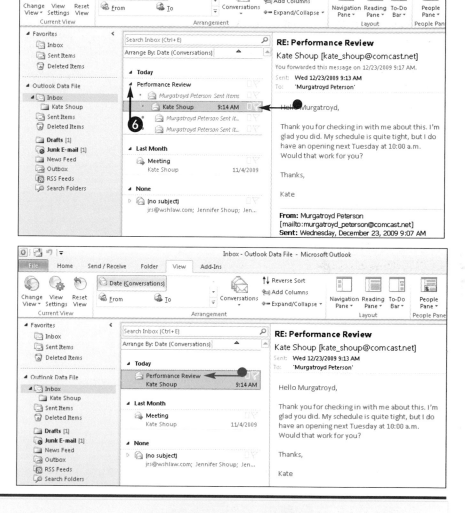

● Outlook compresses the conversation, displaying only the conversation heading.

TIPS

What other view options does Outlook offer?

You can organize your messages using any one of several Outlook views. These include (but are not limited to) Date view, in which messages are organized by date; From view, in which messages are organized by sender; To view, in which messages are organized by recipient; Categories view, in which messages are organized by category; and Importance view, in which high-priority messages are listed first.

Can I limit which messages are included in the conversation?

Yes. By default, Outlook displays all messages from all folders in Conversation view. If, however, you want to view only those messages in the current folder, click the **Conversations** button in the View tab and choose **Show Messages from Other Folders** in the menu that appears to deselect this option. Click it again if you decide that you want to again view all messages from all folders.

Clean Up a Conversation

You may find that as various people contribute to an e-mail conversation, redundant messages begin to appear in your Inbox. To clean up a conversation — that is, to move these redundant messages to the Deleted Items folder — you can use Outlook's Clean Up feature.

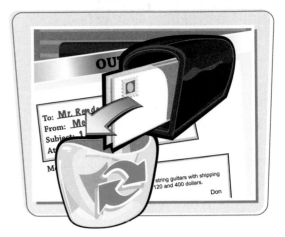

① With your Outlook messages displayed in Conversation view, click a message in the conversation you want to clean up.

② Click the **Home** tab.

③ Click the **Clean Up** button in the Delete group.

④ Click **Clean Up Conversation**.

The Clean Up Conversation dialog box opens.

⑤ Click **Clean Up**.

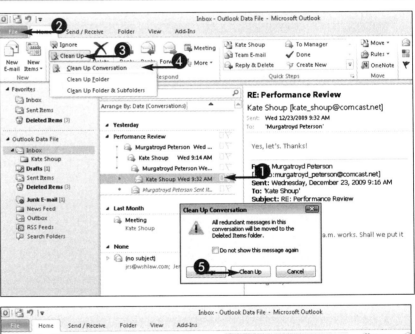

● Outlook removes redundant messages from the conversation.

● Messages are placed in the Deleted Items folder.

Note: To permanently remove the messages, click the **Deleted Items** folder, click the **Folder** tab, and click **Empty Folder**.

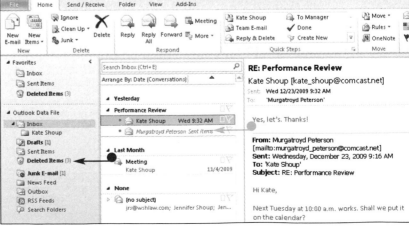

Ignore a Conversation

If you have been included in a conversation of no relevance to you, you can ignore the conversation. When you do, Outlook moves all messages in that conversation to the Deleted Items folder. It also moves any subsequent messages you receive to the Deleted Items folder.

Ignore a Conversation

① With your Outlook messages displayed in Conversation view, click the conversation you want to ignore.

② Click the **Home** tab.

③ Click the **Ignore** button in the Delete group.

The Ignore Conversation dialog box opens.

④ Click **Ignore Conversation**.

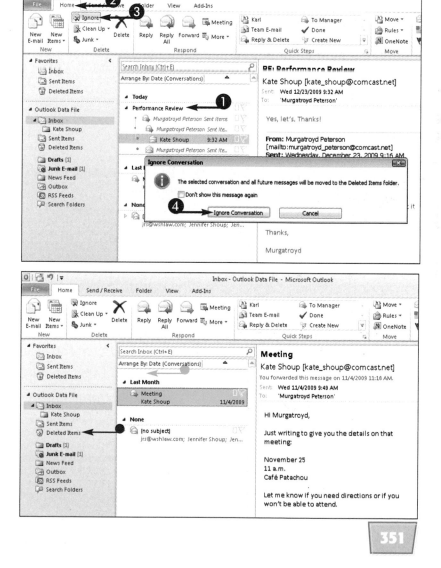

● Outlook removes the conversation.

● The conversation is placed in the Deleted Items folder.

Note: If you realize you have ignored a conversation in error, you can stop ignoring it. To do so, click the **Deleted Items** folder, click the conversation, click the **Home** tab, click the **Ignore** button, and click **Stop Ignoring Conversation**.

Screen Junk E-mail

Junk e-mail, also called *spam*, is overabundant on the Internet and often finds its way onto your computer. You can safeguard against wasting time viewing unsolicited messages by setting up Outlook's Junk E-mail feature. You can target e-mail from specific Web domains and make sure that it is deposited into the Outlook Junk E-mail folder.

View Junk E-mail Options

1 Click the **Home** tab.

2 Click the **Junk** ⊡.

3 Click **Junk E-mail Options**.

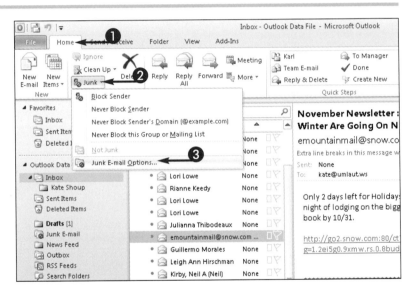

The Junk E-mail Options dialog box appears.

● You can use the various tabs to view junk e-mail settings, blocked domains, and safe senders.

● You can click one of these options to control the level of junk e-mail filtering that Outlook applies.

4 Click **OK**.

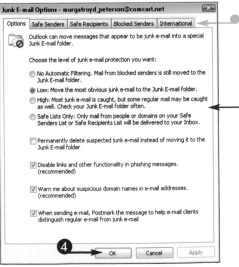

Designate a Message as Junk

① Click the message.

② Click the **Home** tab.

③ Click the **Junk** ▾.

④ Click **Block Sender**.

A prompt box appears.

⑤ Click **OK**.

● Outlook adds the sender's e-mail address to the list of filtered addresses and moves the message to the Junk E-mail folder.

TIPS

How can I restore a junk e-mail to my safe list?

If you accidentally send a message to the Junk E-mail folder, you can correct the action and remove it from the filter. First, click the **Junk E-mail** folder. Then click the message in the folder, click the **Home** tab, and click the **Not Junk** button.

Outlook alerts you that the message will be moved back to its original location and gives you the option of instructing Outlook to remove the sender from the filter list; click **OK**.

Does Outlook empty the Junk E-mail folder?

No. To empty the folder, click it in the Folders list, click the **Folder** tab, and click the **Empty Folder** button. Outlook moves all the items to the Deleted Items folder. To permanently remove the items, you must empty the Deleted Items folder. To do so, click the **Deleted Items** folder in the Folders list, click the **Folder** tab, and click the **Empty Folder** button.

Create a Message Rule

You can use rules to help organize messages that meet a specific set of conditions, such as placing messages from a certain sender or domain directly into a folder of your choosing as soon as the message arrives in the Inbox. Rules are also useful for filtering out unwanted messages.

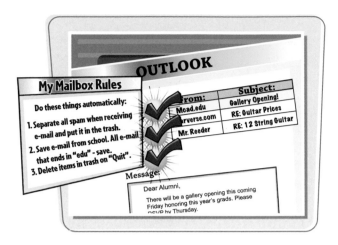

① Click the message on which you want to base a rule.

② Click the **Home** tab.

③ Click **Rules**.

④ Click **Create Rule**.

The Create Rule dialog box appears.

⑤ Click to select the conditions that you want to apply.

⑥ Specify what you want the rule to do when the conditions are met. In this example, select the **Move the item to folder** check box.

⑦ Click the **Select Folder** button.

The Rules and Alerts dialog box appears.

⑧ Click the folder where you want Outlook to move the messages.

⑨ Click **OK**.

⑩ Click **OK**.

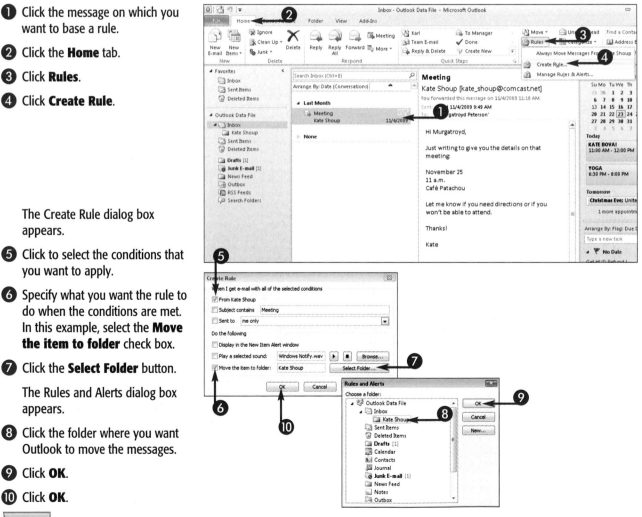

Outlook prompts you to run the rule now.

⑪ Click the check box to select it.

⑫ Click **OK**.

● Outlook moves any existing messages to the folder you specified.

The next time you receive a message matching the criteria you set, Outlook places it directly in the folder you selected.

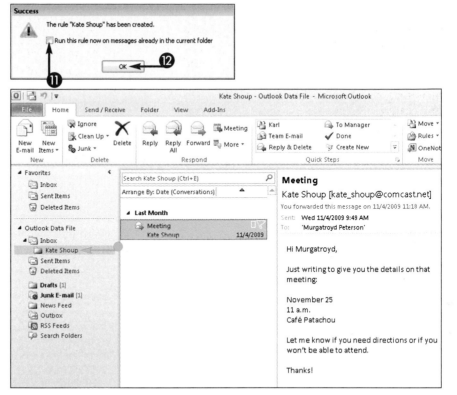

 TIPS

How can I add more criteria to a message rule?

You can click **Advanced Options** in the Create Rule dialog box to display the Rules Wizard. The Rules Wizard includes several sets of criteria that you can specify, such as exceptions to the rule, actions, and even a dialog box for naming the rule. Click the **Next** and **Back** buttons to view all the available criteria that you can specify.

How do I remove a rule that I no longer want?

To delete a rule, click the **Home** tab, click **Rules**, and click **Manage Rules & Alerts** to open the Rules and Alerts dialog box. Next, click the rule you want to delete and click the **Delete** button. (Note that if you have more than one e-mail account, you must first select the correct Inbox for the account that contains the rule.)

PART

VII

Publisher

Publisher is a desktop publishing program you can use to design and produce a variety of publications. You can create anything from a simple business card to a complex brochure. Publisher installs with a large selection of predesigned publications that you can use as templates to build your own desktop publishing projects; additional templates are available on Office.com. In this part, you learn how to build and fine-tune all kinds of publications and tap into Publisher's formatting features to make each document suit your own design and needs.

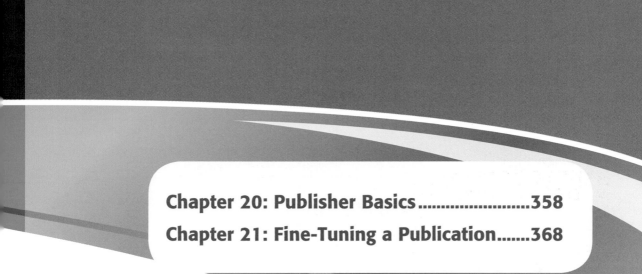

Create a Publication

You can use Publisher to create all kinds of publications, such as brochures, flyers, newsletters, and letterhead stationery. Publisher installs with a wide variety of publication types, including preset designs that control the layout and formatting of the publication. In addition, you can download templates from Office.com. To start a new publication, simply select a design from Publisher's varied list of publication types.

Create a Publication

1 Click the **File** tab.

2 Click **New**.

3 Click a publication category from the list of available templates.

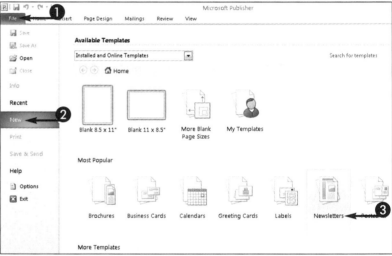

● You can use the scroll bar to scroll through the available publications in the category you chose.

4 Click a publication design.

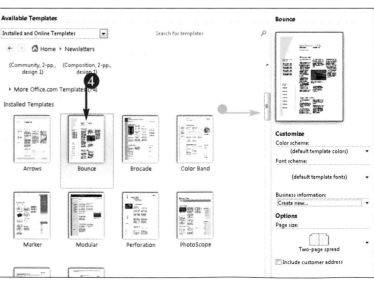

- Publisher displays a preview of the selected design here.

- You can customize a design's color scheme or fonts using these options.

⑤ Click **Create**.

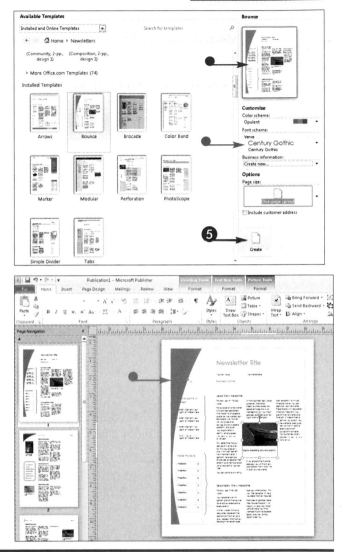

- Publisher creates the publication.

How do I change the design of my publication?

You can click the **Page Design** tab on the Ribbon to access other templates that you can apply to the publication. To change the color scheme, choose a new preset scheme from the **Schemes** group. Click the **Fonts** button to change the font, and click the **Background** button to view and select from available backgrounds.

What design options can I control in a publication?

Two of the most important design options that you can change to customize a publication are the color scheme and font scheme. The color scheme controls the colors used throughout the design. You can select from a wide variety of preset color schemes to create just the look you want. You can use the font scheme to control the font sets used for all of the various text elements in a design template.

Create a Blank Publication

You can create a blank publication, populate it with your own text boxes, and design a layout to suit your project. For example, you might want to create your own brochure or invitation and customize it by adding your own text boxes and art objects. (See the "Add a New Text Box" section, later in this chapter, to learn more about adding text to a blank publication.)

Create a Blank Publication

1. Click the **File** tab.

2. Click **New**.

● If you want to create an 8.5 by 11 publication, click the vertical or horizontal 8.5 by 11 option.

3. Click **More Blank Page Sizes**.

● You can use the scroll bar to scroll through the available page sizes.

4. Click a page size.

● Publisher displays the selected size here.

● You can customize the color scheme or fonts using these options.

● You can click the **Business information** ▾ and choose **Create new** to create a business set. A business set contains your business's name, address, and other information. After you create a business set, you can select it from the Business Information list to apply it to a publication.

5. Click **Create**.

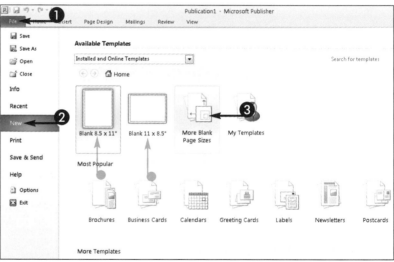

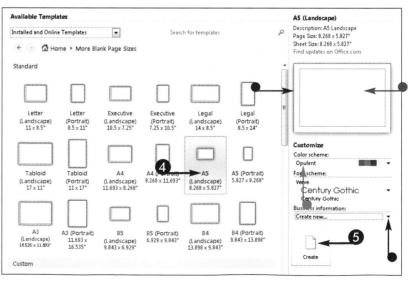

● Publisher creates and opens the blank publication.

You can now add your own text boxes and pictures to the publication.

TIP

Can I create my own templates in Publisher?

To turn a publication you create into a template that you can reuse, click the **File** tab and then click **Save As**. In the Save As dialog box, click the **Save as type** ⬛ and then click **Publisher Template**. Notice that when you select Publisher Templates, Windows automatically opens the Templates folder (●) in the Save As dialog box. Type a name for the file in the **File name** field and click **Save**. To create a new publication based on the template you saved, click the **File** tab, click **New**, click **My Templates**, and click the template in the window that appears.

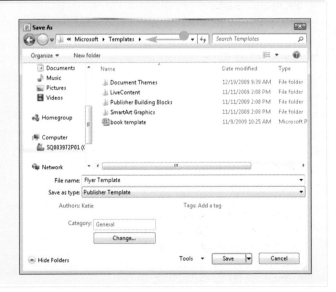

You can use Publisher's Zoom feature to control the magnification of your publication. By default, Publisher displays your document in a zoomed-out view so that you can see all the elements on a page. When you begin working with the publication, adding text and formatting, you can zoom in to better see what you are doing.

Zoom In and Out

Specify a Magnification

① Click the area of the publication where you want to change the zoom magnification.

● When you click an object on the page, Publisher surrounds it with selection handles.

② Click the **View** tab.

③ Click the **Zoom** ▾.

④ Click a percentage.

● You can also type a value in the **Zoom** field.

● Publisher changes the magnification setting for your publication.

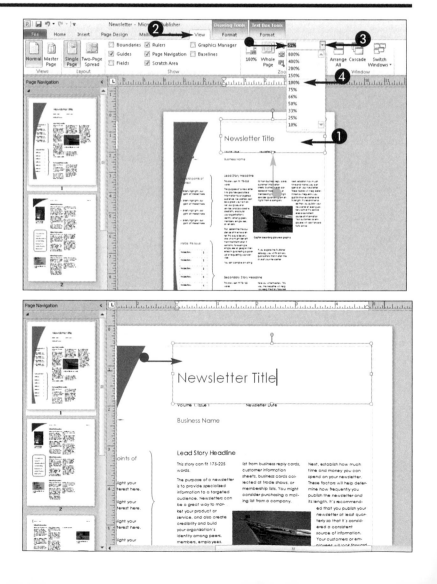

Use Zoom Buttons

1 Click the area of the publication where you want to change the zoom.

2 Click the **Zoom Out** (🔾) or **Zoom In** (⊕) button.

You can click the Zoom buttons multiple times to change the level of magnification.

● You can also click and drag the slider to change the zoom.

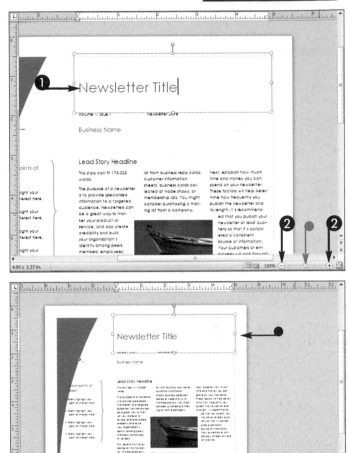

Publisher changes the magnification setting for your publication.

● In this example, the publication is zoomed out.

TIPS

How can I free up more workspace on-screen?

You can minimize the Pages pane to quickly free up on-screen workspace. To do so, click the pane's ≪ button. Alternatively, click the **View** tab and then deselect the **Page Navigation** check box in the **Show** group. To view the pane again, click the **View** tab and reselect the **Page Navigation** check box or click the ≫ button.

Is there a quicker way to zoom my publication?

Yes. There are multiple techniques. One is to press F9 on the keyboard to quickly zoom in and out of a publication. To quickly zoom to 100 percent, you can click the **100%** button in the **View** tab's Zoom group. To quickly view the whole page, click the **Whole Page** button.

When you create a new publication based on a design, Publisher inserts a layout for the text and displays placeholder text in the text boxes, also called *objects* or *frames*. The placeholder text gives you an idea of the text formatting that the design applies and what sort of text you might place in the text box. You can replace the placeholder text with your own text.

Add Text

1 Click the text object that you want to edit.

You may need to zoom in first to see the text object.

● Publisher surrounds the selected object with handles.

● Publisher highlights the placeholder text within.

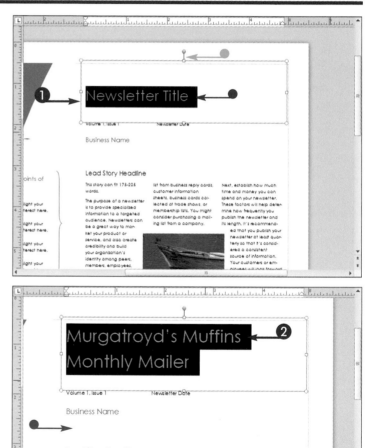

2 Type your own text.

Publisher replaces any placeholder text with the new text that you type.

Note: *To apply formatting to text and to move and resize text box objects, see the next chapter.*

● You can click anywhere outside of the text object to deselect the text box.

You can continue entering text to build your publication.

To edit the text at any time, you can click the text box and make your changes.

Add a New Text Box

You can add new text boxes to a publication and type your own text. For example, you may need to add a new text box to an empty area in your layout to include additional information, or you may need to add new text boxes to a blank publication.

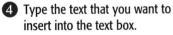

Add a New Text Box

1 Click the **Home** tab.

2 Click the **Draw Text Box** button in the Objects group.

3 Click and drag the text box to the size that you want to insert.

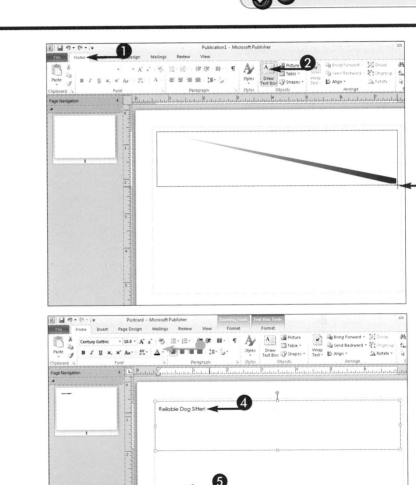

4 Type the text that you want to insert into the text box.

● You can apply formatting to the text.

Note: To apply formatting to text and to move and resize text box objects, see the next chapter.

5 Click anywhere outside the text object to deselect the text box.

Add a Picture to a Publication

You can add digital photographs or other picture files to your Publisher creations. For example, you might add a photo of your company's latest product to a new brochure or include a snapshot of your baby on a family e-mail newsletter.

Add a Picture to a Publication

1 Click the **Insert** tab.

2 Click the **Picture** button in the Illustrations group.

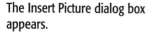

The Insert Picture dialog box appears.

3 Locate and select the picture file you want to use.

4 Click **Insert**.

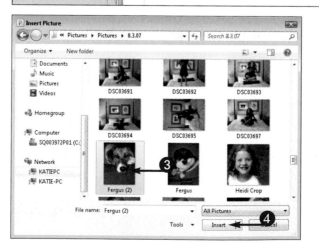

- Publisher inserts the picture file.

- The Format tab appears.

- You can move and resize the picture.

Note: *To learn how to move and resize objects in Publisher, see the next chapter.*

TIPS

How do I fill in an existing picture object?

If you have applied a publication template that includes a picture object in the layout, click the picture object and then click the **Insert Picture** button ([🖼]) to open the Insert Picture dialog box. Locate and select the photo you want to use and click **Insert** to insert the photo.

Can I add clip-art images?

Yes. To add clip art to a publication, click the **Insert** tab and click the **Clip Art Pane** button. The Clip Art pane opens; type a keyword describing the type of clip art you want to insert and click **Go**. The Clip Art task pane displays possible matches; click the clip art that you want to insert. Publisher inserts the clip art and displays the Format tab.

Change the Font, Size, and Color

You can control the font and size of your publication text. By default, when you assign a publication design, Publisher uses a predefined set of formatting for the text, including a specific font and size. You may need to change the font or increase the size to suit your own publication's needs.

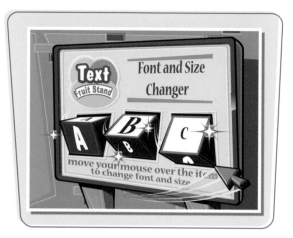

Change the Font

1. Click the text object or select the text that you want to format.

2. Click the **Home** tab on the Ribbon.

3. Click the **Font** [▼].

4. Click a font.

● Publisher applies the font to the text.

Change the Size

1. Select the text that you want to format.

2. Click the **Home** tab on the Ribbon.

3. Click the **Font Size** ⏷.

4. Click a size.

● Publisher applies the font size to the text.

This example applies a 26-point font size to the text.

Note: Another way to change the font size is to click the Grow Font and Shrink Font buttons (A⌃ and A⌄) on the Home tab. Publisher increases or decreases the font size with each click of the button.

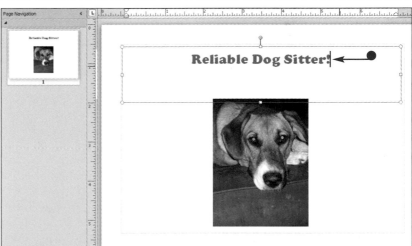

TIPS

How do I apply formatting to my text?

You can use Publisher's basic formatting commands — Bold, Italic, Underline, Subscript, and Superscript — to quickly add formatting to your text. To do so, select the text you want to format, click the **Home** tab, and click the **Bold** (**B**), **Italic** (*I*), **Underline** (U), **Subscript** (X₂), or **Superscript** (X²) button. To undo the formatting, simply select the text and click the appropriate button again.

What is the toolbar that appears when I position my mouse pointer over selected text?

When you select text, Publisher's mini toolbar appears, giving you quick access to common formatting commands. You can also right-click selected text to display the toolbar. If you want to use any of the tools on the toolbar, simply click the desired tool; otherwise, continue working, and the toolbar disappears.

Changing the text color can go a long way toward emphasizing it in your publication. For example, if you are creating an invitation, you might make the description of the event a different color to stand out from the other details. Obviously, when selecting text colors, you should avoid choosing colors that make your text difficult to read.

Change the Font, Size, and Color *(continued)*

Change the Color

1 Select the text that you want to format.

2 Click the **Home** tab on the Ribbon.

3 Click the ▾ next to the **Font Color** button (▲).

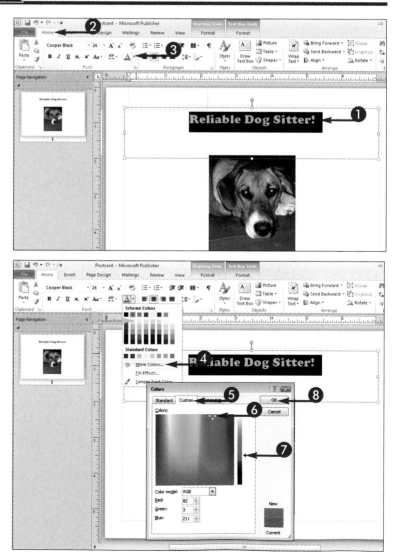

● You can click a color in the palette that appears to apply to the selected text.

4 Click **More Colors**.

The Colors dialog box opens.

5 Click the **Custom** tab.

6 Click a color in the **Colors** field.

7 Click a shade to refine your selection.

8 Click **OK**.

● Publisher applies the color to the text.

This example applies a blue color to the text.

Is there another way to change font characteristics?
Yes. You can also change font characteristics using the Font dialog box. Follow these steps:

❶ Select the text that you want to format.

❷ Click the **Home** tab on the Ribbon.

❸ Click the corner group button () in the Font group.

❹ In the Font dialog box, click the font, style, size, color, underline style, or effect that you want to apply.

❺ Click **OK**.

Apply a Text Effect

In addition to changing the font, size, and color of text in your publication, you can also apply text effects. These include a shadow effect, an outline effect, an emboss effect, and an engrave effect. You apply effects from the Format tab, which appears on the Ribbon when you select text in your publication.

① Select the text that you want to format.

② Click the **Format** tab.

③ Click a button in the Effects group. (Here, the **Shadow** button is clicked.)

● Publisher applies the text effect.

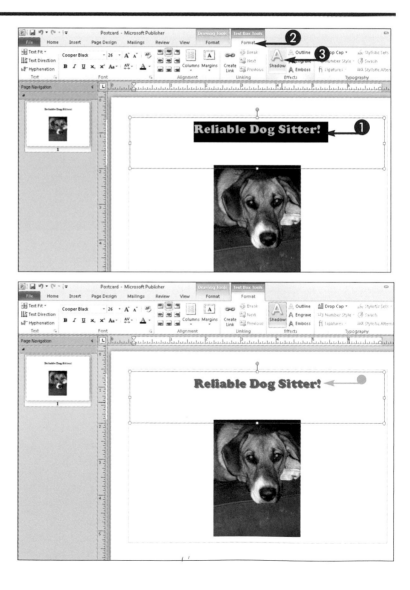

Change Text Alignment

Depending on the publication design that you select, alignment
publication type. You can change the alignment to suit your ow
Publisher's alignment commands to change the way in which te:
horizontally and vertically in a text object box.

Change Text Alignment

1 Select the text that you want to format.

2 Click the **Format** tab.

3 Click a button in the Alignment group. (Here, the **Align Bottom Left** button is clicked.)

● Publisher applies the new alignment.

Add a Border

You can add a border to any object in a publication, including text boxes, clip art, and pictures. You can control the weight and style of the border, as well as the shape and color.

Add a Border

1 Select the object to which you want to apply a border.

2 Click the **Format** tab.

3 Click a border in the Shape Styles list.

● You can click the **Shape Outline** button (🖎) to view available line styles and weights.

● You can click the **Change Shape** (🖼) button to view available shapes for the border.

● Publisher applies the border to the object.

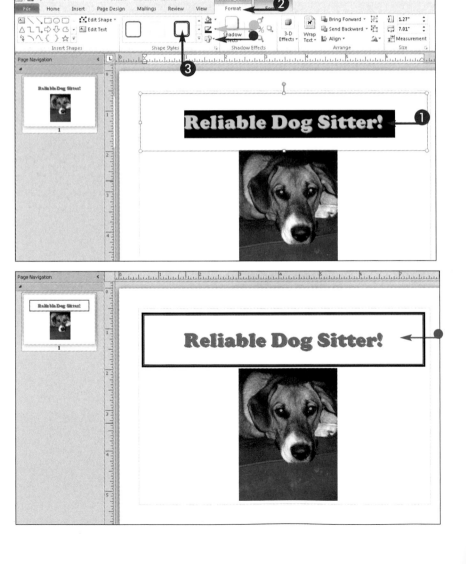

Control Text Wrap

You can control the way in which a text object wraps text around a picture object or any other object in a publication. For example, you may want a column of text to wrap tightly around a clip-art object.

Control Text Wrap

① Click the picture object or other object that you want to wrap text around.

② Click the **Home** tab.

③ Click the **Wrap Text** button.

④ Click a text wrapping option.

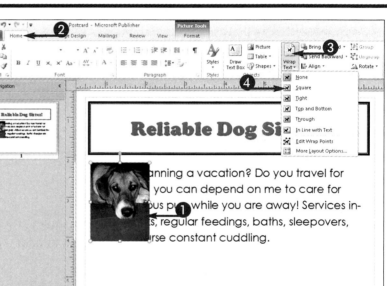

Publisher applies the text wrapping.

● This example applies square text wrapping.

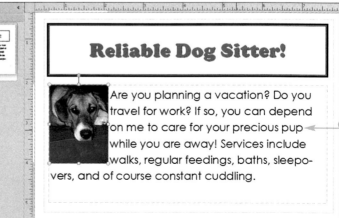

When you add too much text to a text object, it is called *overflow*. You can correct overflow text by connecting the text box to an adjacent text box and flowing the extra text into it. You use the Format tab's Linking tools to navigate and connect text boxes in a publication.

Link Text Boxes

Link Text Boxes

❶ Click the text box that contains the overflowing text.

❷ Click the **Format** tab.

❸ Click the **Create Link** button.

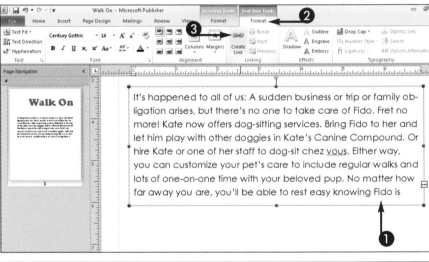

❹ Click and drag to create a new text box for the text overflow (changes to).

- Publisher links the two boxes, and moves any extra text from the first text box into the second text box.

- You can click the **Previous** button to return to the previous text box.

- You can click the **Next** button to go to the next text box.

Break a Link

1 Click the first text box that you want to disconnect.

2 Click the **Format** tab.

3 Click the **Break** button.

Publisher breaks the link.

Are there other ways to handle overflow?

Yes. In addition to correcting overflow text by connecting text boxes and flowing the extra text across them, you can also use Publisher's Text Fit tools to auto-fit your text into the text box. To do so, click the text box to select it, and then click the **Format** tab. Next, click the **Text Fit** button in the Text group and choose **Best Fit**.

Why does Publisher reduce my font size to fit my text in a box?

With some publication designs, Publisher's Autofit feature is turned on by default, and Publisher tries to fit your text into the space provided. To turn this feature off, select the text object to which it has been applied, click the **Format** tab, click the **Text Fit** button, and click **Do Not Autofit**.

Move and Resize Publication Objects

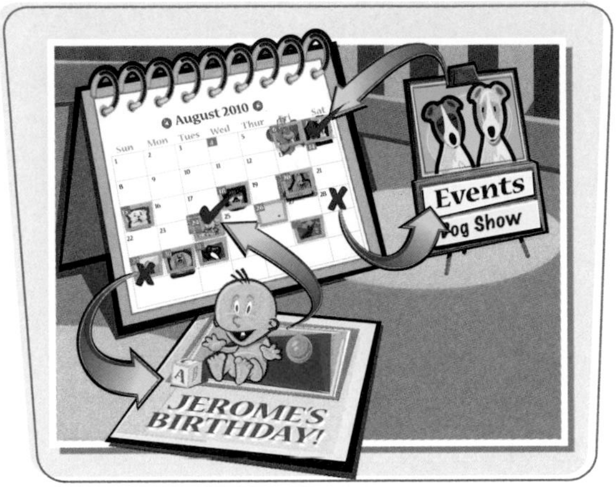

You can move an object to better suit your layout. For example, when building a publication from a blank document, you may need to move text objects or picture objects around to create a better layout. You can also resize objects to improve the appearance of the object or the layout. For example, you may need to resize a text object to fit more text into the box.

Move and Resize Publication Objects

Move an Object

1. Click the object that you want to move.

- Publisher surrounds the selected object with handles.

2. Position the mouse pointer over the edge of the object until it changes from ⇖ to ✥.

3. Drag the object to a new location.

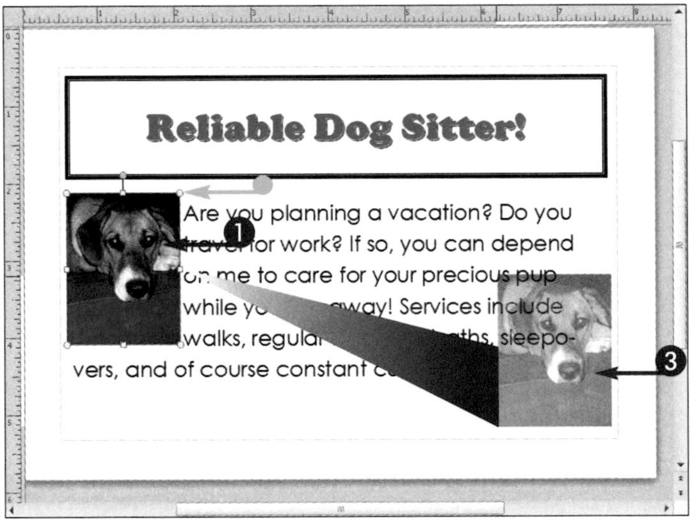

Publisher moves the object.

- This example moves a picture object.

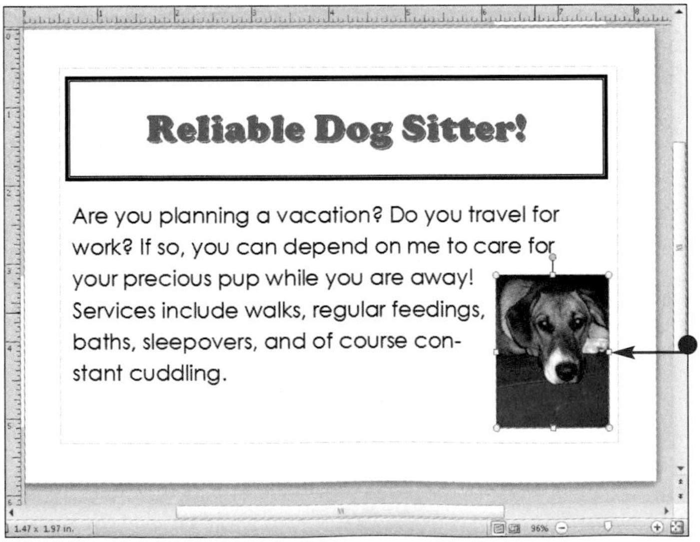

Resize an Object

① Click the object that you want to resize.

● Publisher surrounds the selected object with handles.

② Position the mouse pointer over the edge of the object until it changes from ⌖ to ⤢.

③ Click and drag a handle inward or outward to resize the object.

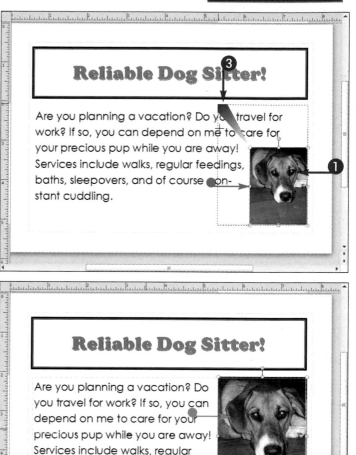

When you release the mouse button, Publisher resizes the object.

● This example resizes a picture object.

Can I rotate an object?
Yes. To rotate an object, click the object to select it, and then click the green rotation handle at the top of the selected object and drag it in the direction you want to rotate the object. When the object has been rotated to the desired degree, release the mouse button.

How do I delete an object that I no longer need?
To remove an object from a publication, whether it is a picture, a text box, or any other object, click the object to select it and press Delete. Publisher removes the object from the page. You can select more than one object to delete by pressing and holding Ctrl while clicking each object.

Edit the Background

You can change the background of your publication page by assigning a new background color, gradient effect, or texture. If you decide you no longer want a background, you can remove it.

Edit the Background

Apply a Background

❶ Click the **Page Design** tab.

❷ Click the **Background** button.

❸ Click the background that you want to apply.

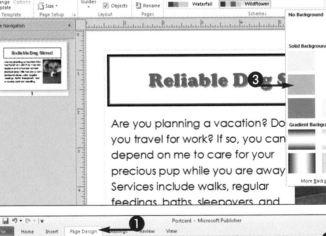

● Publisher applies the background.

Remove the Background

❶ Click the **Page Design** tab.

❷ Click the **Background** button.

❸ Click the option under **No Background**.

● Publisher removes the background.

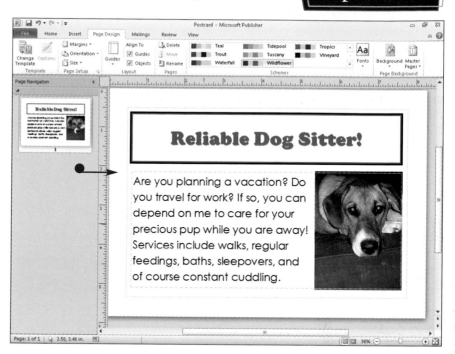

Can I assign backgrounds other than what is shown in the Background menu?

Yes. You can assign a one-color or two-color gradient background using colors you choose; apply a texture background, such as Denim, Canvas, or Granite; apply a pattern, such as Plaid; choose your own photo for a background; or apply your own custom tint. You access these options from the Fill Effects dialog box. To open this dialog box, click the **Page Design** tab, click **Background**, and choose **More Backgrounds**.

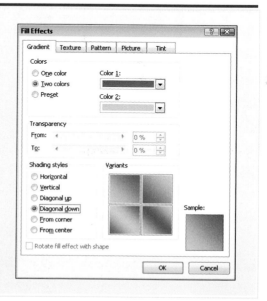

Add a Building Block Object

You can use Publisher's Building Block objects to add all kinds of extra touches to your publication projects. For example, you can add a calendar to a newsletter or a graphical marquee to a letterhead. Publisher's Building Block objects encompass a wide variety of design objects, such as mastheads, borders, boxes, and even coupons and logos.

① Click the **Insert** tab.

② Click a button in the Building Blocks group (here, **Advertisements**).

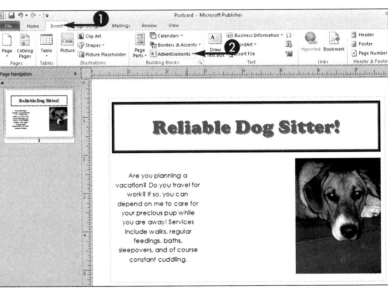

③ Click the Building Block object you want to insert.

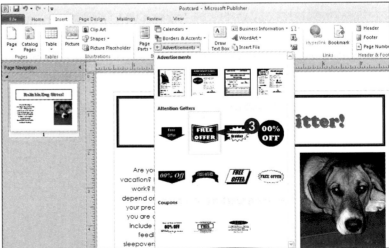

● Publisher adds the object to your publication.

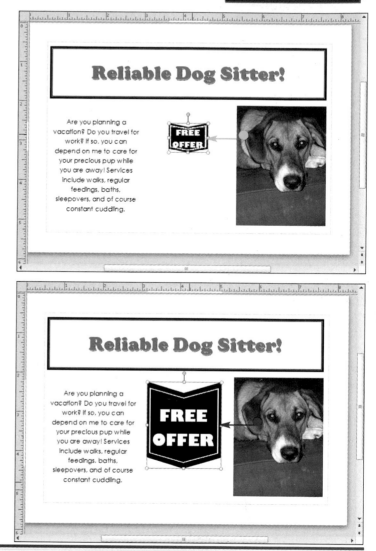

● You can move and resize the object to suit your layout.

Note: *Refer to the section "Move and Resize Publication Objects" earlier in this chapter to learn more.*

TIPS

Can I customize a Building Block object?

Yes. Many of the Building Block objects are composed of simple lines and shapes. You can customize the appearance of an object by selecting individual parts of it and making changes to the selection's formatting. For example, you might change the border or fill color of an object. You can also change the text in a Building Block object by selecting it and typing over it.

How do I select an individual line or fill color to edit?

You may need to ungroup an object to edit individual elements such as lines, fills, and shapes. To do so, click the object, the **Home** tab, and then the **Ungroup** button (⊞). You may need to click the button more than once to free all of the object's individual elements. When you finish making your edits, click the **Group** button (⊞) to turn the elements back into a single object.

Create a Building Block Object

If you find yourself using an object you have created over and over, you can save that object as a Building Block object. For example, if you use the same headline in every publication you create, you can save it as a Building Block object and insert it anytime you need it. Anything you save as a Building Block object is accessible from any other Publisher files you open.

Create a Building Block Object

1 Click the element that you want to save.

2 Click the **Insert** tab.

3 Click a button in the Building Blocks group.

Click **Page Parts** if the Building Block object you want to create is a heading, sidebar, or something similar.

Click **Calendars** if the Building Block object you want to create is a calendar.

Click **Borders & Accents** if the Building Block object you want to create is a border or accent.

Click **Advertisements** if the Building Block object you want to create is a coupon or other advertisement.

4 Click **Add Selection to *Building Block* Gallery**.

Note: *The precise name of this option varies depending on what button you click in Step **3**.*

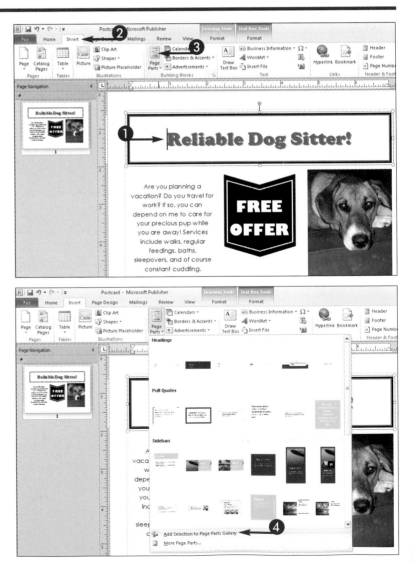

The Create New Building Block dialog box appears.

5 Type a name for the item.

6 Type a description for the item.

7 Choose a category for the item.

8 Enter keywords describing the item.

9 Click **OK**.

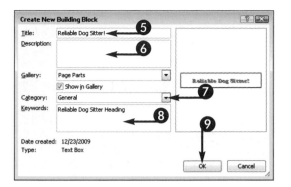

Publisher creates the Building Block object.

● You can view the item by clicking the button you clicked in Step **3**.

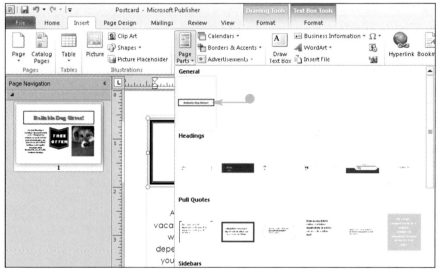

TIPS

How do I remove a Building Block object?

To delete a Building Block object you have created from your list of available Building Blocks, click the **Insert** tab and click the appropriate button in the Building Blocks group. Then right-click the Building Block object you want to delete and choose **Delete**. Publisher asks you to confirm the deletion; click **OK**.

Are there more Building Block objects?

Yes. To access more Building Block objects, click the appropriate button in the Building Blocks group and choose **More *Building Blocks*** from the menu that appears. (The precise name of this option varies depending on what button you click.) The Building Block Library window opens, displaying all Building Block objects of the type you selected. Click an object to add it to your page.

OneNote

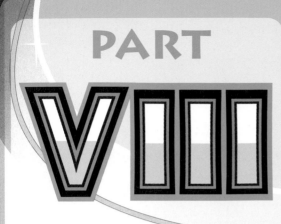

OneNote acts like a digital notebook, enabling you to jot down ideas, sketch out plans, brainstorm business strategies, and compile scraps of information in one searchable, shareable, easy-to-access location. You might use OneNote to take notes during meetings and lectures, collect research materials from the Web, gather information about an upcoming trip, assemble ideas for a home improvement project, and more.

OneNote acts like a binder, with notebooks that you can use to jot down ideas, sketch out plans, and more. By default, OneNote includes one notebook.

1 In the OneNote Navigation bar, click the notebook you want to open.

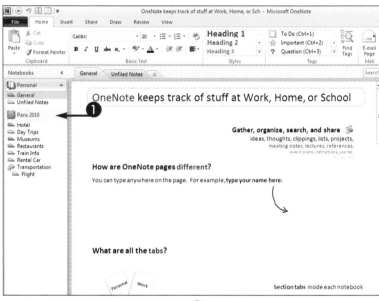

● OneNote opens the notebook you clicked.

2 Click a tab.

● OneNote displays the tab you clicked.

③ Click a page in the tab.

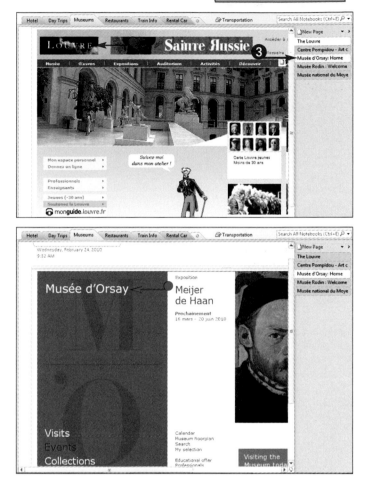

● OneNote displays the page you clicked.

TIPS

How do I display the Navigation bar?

If the OneNote Navigation bar appears minimized on your screen, click the **Expand Navigation Bar** button (▷) to view it. To minimize the Navigation bar, thereby freeing up real estate in the OneNote window, click the **Collapse Navigation Bar** button (◁).

How do I view additional sections?

If OneNote does not display all the sections in a notebook, it displays a tab with a ⊡. Click the ⊡ to reveal links to additional sections in the notebook, and then click the link for the section you want to view.

Type and Draw Notes

As mentioned, OneNote acts like a binder, with notebooks that you can use to jot down ideas, sketch out plans, and more. One way to enter these items is by typing them with your keyboard. Another approach is to use OneNote's drawing tools. When you create an item, also called a *note*, in OneNote, you can move it around the page as desired.

Type and Draw Notes

Type Notes

① With the page on which you want to type open in OneNote, click the **Draw** tab.

② Click the **Select & Type** button.

③ Click the spot on the page where you want to type.

④ Type your note.

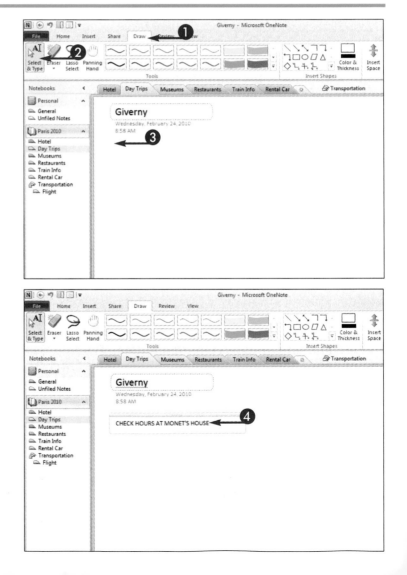

Draw Notes

1 With the page on which you want to draw open in OneNote, click the **Draw** tab.

2 In the Tools group, click a drawing tool.

● Click the **More** button (⊡) to view all available drawing tools.

3 Draw your note.

TIPS

Can I format my typed text?

Yes. In the OneNote Home tab, you can change the text font, size, and color, and apply bold, italics, underline, subscript, or superscript formatting. You can also format text as a bulleted list or a numbered list. You can even apply styles, such as Heading 1, Page Title, and so on. To format text, simply select it and click the appropriate option in the Home tab.

How do I move a note?

To move a typed note, position your cursor over the text to reveal the note container; then move the cursor to the container's header. The cursor changes to ✛; click and drag the container to the desired location. To move a drawn note, press **Shift** while dragging over the drawing to select all its parts. Then position your cursor over the selection. When the cursor changes to ✛, click and drag the selection to the desired location.

Paste a Picture into OneNote

You can paste digital photos you have saved on your hard drive into OneNote. For example, you might paste in a photo of a hotel in which you would like to stay or a photo of an office building in which you are considering renting space. You can move and resize pictures in OneNote much like you do graphics in other Office programs; for help, refer to Chapter 3.

① With the page on which you want to paste a picture open in OneNote, click the **Insert** tab.

② Click the **Picture** button.

   The Insert Picture dialog box opens.

③ Locate and select the picture you want to insert.

④ Click **Insert**.

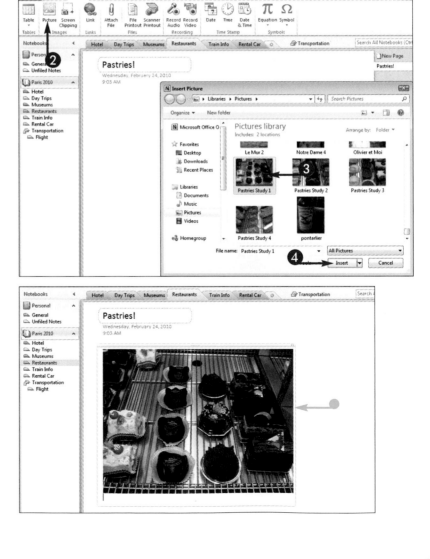

● OneNote inserts the picture.

   You can move and resize the picture as needed.

Sometimes it is helpful to attach a document or other file to a page in OneNote. For example, suppose you have created a spreadsheet for expense account transactions in Microsoft Excel. You can attach that spreadsheet to a OneNote page. When you do, an icon for that file appears on the note; you can double-click the icon to open the file from within OneNote.

Attach Files to Notes

① With the page to which you want to attach a file open in OneNote, click the **Insert** tab.

② Click the **Attach File** button.

The Choose a File or a Set of Files to Insert dialog box opens.

③ Locate and select the file you want to insert.

④ Click **Insert**.

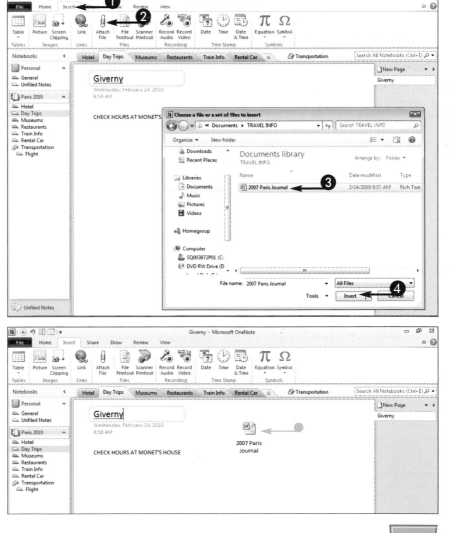

● OneNote inserts an icon for the file.

You can move the shortcut icon as needed.

You can use OneNote's Screen Clipping feature to "clip" portions of Web pages and paste them into OneNote. Screen clippings are especially helpful when you are researching on the Web, planning a trip, or comparing products. For example, you might clip an image of a car you are interested in buying or a price sheet for a service you are considering using.

Insert a Screen Clipping

① In Internet Explorer, open the Web page containing the item you want to clip.

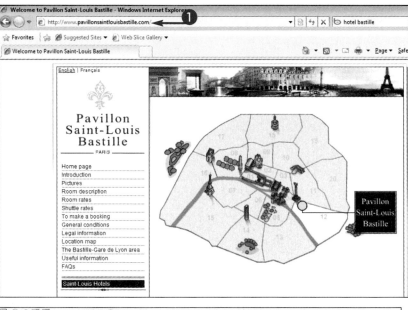

② In OneNote, click the spot on the page where you want to insert the clipping.

③ Click the **Insert** tab.

④ Click the **Screen Clipping** button.

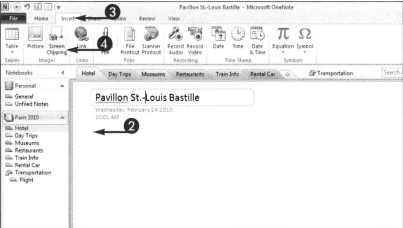

5 In Internet Explorer, click the top left corner of the area you want to clip.

6 Drag the cursor down and to the right until the area you want to clip is selected.

7 Release the mouse button.

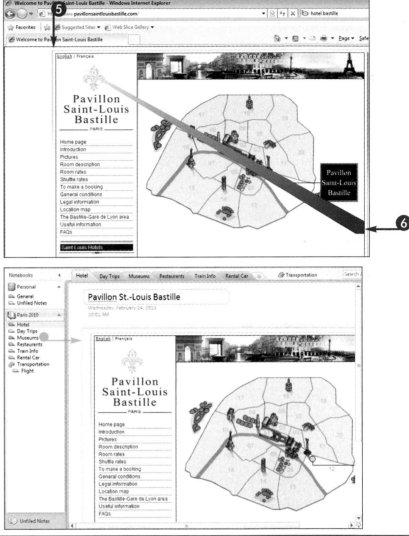

● The clipping is pasted into OneNote.

Note: You can move a screen clipping the same way you move a note. For more information, refer to the tip "How do I move a note?" in the section "Type and Draw Notes," earlier in this chapter.

TIP

Is there a faster way to paste clippings?

Yes. Open the Web site that contains the item you want to clip. Then do the following steps. While holding down [⊞], press [S]. Click the top left corner of the area you want to clip. Drag the cursor down and to the right to select the desired area. The Select Location in OneNote dialog box opens. Click the tab where you want to paste the clipping. Click **Send to Selected Location**. The clipping is pasted into OneNote.

Record an Audio Note

If you are attending a significant meeting or lecture, or even participating in an important telephone conversation or conference call, you can use OneNote to record it and store the recording as part of your notes. Note that in order to record audio, you must have a microphone. Most laptop and tablet PCs come with microphones built in. (Note: You should always ask permission before recording someone.)

1 With the page to which you want to attach a file open in OneNote, click the **Insert** tab.

2 Click the **Record Audio** button.

OneNote begins recording.

● A shortcut icon for the audio file appears.

● The Audio & Video Recording tab appears, displaying playback controls.

Note: You can type notes as you record. When you do, OneNote links the note to the recording, displaying a small icon alongside it. You can click this icon to listen to the audio that was recorded at the time you typed the note.

3 To stop recording, click the **Stop** button.

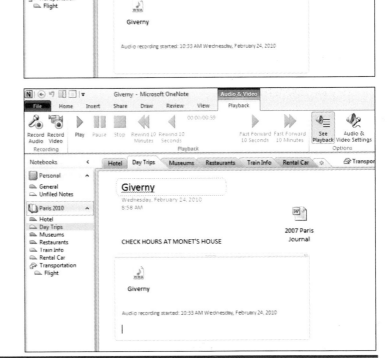

OneNote stops recording.

TIPS

Can I record video notes?

Yes. If your computer features a video capture device such as a webcam, you can record video notes. To do so, click the **Record Video** button in the Insert tab. OneNote launches a video screen in which you can view the footage as it is recorded, displays a shortcut icon for the video recording, and displays the Audio & Video Recording tab. To stop recording, click the **Stop** button in the tab.

How do I play back my recording?

When you create an audio or video recording in OneNote, a shortcut icon for that audio file appears. To play back the recording, double-click the shortcut icon. OneNote plays back the file. It also launches the Audio & Video Playback tab, with playback controls for pausing, stopping, rewinding, and fast-forwarding the recording.

Create a New Notebook

By default, OneNote includes two notebooks: a Work notebook and a Personal notebook. If you want, you can create additional notebooks. For example, you might create a notebook to hold notes for a trip you are planning or a notebook to hold information relating to a home project.

Create a New Notebook

1 Click the **File** tab.

2 Click **New**.

3 Choose where you want to store the notebook.

● Choose **Web** to store the notebook on the Web.

● Choose **Network** to store the notebook on a network.

● Choose **My Computer** to save the notebook on your computer's hard drive.

4 Type a name for the notebook.

● If you want to save the notebook somewhere other than the default, click the **Browse** button and select the folder in which the notebook should be saved.

5 Click **Create Notebook**.

● OneNote creates a new notebook.

● The new notebook contains one section.

● The section contains one page.

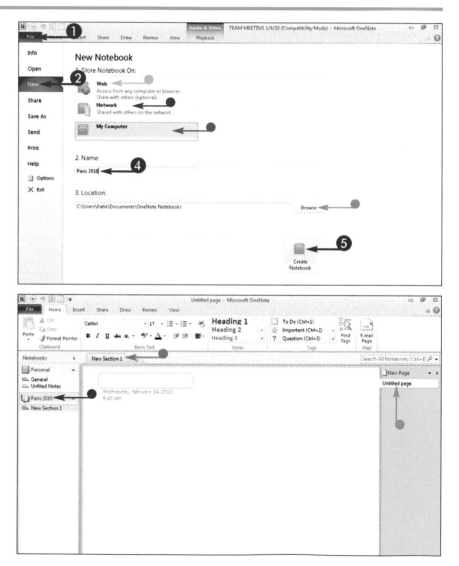

Create a New Section

The notebooks OneNote includes by default — the Work notebook and the Personal notebook — include several sections. You can easily add new sections to these notebooks or to any new notebooks you create. New sections are given names, such as New Section 1, New Section 2, and so on, by default.

Create a New Section

① With the notebook for which you want to create a new section open in OneNote, click the **Create a New Section** tab (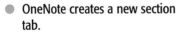).

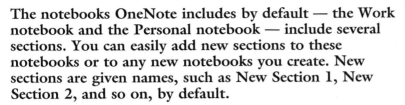

● OneNote creates a new section tab.

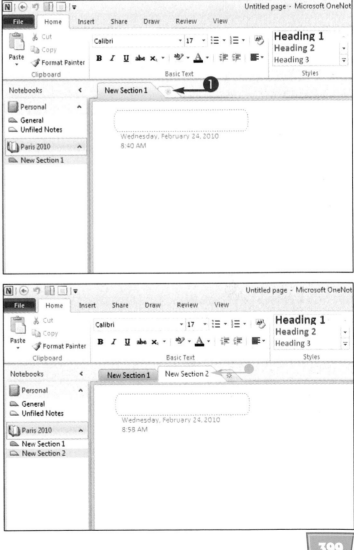

You can easily add new pages to a notebook section. For example, if you are planning a vacation, you might create one page for each phase of the trip. When you create a new page, you can opt to create a subpage — that is, a page on a lower organizational level. You can also choose to use a page template — for example, to create a to do list.

Create a New Page

① Click the **New Page** 🔽.

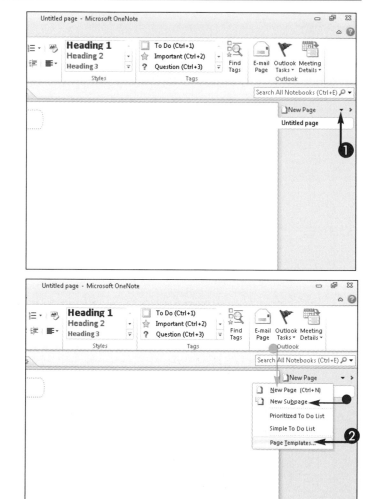

● Choose **New Page** to create a new page in the default style.

● Choose **New Subpage** to create a page on a lower organizational level.

② Click **Page Templates**.

● The Templates pane opens.

❸ Click a category's ▷ to reveal templates available in that category (▷ changes to ◢).

❹ Click a template.

● OneNote creates a new page based on the template you selected.

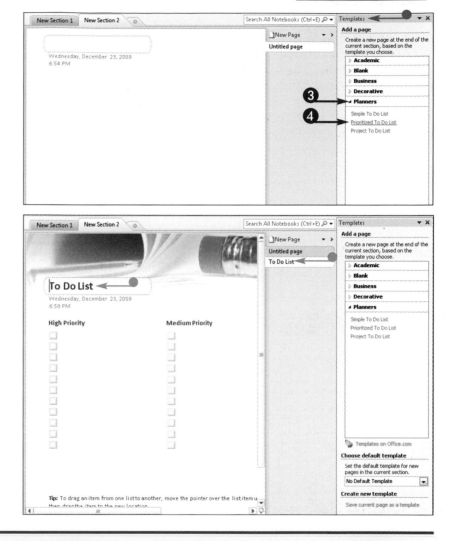

What is the Unfiled Notes notebook?

If you want to create a note but are not sure in which notebook or section it should be filed, you can create the note in the Unfiled Notes notebook. To do so, click **Unfiled Notes** in the Navigation pane; then create new pages and add notes as needed. If you later decide that the page containing the note should be filed elsewhere, you can move it. (See the next tip.)

Can I move pages?

Yes. To move a page to a different section or even to a different notebook, right-click the page in the Page Tabs pane and choose **Move or Copy** from the menu that appears. In the Move or Copy Pages dialog box, click the ⊞ next to the notebook where you want to store the page, click the desired section, and click **Move** (or click **Copy** to copy, rather than move, the page).

Rename Sections and Pages

New sections are given names, such as New Section 1, New Section 2, and so on, by default. Likewise, pages are given default names. You can assign your sections and pages more descriptive names to keep better track of where you have stored various pieces of information. For example, if your notebook relates to a project, you might create sections for each phase of the project and assign section names accordingly.

Rename a Section

1 Right-click the tab for the section you want to rename.

2 Choose **Rename**.

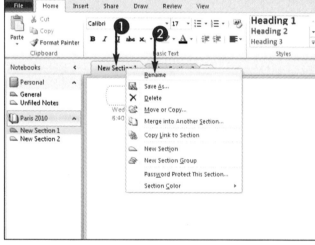

OneNote selects the current section name.

3 Type the new section name and press Enter.

OneNote applies the name you typed to the section tab.

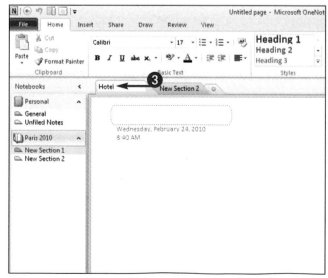

Rename a Page

1 Click in the page's **Title** field.

Note: If the title field already contains text, select the text.

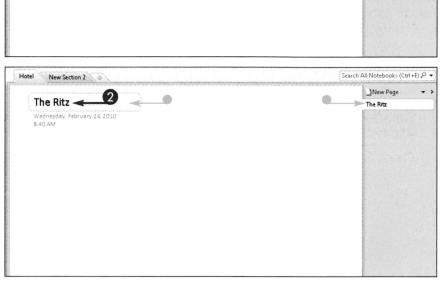

2 Type a new title for the page.

● OneNote applies the title.

TIPS

How do I delete pages and sections?

To delete a page, right-click the page in the Page Tabs pane and choose **Delete** from the menu that appears. OneNote deletes the page. To delete a section, right-click the section tab and choose **Delete** from the menu that appears. OneNote asks you to confirm the section deletion; click **Yes**. OneNote deletes the section and all the pages it contains.

Can I delete a notebook?

Yes. Right-click the notebook in the Navigation pane and choose **Notebook Recycle Bin** from the menu that appears. OneNote places the contents of the notebook in the Notebook Recycle Bin. To remove the notebook completely, you must empty the Notebook Recycle Bin; to do so, click the **Share** tab, click the bottom half of the **Notebook Recycle Bin** button, and choose **Empty Recycle Bin** from the menu that appears.

Group Sections

If your notebook contains several related sections, you can gather those sections into a group to make it easier to locate the section you need. For example, suppose you are planning a vacation and have created a OneNote notebook to keep track of your research. You might gather the notebook's transportation-related sections — one with flight information, one for rental cars, one for train travel, and so on — into a Transportation group.

Group Sections

1 Right-click the blank area to the right of the Create a New Section tab.

2 Click **New Section Group**.

| Hotel | Day Trips | Museums | Restaurants | Train Info | Rental Car | Flight | ☀ |

New Section
New Section Group

Wednesday, December 23, 2009
7:00 PM

OneNote creates a new section group.

3 Type a name for the section group and press Enter.

| Hotel | Day Trips | Museums | Restaurants | Train Info | Rental Car | Flight | ☀ | Transportation |

Wednesday, December 23, 2009
7:00 PM

④ Click a tab.

⑤ Drag the tab to the section group.

The ▷ changes to ▷.

OneNote moves the tab to the section group.

⑥ Click the section group.

Hotel | Day Trips | Museums | Restaurants | Train Info | Rental Car | Flight | ※ | Transportation | Search A

Wednesday, December 23, 2009
7:00 PM

④ ⑤ ⑥

● The section tab appears in the section group.

● Click the **Navigate to Parent Section Group** button (⑤) to return to the regular view.

Transportation: | Flight | ※ | Search A

Wednesday, December 23, 2009
7:00 PM

TIPS

Can I remove a section tab from a group?

Yes. One way to remove a section tab from a group is to open the section group, click the tab you want to move, and drag it to the Navigate to Parent Section Group button (⑤). Alternatively, click the section in the Navigation pane and drag it from the section group to the notebook's main parent section.

Can I change the order in which sections appear?

Yes. To change the order in which sections appear, click the tab for the section you want to move, drag the tab to the desired spot in the order, and release the mouse button. You can also change the order of pages in a section; to do so, click the page in the Page Tabs pane and drag it up or down to the desired spot in the order.

Search Notes

As you enter more and more notes into OneNote, you may find it difficult to locate the information you need. Fortunately, OneNote offers a robust search function. Using it, you can locate any text in your OneNote notebooks — even text found in graphics. If you have enabled OneNote's Audio Search feature, you can even search audio and video for spoken words.

Search Notes

1 Click in the OneNote **Search** field.

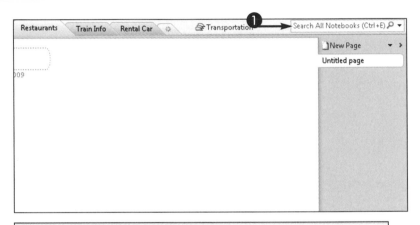

● OneNote displays a list of your notebooks and sections. To limit your search to a particular notebook or section, click it in the list.

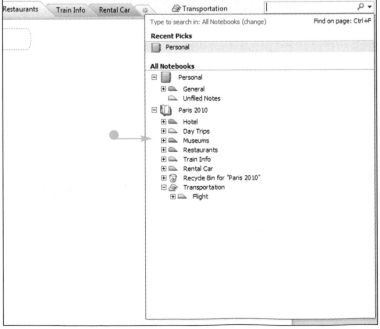

② Type your search text.

Note: As you type, the menu displays potential matches to your search criteria.

③ Click a match to view the page.

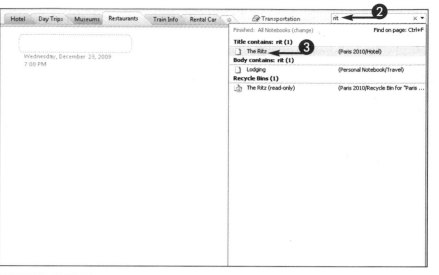

● OneNote displays pages containing the text you typed.

TIP

How do I search audio and video?

In order to search audio and video, you must enable OneNote's Audio Search function. To do so, click the **File** tab and choose **Options**. In the OneNote Options dialog box that appears, click **Audio & Video**, and select the **Enable searching audio and video recordings for words** check box. The Did You Know About Audio Search dialog box appears; click the **Enable Audio Search** button. Finally, click **OK** to close the OneNote Options dialog box.

E-mail a Note Page

You can share pages in your OneNote notebooks with others by e-mailing them. Pages are e-mailed in HTML format, meaning that the message recipient need not have OneNote installed to view them. You can launch the e-mail operation directly from OneNote.

E-mail a Note Page

① With the page you want to e-mail open in OneNote, click the **Home** tab.

② Click the **E-mail Page** button.

● OneNote launches your e-mail program, displaying a new message window containing the OneNote page.

● The message's Subject line contains the page's title.

③ Enter the recipient's e-mail address in the **To** field.

④ Click **Send**.

The message is sent.

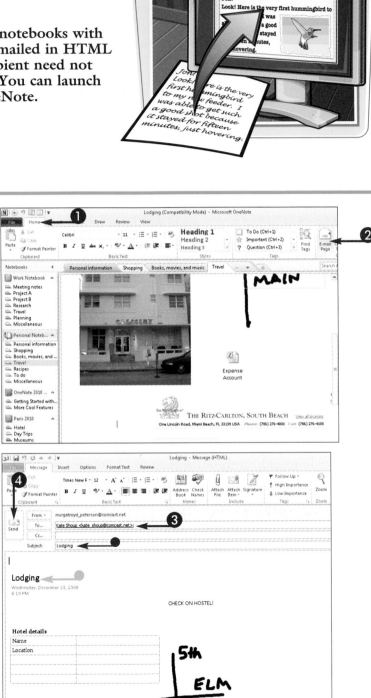

You can convert note pages, sections, or entire notebooks into PDF or XML format. This enables you to distribute them to others who do not have OneNote. You can also publish PDF or XML notes to the Web.

Convert Notes to PDF or XPS Format

① With the page, section, or notebook you want to convert open in OneNote, click the **File** tab.

② Click **Save As**.

③ Click **Page**, **Section**, or **Notebook**.

④ Click **PDF (*.pdf)** or **XPS (*.xps)**.

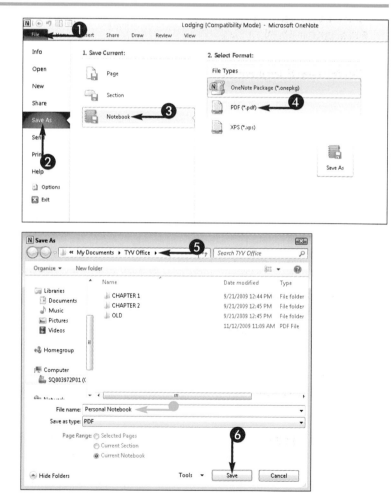

The Save As dialog box opens.

● The name of the page, section, or notebook appears in the File Name field.

⑤ Locate and select the folder in which you want to save the page, section, or notebook.

⑥ Click **Save**.

OneNote saves the page, section, or notebook in the format you specified.

Index

A

absolute cell reference, 192–193
Access, 276–277. *See also* databases; Office applications
alignment, 82, 149–151, 240, 373
animation effects for slides, 260–263, 265
applications. *See* Office applications
appointments, 324–327, 339
arrows in Ribbon buttons, 8
attachments. *See* file attachments
audio recordings in notebooks, 396–397, 407. *See also* sound
AutoComplete, 143
AutoCorrect, 128–129
AutoFill, 146–147
automatic spell and grammar checking, 126–127

B

Background, 159, 380–381
background color, 99, 101, 157
background image, 159, 297
bibliography, 120–121
blog entry, 76–77
borders. *See also* gridlines; lines
    for cells, 156–157
    for images, 44–45
    for pages, 101
    for publication objects, 374
    for text, 100
breaks in pages, 112–113
Building Blocks
    in publication, 382–385
    Quick Parts, 72–73, 108
bulleted lists, 90–91
buttons in Quick Access Toolbar, 10–11
buttons in Ribbon, 8

C

calculations. *See* formulas
calendar (Outlook), 322, 324–329, 338
CD, saving presentation as, 272–273
cell ranges, 149, 166–167, 188
cells
    aligning text or data in, 150–151
    AutoComplete for, 143
    AutoFill for, 146–147
    background color for, 157
    borders for, 156–157
    deleting, 168–169
    deleting contents of, 168
    entering data or text in, 142–143, 146–147
    filtering, 180–181
    finding and replacing, 176–177
    formatting and fonts for, 152–155, 158–161, 169

formulas for. *See* formulas
    indenting text or data in, 151
    orientation of text or data in, 151
    referencing, 188, 191, 192–193
    resizing to fit, 143, 164
    selecting, 27, 144–145
    sorting text or data in, 178–179
    wrapping text or data in, 143, 148
centering. *See* alignment
charts
    in presentation, 244–245
    in worksheet
        axis titles for, 211
        copying to PowerPoint slide, 245
        creating, 204–205
        data in, changing, 215
        deleting, 207
        formatting and fonts in, 212–213
        gridlines for, 214
        layout and style for, 208–210
        moving, 206
        printing, 213
        resizing, 207
        sparklines (data trends) in, 216–217
citations for bibliography, 120, 121
clip art, 32–35, 247, 367. *See also* images
color adjustments to images, 48
color of background. *See* background color
color of text or data, 80, 237, 368–371. *See also* formatting and
  fonts
columns
    in database. *See* fields
    in document, 87, 102–103
    in worksheet, 145, 149, 162–165, 169
comments
    in document, 138–139
    in worksheet, 186–187
    for workspaces, 63
conditional formatting
    for cells, 160–161
    for database fields, 310–311
contacts (Outlook)
    adding sender of e-mail message to, 346
    creating, 330–331
    emailing, 331
    importing, 331
    opening, 322
    scheduling appointments through, 327
    searching, 338
conversations (threads), 348–351
corner group buttons in Ribbon, 8
cross-references in indexes, 115
currency, formatting for, 154–155

Index

Index

Index

formulas in. *See* formulas
gridlines in, printing, 157, 173
inserting in Word documents, 107
naming, 171
print area of, 173
rearranging in workbook, 174
rows in, 145, 162–165, 169
scrolling through, 7, 165

themes for, 159
watch window in, 202–203
zooming, 7
workspaces, 54–57, 62–65

X

XE fields, 114–115
XPS files, 25, 409

WITHDRAWN